A DEEPER CUT

The Political Mind Series
edited by David Morgan

The Unconscious in Social and Political Life (2019)

A DEEPER CUT

Further Explorations
of the Unconscious in Social
and Political Life

Edited by

David Morgan

PHOENIX
PUBLISHING HOUSE
firing the mind

First published in 2021 by
Phoenix Publishing House Ltd
62 Bucknell Road
Bicester
Oxfordshire OX26 2DS

British Library Cataloguing in Publication Data

A C.I.P. for this book is available from the British Library

ISBN-13: 978-1-912691-19-7

Typeset by Medlar Publishing Solutions Pvt Ltd, India

www.firingthemind.com

Tell Them

Tell them (they have names)
and when they turn the bodies over
to count the number of closed eyes.
And they tell you 800,000: you say no. That was my uncle.
He wore bright coloured shirts and pointy shoes.
2 million: you say no. That was my aunty.
Her laughter could sweep you up like
the wind to leaves on the ground.
6 million: you say no. That was my mother.
Her arms. The only place I have ever
not known fear.
3 million: you say no. that was my love.
We used to dance. Oh, how we used to dance.
Or 147: you say no. that was our hope. Our future. The brains of
the family.
And when they tell you that you come from war: you say no.
I come from hands held in prayer before we eat together.
When they tell you that you come from conflict: you say no.
I come from sweat.
On skin. Glistening. From shining sun.
When they tell you that you come from genocide: you say no.
I come from the first smile of a new born child. Tiny hands.
When they tell you that you come from rape: you say no. And you
tell them about every time you have ever loved.
Tell them that you are from mother carrying you on her back.
Until you could walk.
Until you could run. Until you could fly.
Tell them that you are from father holding you up to the night sky.
Full of stars. And saying look, child. This is what you are made of.
From long summers. Full moons. Flowing rivers. Sand dunes.
You tell them that you are an ocean that no cup could ever hold.

JJ Bola
Poet

To exist is the artist's greatest pride. He desires no other paradise than existence, love the existence of the thing more than yourself

Osip Mandelstam
"The Morning of Acmeism"

Contents

Acknowledgements

This is the second book that has developed out of the Political Mind Seminars at the British Psychoanalytical Society. Since the last book we have all been plunged into a catastrophe, in the form of a global pandemic. Lives have been irreversibly altered, affected by death, illness, or economic strife. The after-effects of this trauma will last for a very long time. The economic consequences will probably lead to further polarisation in society between the have-nots and the "have mores". The danger of populism may be used to provide simplistic jingoistic alternatives to real change. While suddenly healthcare workers are the underpaid but appreciated heroes. There has never been a more urgent need for good political leadership and the ability to think.

I am deeply indebted to my colleagues who provide their wisdom and maturity in these pages. I hope others find their thoughts helpful.

I would like to say thank you to Ruth McCall without whose continuous support and intelligence these initiatives would not have happened. Also Freya and Will for their lives, which always inspire me. Also Leo, Alex, Alexa, Mylinh, and Pandora for being in the world. I would also like to express my heartfelt gratitude to Patricia.

Also a thank you to the great Sophie Kemp and Julie Norris at Kingsley Napley for keeping the spirit of Atticus alive.

David Morgan
Lambs Orchard

Permissions

The following have been reprinted with permission.

"Tell Them" by JJ Bola is reprinted with the kind permission of the author.

Chapter One: Understanding right and left populisms by Samir Gandesha is an abbreviated version of Gandesha, S. (2018). Understanding right and left populism. In: J. Morelock (Ed.), *Critical Theory and Authoritarian Populism* (pp. 49–70). London: University of Westminster Press. DOI: https://doi.org/10.16997/book30.d. Licence: CC-BY-NC-ND.

Chapter Two: "Ill fares the land": reflections on The Merchant of Venice—a tale for modern times by Margot Waddell. An earlier version of this chapter was originally published in 2011 as *The Merchant of Venice*: a tale of modern times in: L. J. Gould, A. Lucey, & L. Stapley (Eds.), *The Reflective Citizen: Organizational and Social Dynamics* (pp. 1–18). London: Karnac. This revised version is reprinted with the kind permission of Routledge/Taylor & Francis.

Chapter Three: Psychoanalysis, colonialism, racism by Stephen Frosh was originally published in 2013 in the *Journal of Theoretical and Philosophical Psychology*, 33(3): 141–154. Copyright © 2013, American Psychological

Association, DOI: 10.1037/a0033398. It is reproduced here with the permission of the American Psychological Association.

Chapter Four: Consultancy on deregistration to a care home for the long-stay mentally ill: you can take Stig out of the dump, but can you take the dump out of Stig? by Liz Greenway. An earlier version of this chapter was originally published in 2012 in *Organisational and Social Dynamics, 12*(2): 145–170. This revised version is reprinted with the kind permission of Phoenix Publishing House.

Chapter Eleven: On the psychology of religious fundamentalism by Lord John Alderdice was originally published in 2010 in: P. J. Verhagen, H. M. van Praag, J. J. López-Ibor, J. L. Cox, & D. Moussaoui (Eds.), *Religion and Psychiatry: Beyond Boundaries* (pp. 305–318). Chichester, UK: John Wiley. Copyright © 2010, John Wiley & Sons Ltd. It is reprinted with the kind permission of the publisher.

Chapter Thirteen: Psychoanalytic activism: historical perspective and subjective conundrums by Mary-Joan Gerson was originally published in 2012 in *Psychoanalytic Psychology, 29*(3): 325–329. Copyright © 2012, American Psychological Association, DOI: 10.1037/a0026807. It is reproduced here with the permission of the American Psychological Association.

About the editor and contributors

Professor, the Lord Alderdice, FRCPsych, played a significant role in the negotiation of the 1998 Good Friday Agreement as leader of the Alliance Party of Northern Ireland. He was the first speaker of the new Northern Ireland Assembly until 2004 when he was appointed to the Independent Monitoring Commission tasked by the British and Irish Governments with security normalisation and closing down terrorist activity in Northern Ireland. He was president of Liberal International, the global federation of more than 100 liberal political parties (now "président d'honneur"), and chairman of the Liberal Democrat Party in the House of Lords. His work on fundamentalism, radicalisation, and terrorism in various parts of the world has been recognised with many honorary degrees, prizes, and awards and he is currently direc-tor of the Centre for the Resolution of Intractable Conflict at Harris Manchester College (Oxford, UK), chairman of the Centre for Democ-racy and Peace Building (Belfast, Northern Ireland), and a clinical pro-fessor in the Department of Psychiatry at the University of Maryland (Baltimore, USA).

Dr Elizabeth Cotton is a writer and educator working in the field of mental health at work. Her background is in workers' education and international development. She has worked in more than thirty-five countries on diverse issues such as HIV/AIDS, organising and building grassroots networks, and negotiating and bargaining with employers as head of education for IndustriALL, one of the largest trade unions in the world, reflected in her book *Global Unions Global Business* (Libri). She teaches and writes as an academic at Cardiff Metropolitan University about employment relations and mental health. She is editor-in-chief of an ABS4 British Sociological Association journal, *Work, Employment & Society* and blogs as www.survivingwork.org, a network of 30,000 people. In 2017 she published a national survey about working conditions in mental health, www.thefutureoftherapy.org and her current research is focused on the "Uberisation" of therapy. She set up www.survivingworkinhealth.org, a free resource in partnership with the Tavistock and Portman NHS Foundation Trust and her accompanying book *Surviving Feeling Work in Healthcare: Helpful Stuff for People on the Frontline* (Gower, 2017) was nominated for the Chartered Management Institute's practitioner book of the year.

Dr Tomasz Fortuna trained as a psychoanalyst at the Institute of Psychoanalysis in London. He is a member of the British Psychoanalytical Society and the Hanna Segal Institute for Psychoanalytic Studies. He has worked as a psychiatrist in the NHS for fifteen years, and currently he works at the Portman Clinic with adults, children, and adolescents and is in private psychoanalytic practice. He teaches and supervises in the UK and abroad. His professional interests include the relationship between psychoanalysis and the arts, the understanding of severe emotional disturbance, and criminal behaviour. He has published several articles and chapters, and co-authored the book *Melanie Klein: The Basics*. He was a guest editor of *Empedocles, European Journal for the Philosophy of Communication*.

Professor Stephen Frosh is professor in the Department of Psychosocial Studies (which he founded) at Birkbeck, University of London. He was pro-vice-master of Birkbeck from 2003 to 2017. He has a background in academic and clinical psychology and was consultant clinical psychologist at the Tavistock Clinic, London, throughout the 1990s. He is the author of many books and papers on psychosocial studies and on psychoanalysis. His books include *Hauntings: Psychoanalysis and Ghostly Transmissions, Feelings, A Brief Introduction to Psychoanalytic Theory, Psychoanalysis Outside the Clinic: Interventions in Psychosocial Studies, Hate and the Jewish Science: Anti-Semitism Nazism and Psychoanalysis, For and Against Psychoanalysis, After Words: The Personal in Gender, Culture and Psychotherapy. The Politics of Psychoanalysis: An Introduction to Freudian and Post-Freudian Theory, Sexual Difference: Masculinity* and *Psychoanalysis, Identity Crisis: Modernity, Psychoanalysis and the Self.* His most recent book is *Those Who Come After: Postmemory, Acknowledgement and Foregiveness* (London: Palgrave, 2019). He is a fellow of the Academy of Social Sciences, an academic associate of the British Psychoanalytical Society, a founding member of the Association of Psychosocial Studies, and an honorary member of the Institute of Group Analysis.

Samir Gandesha is currently an associate professor in the Department of the Humanities and the director of the Institute for the Humanities at Simon Fraser University, British Columbia, Canada. He specialises in modern European thought and culture, with a particular emphasis on the relation between politics, aesthetics, and psychoanalysis. He has contributed chapters to numerous volumes and also papers to a wide range of journals.

He is co-editor with Lars Rensmann of *Arendt and Adorno: Political and Philosophical Investigations* (Stanford, 2012), and co-editor with Johan Hartle of *Spell of Capital: Reification and Spectacle* (University of Amsterdam Press, 2017) and *Aesthetic Marx* (Bloomsbury Press, 2017) also with Johan Hartle.

He is editor of *Spectres of Fascism: Historical, Theoretical and International Perspectives* (Pluto, 2020), and co-editor (with Peyman Vahabzadeh) of *Crossing Borders: Essays in Honour of Ian Angus, Beyond Phenomonology and Critique in Honour of Ian Angus* (Arbeiter Ring, 2020). In the spring of 2017, he was the Liu Boming Visiting Scholar in Philosophy at the University of Nanjing and visiting lecturer at Soochow University of Science and Technology in China. In January 2019, he was visiting fellow at the Hochschule für Gestaltung in Karlsruhe, Germany, and in February of the same year, he was visiting lecturer at Faculdade de Filosofia, Letras e Ciências Humanas—FFLCH-USP (Universidade de São Paulo, Brazil).

Dr Mary-Joan Gerson is adjunct clinical professor, consultant in psychoanalysis, and former director of the Advanced Specialization in Couple and Family Therapy at the New York University Postdoctoral Program in Psychotherapy and Psychoanalysis. She is founding president of Section VIII, Couples and Family Therapy, of Division 39 (Psychoanalysis), as well as founding co-chair of the Committee on Psychoanalysis and Health Care, and the Committee on Psychoanalysis and the Community, for Division 39 (Psychoanalysis) of the American Psychological Association.

She is author of *The Embedded Self: An Integrative Psychodynamic and Systemic Perspective on Couples and Family Therapy*, published in 2009 by Routledge Psychoanalysis. Her numerous publications have appeared in such journals as *Contemporary Psychoanalysis*, *Psychoanalytic Psychology*, *The Journal of Psychotherapy Integration*, *Social Science and Medicine*, and *Family Systems Medicine*.

Mary-Joan Gerson has been awarded a Fulbright Specialist Award, which took her to Namibia in August 2013 to consult with psychologists and other healthcare workers at the University of Namibia and government ministries. Dr Gerson was recently awarded the Florence Kaslow Distinguished Contribution to International Family Psychology Award (2012), by Division 43 (Family Psychology) of the American Psychological Association.

Liz Greenway has worked for more than fifteen years as a psychotherapist in GP surgeries, charities, and private practice with a broad range of individuals including those on the edge of society who are homeless, entrepreneurs, elderly, working professionals in government, law, health, charities, social care, education and corporate environments, actors, stay-at-home parents, family businesses. As a psychodynamic organisational therapist, integrative psychotherapist, and cognitive analytic therapy practitioner she has substantial experience across private, public, and voluntary sectors, and in group relations. Her organisational consultancy, reflective practice, and professional role consultation considers dynamic issues beneath the surface and relationships at work in context. She has also worked in clinical commissioning groups. She has a background in adult education. She is published in the *Organisational and Social Dynamics* journal and received, for scholarly excellence, Best Paper Award from the University of Missouri's Center for the Study of Organizational Change in 2014. She has a chapter in the recently published *Psychoanalytic Thinking on the Unhoused Mind* (Routledge, 2019). She has presented her work at various conferences. Additionally, she is a doctoral candidate in consultation and the organisation at the Tavistock and Portman NHS Foundation Trust for which the subject of her research is the impact of challenging work contexts on professionals in role, a concept of broad application in working life. She remains particularly interested in enabling environments to facilitate creativity, sustainability, and recovery.

Roger Hartley is a retired civil servant. His postgraduate research was in the sociology of literature, on George Orwell. He then taught English literature and cultural studies at the University of Sussex, and subsequently was a civil servant for some twenty-three years in Whitehall. He has a long-standing interest in psychoanalysis, which includes an analysis with Donald Meltzer in the 1980s.

David Morgan is a consultant psychotherapist and psychoanalyst, and a fellow of the British Psychoanalytical Society. He is a training analyst and supervisor at the British Psychoanalytic Association and at the British Psychotherapy Foundation, and a lecturer recognised nationally and internationally. He is the editor of *The Unconscious in Social and Political Life* (2019), and co-editor (with Stanley Ruszczynski) of *Violence, Delinquency and Perversion* (2007), and has authored many chapters and papers. He is currently a director of Public Interest Psychology Ltd, as well as a member of the IPA committee on Humanitarian Organisations. He is the chair of The Political Mind Seminars, co-chair and editor with Kurt Jacobson of the Psychoanalysis and Public Sphere Conference and the *Free Association* journal, and was chair of Frontier Psychoanalyst, a radio broadcast series on Resonance FM. He is also a member of the Think Tank on Resolution of Intractable Conflict.

Luisa Passalacqua, MA, MNCS, is an integrative counsellor and an independent researcher and consultant in psychological anthropology with a background in occupational and organisational psychology as well as anthropology of art. Her experience ranges from professional training and continuing education to arts therapies, which she has practised privately as a qualified dramatherapist, having been a member of the British Association of Dramatherapists (UK) and the North American Drama Therapy Association (USA) for many years. She has published several arts therapies-related articles in the journal *Arti Terapie*, one in *The Dramatherapy Journal* (1995), and the book *Guarire con le Arti Drammatiche [Healing through Dramatic Arts]* (2008). She is currently interested in the "unrepresented" escaping the verbal mapping of daily life, particularly invisible interpersonal processes that culminate in the creation of narratives as they become social and political, which she shows on screen using audio-visual media. Her first ethnographic film *Red on White* (2020) is on pre-adolescent girls' corporeality, and will be followed by *S(e)oul* (in production) on urban shamanism. She is currently working on her next essay, *The Science of Forgiveness*.

Dr Kate Pugh is a consultant psychiatrist in psychotherapy working in the NHS alongside practising as a psychoanalyst. She teaches psycho-analytic concepts to mental health workers in London and abroad.

Dr Marco Puricelli is a psychologist and psychotherapist. With a background in psychological science and techniques, neural networks (which he had studied since his master's degree in engineering for the environment at Politecnico University in Milan), as well as neuropsychology and clinical psychology, he qualified in Adlerian-oriented psychotherapy in Turin, with a thesis in the psychology of religion. He contributed to *Forms of Intersubjectivity—the Explicit and Implicit in Interpersonal Relations*, edited by Lucia Carli and Carlo Rodini (2007) and his article with Lucia Carli, "The Contribution of Nonlinear Dynamics to the Notion of Change", was published in the *Italian Journal of Psychology* (2014). He is the author of *Dio o super-dio? Vere e false rappresentazioni di Dio [God or Super-Ego? True and False Representations of God]* (2011), *Rappresentazioni di Dio: deformazioni e negazioni [Depictions of God: Deformations and Negations]* (2013), and *Traumi infantili e genesi* *dell'odio verso se stessi e gli altri [Childhood Trauma and the Source of Hatred towards Self and Others]* (2015). Marco consistently applies Alice Miller insights into his daily clinical practice, integrating her thoughts and intuitions with other psychotherapeutic techniques.

From 2010 to 2017 he was a teaching assistant for dynamic psychology and advanced dynamic psychology at the faculty of psychology at the Bicocca University of Milan. He currently works as a psychotherapist in private practice in Milan, mainly with adults, while he is referent counsellor for teenagers and adolescents in a public clinic in Gallarate (not far from Milan).

He leads lectures and seminars in the psychology of religion.

Dr Edgard Sanchez Bernal is a consultant psychiatrist and a psychoanalyst and a fellow of the British Psychoanalytical Society. He works in the NHS for South London and Maudsley NHS Trust, based at King's College London Student Services. He also works at his private practice. He has written papers on clinical issues including free association, transference, termination in psychoanalytic settings, and deliberate self-harm. He is a founding member and co-chair of the Freudian Study Group.

Elisabeth Skale, MD, is a psychiatrist, a member and training analyst at the Vienna Psychoanalytic Society, a coordinator of the Department of Theory/History/Culture of the Vienna Psychoanalytic Academy, as well as Austrian consultant of the European Psychoanalytic Film Festival. She has written papers on clinical and technical issues of psychoanalysis. She currently works in private practice and the Vienna Psychoanalytic Clinic.

Professor Mark Stein is chair in leadership and management at the University of Leicester, UK. He has been a senior lecturer at Imperial College London and a research fellow at the London School of Economics and Brunel University. He has also had a long-standing connection with INSEAD, France, where he has been an adjunct professor and visiting scholar. For many years Mark has also been connected with the Tavistock Institute and Clinic. He was employed by the Tavistock Institute as a researcher and consultant; undertook observational studies at the Tavistock Clinic; and has also been on the staff of group relations events at the Clinic and Institute, including the "Leicester Conference". Mark was awarded the Gavin Macfadyen Memorial Essay Prize for the paper on the gang published in this volume. He has also received an Emerald Citation of Excellence; the "Group & Organization Management" best paper prize; the Richard Normann Prize; and the iLab Prize for innovative scholarship.

Margot Waddell is a fellow of the Institute of Psychoanalysis and a child analyst. She has a background in classics and English literature. She has taught at the Institute over many years and is currently the chair of publications there. She has worked for more than thirty years as a consultant child and adolescent psychotherapist at the Tavistock Clinic, London, where she continues to contribute as a visiting lecturer. She has edited the Tavistock Clinic Book Series since its inception in 1998. An extended version of her book *Inside Lives: Psychoanalysis and the Growth of the Personality* was published by Karnac in 2002, *Understanding 12–14-Year-Olds* was published by Jessica Kingsley in 2005, and her latest book, *On Adolescence: Inside Stories*, was published by Routledge in 2018.

Introduction

David Morgan

An olive grower sat outside his olive grove in the sunshine drinking ouzo when a scion of a vast olive oil company offered to help him organise his rather scruffy olive grove into a multimillion dollar enterprise. The owner of the grove replied, "Ah yes, I can get rich so then I could sit in the sunshine drinking my ouzo."

This is a celebration of Epicurean philosophy about life's pleasures versus the attractions of material riches. I often think about this while sitting out the current pandemic in 2020. Politics has changed a great deal since the publication of *The Unconscious in Social and Political Life* (Morgan, 2019). We have now been forced indoors to avoid the threat of death and if fortunate enough re-discovered important truths about what is necessary in life. The question being, should we return to "normal" with all that entails for climate change and society as a whole?

The olive grower in the story is able to manage the externalisation of the greed of the businessman, reminding him of pleasures other than economic expansionism and growth. Something we need to reflect on seriously in the face of this virus rather than being sucked into the excesses of unfettered consumerism once again. The themes in Margot Waddell's thoughtful chapter, "'Ill fares the land': reflections on

The Merchant of Venice—a tale for modern times", which investigates the relationship between internal and external reality, chime here.

Psychoanalysts try to bring much-needed nourishment to the minds of their patients, some of whom are psychotic and severely disturbed. Many valuable theories around psychosis and its causes, such as trauma or unrecognised transgenerational pain, can be applied to understanding some of the current political and social malaise that confronts our time. Take for example a banker patient who worked six days a week, neglecting his children to do so despite having made enough money for several lifetimes. He had panic attacks on Sundays. He tried to make me come to his office saying his time was money and offered me a ton of money to do so. I suggested that he was anxious that I was only interested in his money and did not value the space in which I practised, and bribing me was a way to see if this was true. A reflection of his own battle with finance that had taken over everything in life that was precious. I was surprised to discover that he had seen his parents almost starve and that he had dedicated himself to ensure that this would never happen to him. Although, as we can see, at a different level he was starving.

Another example is Ms M, a creative person whose work always contained images of ice. She broke down with the illusion (with climate change maybe not so much of an illusion) that the next ice age was coming, and she stood outside the Ministry of Defence haranguing passersby. When I saw her for inpatient therapy, it was clear this was a strong delusion. She would listen to the shipping forecast expecting a special, personal message to tell her that the next ice age was starting. My immediate thought on seeing her was, what had been the last ice age? What emerged in our work was the belief that she was defending herself with this delusional messianic belief system and she would save the world by cutting her wrists. Very early in her life, her mother had a post-puerperal psychosis and had become cold and unavailable to her child. I think my patient believed she was responsible and guilty for this frozen mother and had developed her delusional belief in response; all her defences had to be directed at preventing the ice age she had been through from happening again.

I saw her for many years, in and then outside hospital. As in the story of the ice queen, something defrosted and the pain surrounding her about her early years manifested itself. This included her fury for what she felt were "the icy attitudes of psychoanalysts toward their patients who they reify with their cold theories". I was able to explore this belief system that existed between us; it was something that resonated deeply with me, as in my own analysis I had originally found the regimented aspect of analysis and training difficult and relentless.

This meant I had some empathic regard for the patient's need to hate what was felt by her to be a frozen, cruel, and cold analyst, with his icy theories and setting. At times it would become too much for her (or me) and she was admitted to a ward that was psychoanalytically orientated, where I could continue to see her. This was difficult and exhausting work. Eventually, through a combination of medication and then just therapy, she was able to achieve some stability in her life, free from her overriding delusional system.

If you want people to behave thoughtfully to others, then you have to give them the experience of being thought about, otherwise enactment becomes the only means of communication, where people are only taken seriously due to the thoughtless violence of their actions—the latter an enactment of their own experience of a neglectful world. There was an infamous case in the 1990s of a very distressed man who had been refused admission by several hospitals and who was driven to attack and kill a man who refused to provide him with a light for his cigarette. This refusal led to an enactment of his many years of neglect and rejection. The light for the cigarette concretely represented all this man had suffered and his painful rejection at the hands of uncaring institutions.

Hanna Segal (1957) located the provenance of psychosis in the inability to properly construct a system of mental symbolisation. For the patients she analysed, symbols and the actual things they represented were jumbled and undifferentiated, so that merely uttering a person's name might inflict upon them concrete physical harm; or like a patient I saw who took as an insult her father's gift of a bunch of bananas when visiting her in hospital, suggesting that she was mad. Another young woman, having been told when given a hand-me-down coat by her mother that she "would grow into it", actually waited for many years for buttons to appear on her body.

Early psychoanalytic papers often involved the analysis of a particularly relentless, cruel superego formation that constantly reappears, seemingly destroying progress, with the accompanying extreme loss of any good object relationship. The ward, at times of acute crisis, used to provide some respite, to both analyst and patient, from this relentless-ness. Dr Murray Jackson writes compassionately about this inpatient work in *Unimaginable Storms* (1994) and *Weathering the Storms* (2001), both superlative accounts of the profundity of good analytic inpatient work within the confines of an old mental hospital, as in his justly famous Ward 6. Within this book, Kate Pugh's thoughtful chapter on the politics of psychiatry in the UK shines a light on the ongoing problems with mental health services, as does Liz Greenway's reflective explora-tion of policies and provisions for mentally ill patients.

Whether inpatient or outpatient, the psychotic patient brings extreme states to the awareness of the analyst. This, I feel, is an exploration of the analyst's capacity to bear unspoken unsymbolised cruelties, but also an exploration of the analyst's ability to find internal or external help from others, in ways the patient or their objects were unable to find. The question being, do you (the analyst) have any more resources than I (the patient) to manage these extremes?

Guilt and psychosis are closely related but often reside in the trans-generational history of the people I see, manifesting as apparent delu-sional systems when in fact it is often someone having someone else's experience that is unrecognised. Like Christopher Bollas's idea of the unthought known, which I find useful: "The primary repressed must be that inherited disposition that constitutes the core of personality, which has been genetically transmitted, and exists as a potential in psychic space" (Bollas, 1989, p. 78). As a result of working with patients I devel-oped the idea of a research project looking for severe trauma in previ-ous generations of family members of people presenting with apparent delusional belief systems—there was often a strong correlation. The core issue here is that unrecognised painful trauma leads to cruel, icy, suicidal beliefs and powerful psychotic delusions. Luisa Passalacqua and Marco Puricelli's gripping chapter, "Alice Miller on family, power, and truth" includes a look at the long-lasting effects of trauma on individuals.

One method of managing painful insight into one's own internal world is to externalise/project the unthought known issues into some-one or something else. Usually this is another person's mind, which is filled with the thoughts and insights that are being repudiated. This is a ubiquitous aspect of what Melanie Klein (1946) described as the paranoid–schizoid position. The beginnings of maturity, or what she calls the depressive position, is the recognition that what we have previously projected also belongs to us and then we might begin to face the guilt, if we can. The most pernicious aspect of this is a cruel superego formation, an amalgam of severe transgenerational trauma and unprocessed aggression.

Psychoanalysts are therefore familiar with these concepts within the consulting room and within the individual, but realising how deep-seated these psychotic mechanisms are at a collective level is much less recognised. Yet entire societies continue to function at a paranoid–schizoid level, risking splits and projections that can only dangerously reduce the safety of the world. My own chapter looks at the psychological dimensions of defying a perverse or corrupt authority through the actions of the whistleblower. While Lord John Alderdice investigates the psychology of religious fundamentalism and its relationship to group psychology.

The human capacity for a sense of guilt is indicative of individual emotional growth: a defective sense of guilt is not linked to intellectual capacity or incapacity but rather the capacity for guilt is linked to the tolerance of ambivalence within the self. In successful analyses of individuals oppressed by guilt, there is a lessening of guilt, though for some the source of guilt cannot be reached, and for those individuals who feel that they are not able to explain this, it can make for a feeling of madness. I think this can also pertain at the societal level (Winnicott, 1959, p. 44). Mary-Joan Gerson brings us a call to arms to engage with the world outside our consulting rooms, using what we have learned from individuals and applying it to the wider community.

I feel that the ethics of migration involve bringing about an awareness of collective guilt in the West that we wish to obviate by locating it outside ourselves. I suggest that the migrant is a repository of our own fears, carrying a reminder of Western hegemony and the dreaded retaliation or insight it could bring about. We can experience these reminders as persecuting because they remind us of aspects of our cultural history we choose to turn a blind eye to. Tomasz Fortuna's stimulating chapter, "Diversity: notes from the inside and the outside", looks at the links between the internal experience of difference and its external manifestations.

People migrate owing to a need to survive, to find food, and to avoid danger and death by moving towards opportunities for life that many of us here, through luck and, arguably, an aggressive foreign policy, possess. With the history of privilege many of us from the developed West have benefited from, we can feel we are winners of the global quasi "Hunger Games" we live in. Of course the winners want to keep the upper hand and control the fruits of conquest as they, we, always have done. However, I want to suggest that we can think about a global ethical depressive position. Having dominated much of the world through using internal processes of splitting and projection that allow aggressors to attack and exploit, often in the name of survival, I think it is important that we realise that the victims of this exploitation have rights and needs, and that they are the reminders of our collective guilt. We are dangerously distracted from the real causes of our current problems in the West and encouraged to focus on the victims.

The birth of the "Other" in our midst is a reminder of the moral dilemma and the Other is so easily reified, asset-stripped, and turned into a threat. I believe from my work with migrants and asylum seekers that certain historical or cultural factors cause an inhibition of our capacity to think through the significance to us of refugees and immigrants. Central here is the repudiated awareness of our own implication in the horrors the migrant is fleeing, which leads to our unconscious guilt for the depredations of the Western colonial past and our wish to retain power and commodities in the new global economy. Stephen Frosh tackles these issues head on in his insightful exploration into postcolonial thought from a psychoanalytic viewpoint.

The migration debate in Britain is usually dominated by the reporting of economic and cultural concerns. On the surface, the debate appears to be about immigrants and the question of what they claim in state benefits, wages they undercut, jobs they steal, overuse of social resources, and whether the national identity will be diluted and multiculturalism made untenable when "swamped" by the Other. The understanding of the "Return of the Oppressed" can provide an ethical dimension to understanding this propaganda. Roger Hartley's nuanced take on "George Orwell: politics and the avoidance of reality" resonates here.

Right-wing populist politicians can rely on the paranoid–schizoid fears that reside in us all. We all retain the infantile traces of absolute dependency on the maternal provider and, as we grow up, this easily relocates itself onto the nation state and government. When politicians tell us our nation state is at risk, we experience infantile anxieties easily converted into blame and resentment. The main purpose of the anti-immigration rhetoric is to deprive the Other of inclusion and political membership. This excluding political rhetoric insists that some people are more significant than others.

As psychoanalysts, surely we do not believe a person's life chances should be determined by arbitrary features such as race, ethnicity, gender, or sexuality, and in a thoughtful, depressive-position world such factors would not determine life chances. The West wants to keep its upper hand. Having exploited, we must now realise that the victims of this exploitation have rights and, I argue, they are the reminder of our collective guilt and a distraction from the true threat in the world, which is the cause, rather than mass migration, which is the symptom.

So, if we dare to think about it ethically, we can see that one main issue underpins this twenty-first-century manifestation of economic anxiety, and the paranoia it induces: power. These hapless immigrants are excluded from the democratic process, which is analogous to men wielding political power over women, the injustice of the white population of South Africa that exercised political power over the black population; that is, coercive power over the excluded, with no opportunity for them to participate as equals. We all agree here, I imagine, that no person is more morally significant than any other, but it was and is this belief in such an insignificance that was projected by the powerful into the excluded to justify the continued exercise of power.

By dividing human societies between those who carry particular attributes, accidents of birth, geographical placement, wealth, education and so on, we create the lucky ones and the unlucky ones, to continue the analogy of the *Hunger Games*. The lucky ones have not earned these attributes, do not "deserve" them, and do not merit special treatment or reward.

We are in a period of time when the West is dominated by neoliberalism and the rise of the right wing. Anxieties around survival lead to a massive split between the "have mores" and the have-nots. Samir Gandesha explores these effects on both right and left populisms in the opening chapter and Elisabeth Skale looks in detail at the rise of the new right from a psychoanalytic perspective in Chapter 14.

We need international solidarity of government, to stop crippling developing countries by stealing their natural resources and stop imposing punitive austerity on developing countries as part of World Bank loans to simply keep the country alive. Edgard Sanchez Bernal's powerful chapter gives us a Third World perspective on power and the manipulation of the masses. Let's say goodbye to unregulated capitalism once and for all. Relentless production takes the place of meeting the needs of the global population, it exploits both the individual and the planet. This is given centre stage with Elizabeth Cotton's informative study of the role of trade unions and the psychodynamics of solidarity in modern society.

Perhaps we need to stop pretending that there is such a thing as a free market. It is a false entity because it's not free, it is always political and involves an abuse of power. Hopefully this book and its sister publication, *The Unconscious in Social and Political Life* (2019), will contribute something, however small, to a move to something better.

References

Bollas, C. (1989). *The Shadow of the Object: Psychoanalysis of the Unthought Known*. New York: Columbia University Press.

Jackson, M. (1994). *Unimaginable Storms: A Search for Meaning in Psychosis*. London: Karnac.

Jackson, M. (2001). *Weathering the Storms: Psychotherapy for Psychosis*. London: Karnac.

Klein, M. (1946). Notes on some schizoid mechanisms. *The International Journal of Psychoanalysis, 27*: 99–110.

Morgan, D. (2019). *The Unconscious in Social and Political Life*. London: Phoenix.

Segal, H. (1957). Notes on symbol formation. *The International Journal of Psychoanalysis, 38*: 391–397.

Winnicott, D. W. (1959). Psycho-Analysis and the Sense of Guilt. *The Collected Works of D. W. Winnicott: Volume 5, 1955–1959*. L. Caldwell & H. Taylor Robinson (Eds.). Oxford: Oxford University Press.

CHAPTER ONE

Understanding right and left populisms

Samir Gandesha

We appear to be living in an age of populism. Over the past three decades, we have witnessed the rise of right-wing populist parties throughout Europe such as Haider's Freedom Party of Austria, Victor Orban's Fidesz Party in Hungary, and the Polish Law and Justice Party. In one of the most disturbing developments, a long-standing taboo in Germany was recently broken with the neo-Nazi Alternative für Deutschland having just joined a coalition government with an FDP premier in the state of Thuringia.

Such a development hasn't been confined to Europe but is a global phenomenon as evinced, for example, by the electoral triumphs of Narendra Modi in India in 2014 and that of Recep Tayyip Erdoğan in Turkey as early as 2003. But no phenomena more clearly evince this thesis than the stunning victory of Donald J. Trump in the 2016 American presidential election and the triumph of the Leave campaign (from the European Union) led by the United Kingdom Independence Party (UKIP).

But there has also been a populism of the left. The Arab Spring was widely regarded as a broad-based, if short-lived, popular revolt and therefore as a kind of "populism in the streets" in 2011. The events of

Tahrir Square profoundly inspired the Occupy Movement. Radiating out beyond Zuccotti Park, the movement spread through much of the Western world. Arguably, the Occupy Movement's most significant and enduring effect was to be felt five years later in the rising support for Bernie Sanders and Jeremy Corbyn.

Latin America, moreover, has seen a dramatic revival of populism in the Bolivarian model in the Chávez/Maduro regime in Venezuela and in Evo Morales in Bolivia, as well as in the Kirchner governments in Argentina. The dramatic global rise of populist parties and movements has resulted in a burgeoning scholarship on this most slippery of political concepts.

But can we understand populism with more precision? How can we account for its recent pervasiveness? I will focus on two exemplary accounts of populism before trying to arrive at some conclusions of how to understand the difference between right and left forms of populism in the context of neoliberal globalisation.

The first account is a recent widely cited and discussed empirical study by Norris and Inglehart (2016). The second is a more theoretical account of populism by Ernesto Laclau articulated over several decades, occasionally in collaboration with Chantal Mouffe (Laclau 1977, 2005; Laclau & Mouffe, 1985). If Norris and Inglehart struggle to come to terms with the populism of the left, then Laclau struggles to come to adequate grips with the populism of the right. The former draw upon a somewhat narrow definition of populism, emphasising its anti-establishment, authoritarian, and nativist dimensions; the latter understands populism as a logic constituted by the establishment of an "equivalential chain" of different demands. It appears to suggest that populism is a democratic, horizontal, and egalitarian discourse.

Populism explained: economic insecurity or cultural backlash?

A paper widely discussed in the media by Pippa Norris of Harvard University and Ronald Inglehart of the University of Michigan suggests—following Cas Mudde—that populism shares three distinct elements: 1) anti-establishmentism, 2) authoritarianism, and 3) nativism (for the most recent discussion see Mudde, 2020). The first contrasts with the established structures of representative democracy; the second with the principles of liberalism (in particular with the protection of minority rights) and emphasises the direct expression of popular will via charismatic leadership, referenda, and plebiscites that circumvent the typical checks and balances of liberal democracy; and the third contrasts with cosmopolitanism.

Building on Mudde's conceptualisation, the authors develop a heuristic model of populism based upon two distinct axes: economic and cultural. The former has to do with the level of state management of the economy, and the latter has to do with "conservative" versus "progressive" values. The authors suggest three possible analytical types of explanation for the rise of populism: 1) the rules of the game, 2) the "supply side" of the market of party politics, and 3) the "demand side" of party politics. They gear their explanation to the third dimension and suggest that this can be understood to have two distinct—though not mutually exclusive—causes. The first is that populism emerges in response to economic insecurity, and the second is that populism appears as a backlash by older white males to the erosion of traditional cultural values.

Norris and Inglehart (2016, p. 5) argue that the latter is the most convincing argument: "We believe that these are the groups most likely to feel that they have become strangers from the predominant values in their own country, left behind by progressive tides of cultural change which they do not share ... The silent revolution of the 1970s appears to have spawned an angry and resentful counter-revolutionary backlash today."

While the empirical data the authors cite to support their argument is indeed impressive, it is possible to raise significant objections about the way they frame this evidence. First, the separation of "supply" and "demand" explanations seems deeply dubious. In strictly economic terms, according to Say's law of markets, for example, aggregate production necessarily creates an equal quantity of aggregate demand.

A second objection arises from the cultural backlash argument: by mischaracterising Mudde's definition as inherently authoritarian and nativist, Norris and Inglehart bias their conclusion towards culturalist explanations.

A third objection is that it is deeply debatable that "progressive values" are on the ascendant. Indeed, today it is far from clear what comprises "progressive values", as we saw in the recent Democratic presidential nomination pitting Hillary Rodham Clinton against Bernie Sanders. This opposition has been echoed in debates between political theorists in terms of the relative priority between a "politics of recognition" versus a "politics of redistribution".

Whether populism can be understood exclusively in terms of traditionalist backlash is also debatable. If this was the predominant measure of populist politics, one could expect recent immigrants—who themselves hold traditional values—to the US, the UK, and other parts of Europe to join in these movements. However, far from this being the case, they are often, in fact, the *very targets* of the backlash.

Finally, one wonders whether the authors don't seriously underestimate the threat right-wing populism poses to the institutions of liberal democracy in the United States. A worrying inference that the authors explicitly draw from their progressivist premises is that populism will eventually die out. The study therefore fails to sufficiently appreciate the ways in which populist governments seek to institutionalise their agendas, thereby changing the rules of the game. This has become most drastically evident in the case of Poland, for example, in which Andrzej Duda (leader of the right-populist Law and Justice party) has significantly limited the autonomy of the judicial branch of government. Other such examples abound.

Understanding populist reason

In his hugely influential yet profoundly controversial work with Chantal Mouffe entitled *Hegemony and Socialist Strategy*, Laclau seeks to develop his analysis of populism so as to generate a new post-Marxist politics. In other words, Laclau is developing in a British context a political strategy that is germane to a context that has seen the rise of what Stuart Hall (2017) has called "authoritarian populism" in the form of Thatcherism. *Hegemony and Socialist Strategy* differs from Laclau's earlier work in at least two ways: 1) it breaks with Althusserian Marxism, particularly that of Nicos Poulantzas, insofar as it no longer accords the working class a privileged role in social transformation; and 2) it provides a discursive account of the social. As he and Mouffe argue (1985, p. 84): "In our view, in order to advance in the determination of social antagonisms, it is necessary to analyse the plurality of diverse and frequently contradictory positions, and to discard the idea of a perfectly unified and homogenous agent, such as the 'working class' of classical discourse. The search for the 'true' working class and its limits is a false problem, and as such lacks any theoretical or political relevance."

The continuity, however, lies in the fact that Laclau insists upon the centrality of the concept of hegemonic articulation of heterogeneous political demands as the basis of a leftist political strategy.

In *On Populist Reason* (2005) Laclau argues against those political theorists who claim that populism is an irrational political discourse by reconstructing and foregrounding, as the title suggests, populism's own distinctive reason. Its logic is that of an "antagonistic synthesis", but now understood as an equivalential articulation of differences, that is, a linking together of what different political demands share in common in relation to a common "antagonistic frontier". For Laclau, all democratic politics are, in fact, populist. In other words, if we assume that society is inherently heterogeneous, politics must entail the hegemonic articulation of a multiplicity of political demands in a manner that is always provisional and open to revision. A given hegemonic equivalential articulation of differences is always shifting, temporary, and open because it is based on a logic of the empty signifier.

The key difference from his previous work is Laclau's attempt to conceptualise the affective dimension of politics via Lacanian psychoanalysis. John Kraniauskas understands this as the articulation of a Gramscian Lacan in contradistinction to Žižek's Hegelian Lacan. While the latter takes, as its point of departure, the understanding of the "desire of the Other" (the impossible-because-unattainable desire for intersubjective recognition), the former can be understood in terms of political desire.

For Laclau, political desire is geared to what Lacan calls the "objet petit a", meaning a partial object that is a fragment of the Real (that which eludes symbolisation yet is caught within the symbolic order). The "objet petit a" is often symbolised by the bountiful breast and, as such, promises a return to an original plenitude prior to the symbolic order based on the split between signifier and signified.

Political desire, then, is established through the Name or the coincidence of signifier and signified that is only set retroactively. The key point Laclau is making here is that this Lacanian understanding of political desire enables an alternative to Freud's, the latter being mass politics grounded in the love of an authoritarian leader who represents the imago of the father. In contrast, political desire grounded in the utopian logic of the "objet petit a" is characterised by the horizontal relations between brothers (and presumably, sisters).

Several criticisms can be made of Laclau's approach to populism. Critics have drawn attention to its formalism, stemming from its reliance on structural linguistics in which signification is understood by way of a system of differences with no positive terms. This formalist premise is the basis for his understanding of the figure of the people as an empty signifier that can take on radically divergent contents. What the approach seems to elide is the historical continuity of this figure.

Second, it appears that Laclau thinks either we must conceive of necessity in reductive terms, that is, of a closed historical totality, or the social dissolves completely into an infinite, deconstructive play of radical difference. This is untenable.

Third, Laclau also downplays the role of institutions in historical change and continuity. Can we understand the mechanism of articulation other than through institutions such as the state, political parties, trades unions, and the whole host of organisations and associations that comprised what Gramsci called "civil society"?

Finally, and most importantly for our purposes, the above questions are raised by the Freudian/Lacanian psychoanalysis upon which Laclau depends to ground his account of populism; in particular, to rescue populism from the "denigration of the masses" of figures like Gustav Le Bon. Laclau's engagement with Freudian social psychology, however, must be regarded as a missed opportunity, since he ignores the problem that occupies such an important role in *Group Psychology and the Analysis of the Ego* (1921c), namely the phenomenon of the regression of the group through a libidinal cathexis in the figure of the leader possessed of (real or imaginary) strength. Such an investment constitutes what Erich Fromm called an "escape from freedom".

Differentiating right and left populisms

According to David Harvey (2005), neoliberal globalisation is comprised of four processes: accumulation by dispossession; deregulation; privatisation; and an upward redistribution of wealth. Taken together, they have increased both economic insecurity and cultural anxiety via three features in particular: the creation of surplus peoples, rising global inequality, and threats to identity.

The anxiety wrought by neoliberal globalisation has created a rich and fertile ground for populist politics of both right and left. Neither Norris and Inglehart nor Laclau adequately account for such insecurity in their theorisation of populism. As we have seen, populism can be understood as a mobilising discourse that conceives of political subjectivity as comprised of "the people". Yet this figure of "the people", as Agamben (2000) has indicated, is deeply ambivalent insofar as it can be understood, both in terms of the body politic as a whole (as in the US Constitution's "We the People"), or in terms of what Rancière (2004, p. 12) calls the "part that has no part", or the dispossessed and the displaced, as in "The people united shall never be defeated", or in the Black Panthers' famous slogan: "All Power to the People".

In this dichotomy, the figure of "the people" can be understood in terms of its differential deployments by right and left, which themselves must be understood in terms of the respective enemies through which "the people" is constructed, and this is the decisive dimension of populism.

Right populism conflates "the people" with an embattled nation confronting its external enemies: Islamic terrorism, refugees, the European Commission, the International Jewish conspiracy, and so on. The left, in marked contrast, defines "the people" in relation to the social structures and institutions, for example, state and capital, that thwart its aspirations for self-determination—a construction which does not necessarily, however, preclude hospitality towards the Other.

In other words, right-wing or authoritarian populism defines the enemy in personalised terms, whereas while this is not always true, left-wing populism tends to define the enemy in terms of bearers of socio-economic structures and rarely as particular groups. The right, in a tradition stemming back to Hobbes, takes insecurity and anxiety as the necessary, unavoidable, and, indeed, perhaps even favourable product of capitalist social relations. It transforms such insecurity and anxiety into the fear of the stranger and an argument for a punitive state. In contrast, the left seeks to provide an account of the sources of such insecurity in the processes that have led to the dismantling of the welfare state, and corresponding phenomena such as "zero hours" contracts, the casualisation of labour, and generalised precarity. It then proposes transformative and egalitarian solutions to these problems. This was, of course, reflected in the ultimately ill-fated leadership of Jeremy Corbyn which emphasised that it was "for the many and not the few" as well as in Bernie Sanders' campaign for the Democratic Party's presidential nominee which stands for the majority of "working class Americans". In this, left populism presents the best possible answer to the xenophobic populism of the right.

References

Agamben, G. (2000). What is a people? In: *Means without End: Notes on Politics* (pp. 29–36). Minneapolis, MN: University of Minnesota Press.

Freud, S. (1921c). *Group Psychology and the Analysis of the Ego. S. E.*, 18. London: Hogarth.

Fromm, E. (1941). *Escape from Freedom*. New York: Farrar & Rinehart.

Hall, S. (2017). The great moving right show. In: *Selected Political Writings: The Great Moving Right Show and Other Essays* (pp. 172–186). Durham, NC: Duke University Press.

Harvey, D. (2005). *A Brief History of Neoliberalism*. Oxford: Oxford University Press.

Kraniauskas, J. (2014). Rhetorics of populism: Ernesto Laclau: 1935–2014. *Radical Philosophy, 186* (July–August): 29–37.

Laclau, E. (1977). *Politics and Ideology in Marxist Theory: Capitalism, Fascism, Populism*. London: New Left.

Laclau, E. (2005). *On Populist Reason*. London: Verso.

Laclau, E., & Mouffe, C. (1985). *Hegemony and Socialist Strategy: Towards a Radical Democratic Politics*. London: Verso, 2001.

Mudde, C. (2020). Populism in the twenty-first century: An illiberal democratic response to undemocratic liberalism. https://sas.upenn.edu/andrea-mitchell-center/cas-mudde-populism-twenty-first-century

Norris, P., & Inglehart, R. (2016). Trump, Brexit, and the rise of populism: Economic have-nots and cultural backlash (pp. 1–52). Cambridge, MA: Faculty Research Working Papers Series, John F. Kennedy School of Government, Harvard University, August.

Rancière, J. (2004). *The Politics of Aesthetics*. G. Rockhill (Trans.). New York: Continuum.

CHAPTER TWO

"Ill fares the land": reflections on *The Merchant of Venice*—a tale for modern times

Margot Waddell

> *Ill fares the land, to hastening ills a prey*
> *Where wealth accumulates and men decay.*

The title of the late Professor Tony Judt's final book could not be more apt, introducing, as it does, a powerful and persuasive treatise on present discontents. It is about the actual cost of the pursuit, both individually and collectively, of material self-interest. The title is taken from Oliver Goldsmith's poem, written in 1770, "The Deserted Village", to which I shall return.

The financial, institutional, organisational, and personal predicaments of our time are no new ones, in other words. As my own title suggests, I shall be drawing on *The Merchant of Venice* (first staged in 1605) as another tale of modern times, especially of our own particular time. At the heart of the play is a stark social and psychological polarisation: that between the raw materialism and greed of Venice's Rialto on the one hand, and the apparently reflective, generous thoughtfulness of Belmont on the other. (Belmont has, as in most of Shakespeare's comedies, the important status of being "somewhere else"—a world apart, as it were, on the shores of Illyria, for example, or Bohemia, or the Forest of Arden, or the Duke's Oak near Athens.) Among other things, this is a play about two worlds: one that knows much *about* wealth—in those days, trade routes, the market, profits, and usury; in these, about financial globalisation, internet culture, international banking, offshore tax havens, and fraud. Each lacks an internal moral compass of a kind that marks a culture of learning from emotional experience, and also one that demonstrates the difficulties of sustaining such a stance and not betraying hard-won values. In psychoanalytic terms, that very distinction is all pervasive and was especially central to the thinking of the psychoanalyst Wilfred Bion. It constitutes the contrast between knowing *about* things and knowing and learning from experience. The distinction brings to the fore Oscar Wilde's well-known insight into the characteristics of those who know the "price of everything and the value of nothing".

The mercantile opportunism and decadent values of the Rialto (it is silk and spices that the merchant, Antonio, stands to lose) are, currently, all too familiar, though perhaps less specifically identifiable in the current "language" of the globalised economy. What needs to be considered is what kind of relationships, individual and collective, support, in some, the development of the personality, the growth of the mind; what kinds engender in people the courage to be themselves and, for example, to combat decadence in the name of fair trade; in others, quite the reverse. How can the modesty of the former modify or modulate the latter? I do not think it is merely fanciful to find these themes to be as central to *The Merchant of Venice* as to our own parlous times. Nor do I find it fanciful to "to see" played out in the plot some of the themes that are central to the processes of psychic development during the adolescent years, in particular.

The themes are embedded in perennial conflicts, differently weighted and freighted: those between man as an individual and as a social animal; between the human potential for growth and development and the social, political, and cultural vagaries and necessities that impact upon that. Such is the stuff of a range of psychoanalytic thinking. Such, too, is the subject of political philosophy over the years, and such are the conflicts that are epitomised in this much misunderstood play of Shakespeare's. (The play is usually designated a "comedy" but it certainly has much in common with the "problem" plays.) It is my reading of those conflicts that I shall be exploring, along with some of Judt's insights into the plight of a society in which "the language of politics itself has been vacated of substance and meaning" (2010, p. 165).

Intrinsic to many of Shakespeare's dramatic narratives is the quest to achieve sufficient self-knowledge to ensure the future of the social fabric, whether personally, in terms of integrity, humility, love, and honour (usually represented, symbolically at least, by marriage) or, more publicly and historically, in terms of kingship and succession—as in the history plays. Usually the two are inextricable. *The Merchant of Venice* is also, importantly, about the failure, in some, of such a quest. It explores the *in*capacity to hold out against forces of, for example, greed, perversion, envy, power, prejudice, hatred, vengeance, and ignorance.

In the crudest terms, *The Merchant of Venice* addresses the relationship between internal values and principles and external societal and cultural mores, rules, and conventions. It is about internal and external reality, in other words, and the relationship between the two. It is about harmony and dissonance; love and hate; about the process of coming to know oneself and others and the difficulties of so doing; about the differentiation between kinds of knowledge—the genuinely exploratory and truth-seeking purpose of its acquisition, what Bion (1962) was to designate K, on the one hand, and the questionable use to which it can be put, on the other, -K in Bion's terms. As he was memorably to say, "You can't see the wisdom for the knowledge" (p. 46). The unifying distinctions in this series of dualities are played out in the polarised cultures of Belmont and Venice. The former is a culture of thought and what the psychoanalyst Donald Meltzer (1988) called "aesthetic reciprocity", the latter of action, of bartering, dealing, gambling, and chancing. As J. S. Mill so wisely put it: "No great improvements in the lot of mankind are possible, until a great change takes place in the fundamental constitution of their modes of thought" (quoted in Judt, 2010, p. 151).

One of my focuses will be on the shape and form of the adolescent process as represented in the play. Although there was no conception of "adolescence", as such, in Elizabethan times, the prerequisites for, and the nature of, the transition from parental authority to sexual and coupled maturity lies at the heart of many of Shakespeare's plays, engaging as they so often do with the meaning of that "maturity" and with the move, at whatever age or stage, towards adulthood. This is a move, if not blighted by adverse forces from within and without, that can be described in terms of the development of inner capacities, be they for separation, marriage, for selfhood, kingship, succession, or, more generally, for valued contributions to the common weal.

Although growing up is a lifelong process, what is involved in that process is intensified, perhaps even caricatured, certainly epitomised, during the adolescent years. There is a chronic and contradictory pull, both personal and cultural, between progression and regression. Yet such "pulls" may not be as contradictory as they can seem. For the catastrophic anxiety that attends any development in the personality is inevitably also related to the painful relinquishment of aspects of the self that need to be left behind in order to move on, developmentally. It involves the capacity to explore, or to get to know, aspects of that self which may, hitherto, have been felt to characterise other people, and to find a way of accommodating them in the increasingly, though perhaps resistantly, "known" personality.

What all of us encounter in the course of growing up is a fundamental, both institutional and personal, resistance to change, however awful the status quo may be felt to be. I am exploring the interplay of factors that both promote and prevent change. I am seeking to link the action of *The Merchant of Venice* to all ordinary attempts to hold out for what might be termed one's "best self", attempts that are based in coming to know oneself and others (Bion's K), under the guidance of what I would describe in terms of Keats' "thinking principle" (also invoked by Bion), here represented by Portia. This is a thinking principle that is neither perfect, nor static, but willing (up to a point) to "work and to be wrought upon" (Keats, "*Ode to Psyche*"). *The Merchant of Venice* is a narrative of love and hate, of cultural prejudice, of gain and loss. A crucial question is that of the relationship between adolescent development as understood psychoanalytically and the nature of political, economic, and cultural reality; of group functioning and collective and organisational thinking and practice, secondary and tertiary education in particular. Psychoanalytic theory gathers up, and draws upon, insights that have found poetic form, indeed, artistic form more generally, and have been expressed in literary terms over the centuries, as is so clear in "The Deserted Village". What can we, in these exceedingly parlous days, *learn* from this play and from thinking, from a psychoanalytic stance, about ourselves in relation to it?

Another significant aspect of the comedies is that they explore issues that need to be resolved before the kind of marriage that betokens growth and development can come about—one that symbolically offers some sense, albeit imperfect, of birth and renewal. Can the necessary conditions for faith in the future be safeguarded? How can that future be established, or, in the current climate, be refound and promoted? *The Merchant of Venice* has much to say, as does Judt himself, about the necessary conditions for such faith, about the ongoing march of society and how that can be re-established. Pre-eminently, the play has much to convey about prejudice and racism, both overt and covert. As Judt says, drawing on Pope John Paul II, "Humans need a language in which to express their moral instincts" (p. 180). With integration and self-knowledge as common goals, psychoanalytic practice and artistic expression share a number of congruencies. They go some way to providing such a language "… we need to ascribe meaning to our actions in a way that transcends them" (p. 180). One aim of the psychoanalytic way of thinking could be described as seeking to make available to the patient, client, or organisation more and more aspects of the self, whether in group or in individual modes of functioning; or for the artist, the parent, the teacher, the sociologist, or the moral philosopher, the seeker after truth.

Yet any such task occurs in a particular culture and in a particular climate of thought. The effort, for example, to establish true values, as opposed to counterfeit ones, is especially hard in a setting where external appearance, the trappings of wealth, of luxury and of power, and, currently, of "fake news", celebrity, lies, and corruption, have influence and their domination holds sway. This is all too evident in social and political terms, but individually too, these forces threaten internal values of truth, of meaning, and the capacity to think for oneself.

Here are the opening lines of the play:

> Antonio: In sooth I know not why I am so sad,
> It wearies me, you say it wearies you;
> But how I caught it, found it, or came by it,
> What stuff 'tis made of, whereof it is born,
> I am to learn:
> And such a want-wit sadness makes of me,
> That I have much ado to know myself. (ll.1–7)

Thus speaks the eponymous Merchant of Venice—"I am to learn. ... I have much ado to know myself." In the course of the play, the audience learn extensively about the complacent, primitive, vengeful, infantile, and increasingly reactive aspects of human nature that Shakespeare describes, ones that we are assaulted with on a daily basis, whether personally, politically, or professionally. We learn about the propensity to disown and find in others attitudes, thoughts, and feelings that do not sit comfortably with preferred self-conceptions (the psychoanalyst Melanie Klein called this "projective identification"). At first, Antonio seems to believe himself (we might venture omnipotently), to be totally "insured" against any experience of loss. This is expressed by his friends', also denizens of the Rialto, suggestion that he is anxious about the trading vessels, or, perhaps, anxious about love. He just finds himself mysteriously depressed. The threatening allusion is to how a wealthy, proud ship, laden with the luxury goods of the dominant mercantile world, can possibly become "worth nothing". "All his fortunes are at sea." But it is his emotions, too, that are imperilled: the potential wreck or wrack is also a personal issue of being completely "at sea". In Antonio's case, this is in terms of his passion for the young, and, at this stage, careless, risk-taking Bassanio. Yet, as W. H. Auden (1962), looking back on the whole play, puts it:

> It occurs to us that we have seen two characters do this, [hazard all he hath], Shylock, however unintentionally, did, in fact, hazard all for the sake of destroying the enemy he hated, and Antonio, however unthinkingly he signed the bond, hazarded all to secure the happiness of the friend he loved. Yet it is precisely these two who cannot enter Belmont. Belmont would like us to believe that men and women are either good or bad by nature, but Shylock and Antonio remind us that this is an illusion: in the real world, no hatred is totally without justification, no love totally innocent ... (p. 154)

And this is a lesson that everyone, but Portia in particular, has yet to learn.

Commenting on usury, Auden points out that:

> Like prostitution, usury may corrupt the character, but those who borrow upon usury, like those who visit brothels, have *their* share

of responsibility for this corruption and aggravate their guilt by
showing contempt for those whose services they make use of.
As he says, the commodities with which the Venetian merchant
deals are not necessities, but luxury goods, governed by social
prestige—there is no question of a Just Price. (p. 152)

In the world of pyramid lending, hedge funds and international turmoil, the question of a "just price" has not, until recently, been on the
agenda. In the *Merchant of Venice* the nature of such deals is, essentially,
the main axis of the Christian/Jew theme in which, as the play proceeds,
the similarities between the Christian, Antonio and the Jew, Shylock
become increasingly striking. This highly emotive and, apparently, ever
more polarised racial issue represents matters of internal conflict as well
as external political and religious controversy. It also, even now, functions as the repository for so much else. Painful feelings—for example,
of envy, of jealousy, of hatred, and of desire for revenge—are shown to be
easily locatable in others, and they stir in the individual the impulse to
persecute them there, rather than to learn about them in the self.

This is the stuff, the daily bread, of contemporary social-political
life. Here we come to know the wisecrack and the bully mentality—a
modern, political, version being, perhaps, a "flip flop" stance of assuring
one thing and doing the opposite. Through the play, we come to learn
about the need to find scapegoats; about the difficulty of acknowledging
and tolerating these unacceptable characteristics and about the necessity of so doing. We learn about the danger of believing our own stories
and vilifying anyone who does not share them. We learn much about
the sadomasochistic bind; we also learn much about those who would
always rather mock and persecute someone else than take in, or take
on, the true measure of their own anxiety and sense of social exclusion;
or about those who would rather "talk dirty" than engage with genuine pain; about those who feel so wronged and persecuted, abused and
bereft, that all they can do, in an attempt to assuage such humiliation,
is to inflict it on others (Shylock)—and this only eventually, after, in his
case, the unspeakably bitter loss of his daughter, Jessica. For Jessica has
eloped, to Shylock's absolute horror and devastation, with the Christian,
Lorenzo. She takes with her not just considerable amounts of her father's
money, but the precious ring given to him by his beloved late wife, Leah.
It is this concatenation of losses that converts the "principle" of the bond

into a deadly serious actuality—a life and death issue of what amounts to ritual murder.

We learn, too, about those who need to enact their adolescent rebellions before they are, belatedly, able to take in something of an adult sense of responsibility and an awareness of truth and beauty (Lorenzo and Jessica). This couple, in Portia's absence, are left in charge of Belmont, entrusted to care for it, even to "husband" it, and to learn from the experience of so doing. That is, in the course of the play, the couple learn to discriminate between their adolescent/infantile, prodigal, and cruel selves, and some much deeper and more harmonious capacity to acknowledge the wonder and modesty of genuine love. Their earlier crudity and cruelty have become transformed into the beautiful poetry of a declaration of their mutual love:

> The moon shines bright. In such a night as this,
> When the sweet wind did gently kiss the trees
> And they did make no noise, in such a night … (V, I, 1–3)

This capacity is so far from that which is carried on the "strumpet wind", that of the chancer mentality of Antonio's limited knowledge of himself, or, at this point, of the world.

Later on, in the trial scene, as the complexities and the questionable devices of Portia (now disguised as a young male advocate) make clear, it becomes evident that the road to wisdom is in no sense a straight one. Even she has to encounter in herself, as well as in the cut and thrust of realpolitik, unexpected emotional realities: those of the ugliness of jealousy, the fear of loss of face as well as of goods, and the possibility of anticipated abandonment and betrayal. She had not expected the pain and harshness of such feelings, ones which confronted her with the necessity of "thinking under fire" (in Bion's terminology). Having been brought up in the harmonious setting of Belmont, far from the tough realities of the Rialto, she had not experienced such feelings in herself before, nor had she had to draw on methods—the silver-tongued sophistry of the clever lawyer—which, hitherto, she had neither registered nor needed.

But more: to the internal consideration had to be added serious external ones—those of the maintenance of the economic and social fabric of the city state. An often missed detail is that of how Portia spends the time between the trial scene and her return from Venice to Belmont. She wanders with her "waiting woman" Nerissa, we are told, among holy crosses where she kneels and prays, "for happy wedlock hours" (V, i, L, 32), accompanied by a holy hermit. Perhaps this attests to her need to reflect on the relationship between the public events of the cross-dressed Balthazar version of herself and the private reality of her love for Bassanio. As so often in Shakespeare, despite formal marriage, this relationship is still unconsummated. There remain elements, in terms of trust and commitment, as yet unresolved on either side. Before any such commitment can be made, Portia needs to let Bassanio go to Antonio to establish the status and meaning of their relationship, just as she needs to commune with herself about the significance of the internal and external events of the world in which she now finds herself. One wonders too, in the light of the leaden casket signifying death, whether the facing of that ultimate dimension of things is also a necessary component of maturity—not so much, these days, in terms of denial of ageing, as of the acceptance of death as part of the life cycle. Portia's father's will had stipulated that her future husband be he who rightly chooses among the three caskets, that is, the one that contains her own portrait—neither golden, nor silver, but leaden.

There is a certain something that underlies Portia's role in the play and which finds expression in her relationship with Nerissa—a something that psychoanalysts find very difficult to pin down, but one that also pervades a true analytic relationship. It is this: it may slowly become possible for one person to take in and to think about those very issues or contradictions that have hitherto been felt, consciously or unconsciously, to be impossible to engage with, or indeed, may not even have been known about. The process was designated by Meltzer (1978) as "the most important and most mysterious concept in psychoanalysis"—introjective identification (p. 459). For example, it is possible with one part of the self to betray that to which, with another part, one feels oneself to be utterly committed. Bassanio and Gratiano are tricked/persuaded by Balthazar/Portia and Nerissa to give away the rings that the young women had entrusted to their new husbands. But Portia and Nerissa come to see the wisdom of Portia's father's will. In the process, they grow up from being boisterous girls to being capable of a true marriage; from being able to understand not just flirtation and infatuation also passion and commitment. After all, they go through a great deal together in the course of the play, and much can be learned about their mutual development as the swift repartee of the early prose blossoms, towards the end, into the beauty of the poetry of their respectively deepened perceptions and pledges.

What may, this being comedy, look like some kind of merely manipulative testing of Bassanio and Gratiano (the issue of giving away the rings) can, in fact, represent a serious test of commitment, which, at this point, both young men fail. Shakespeare seems to be suggesting something of the awesome nature of the true *internal* commitment that needs to be made and how hard it is to develop such a capacity, and, in turn, what an impact it might have on the public weal; the values of Belmont possibly moderating the Rialto.

The allusion made earlier to a narrative of love and hate, of gain and loss engages with something that is repeatedly found at the heart of the psychoanalytic relationship, and is enshrined in its practice. Yet, Bion's early work notwithstanding, the thinking has tended to be limited by being held within the consulting room and its "internal world" focus. It needs further to be widened to embrace the social, political, and cultural setting more explicitly. This is something that Bion himself always wanted to return to and which seems so pressing, indeed crucial, in current times.

The Merchant of Venice explores, powerfully and inescapably, different kinds of loss and the nature of their impact, both personally and societally. Among these losses are the wreck of Antonio's ships, of Bassanio's and Antonio's special relationship, of Shylock's devotion for his daughter, Jessica, and, ultimately and drastically, the threat of the loss of the merchant Antonio's life. In the internal world, then, this play does present a life and death issue—the conflict of those elements that are on the side of personal and collective psychic life or, by contrast, that of death, both actual and symbolic. In the play, these become life and death issues, but, in Shakespeare, they also, metaphorically, represent the life of the mind and its all too possible slow and incremental demise. It represents, too, the life of a society—one that might manage to be prosperous without becoming decadent. Its demise, here, lies in the danger of wholly succumbing to the values of the Rialto, a culture, as already noted, dedicated to outward show where, indeed, "wealth accumulates and men decay"; a culture also dedicated to an investment in economic risk, one that, as becomes so clear in the trial scene, is willing to collude with whatever is deemed legally "necessary" to uphold trading relations with the rest of the mercantile world. This is by contrast with the empire of the "soul", one that is dedicated to those inner principles that Portia, with her better self, seeks to uphold, despite finding herself in so complex and compromising a position, a position of which the trial scene is so powerful an emblem. Initially it was Antonio's body that was forfeit. In the end, as he so clearly states, it is his soul:

> … I once did lend my body for his wealth …
> I dare be bound again
> My soul upon the forfeit. (V, ii, 249–253)

This contrast between the Merchant at the beginning and at the end of the play is a central theme: some of the characters, through their contact with what is represented by Portia and Belmont, *do*, like Portia herself, eventually learn something crucial about themselves, a shift *does* occur from a predominantly –K frame of mind to a K one. For Belmont favours those states in which emotions, genuinely undergone, can, despite resistance, be known and thought about truthfully—especially those of mercy, grace, and forgiveness. Some characters become truly capable of gratitude and sincerity, if only in the last Act. The play engages, then, with the possibilities of putting a cycle of competition and revenge to rest. If this is to be done at all, it is to be through internal changes of a kind that bear on external relationships.

The Merchant of Venice takes on some of the ugliest aspects of human nature—the most primitive, ignorant, prejudiced, and vengeful—and makes it clear that those very aspects have to be recognised and are, on some level, present and active in even the most apparently acceptable aspects of human nature and discourse more generally. They have to be faced, recognised, and owned if there is to be any fruitful integration of a constructive rather than a destructive kind. What *appears* to be so polarised—the values of a notional Belmont versus those of, all too real, Venice; what the Jew versus the Christian stands for—become, as the play proceeds, but different aspects of one and the same and, as Auden (1963) points out, the attraction to Belmont is *also* questionable. The apparent polarisations do not stand up to scrutiny. They can slide into a kind of reflexivity, the one of the other.

There is a sense that those internally repudiated and split-off parts of the self have to be faced for what they are before any honest union can occur, and this is true for almost every character in the play. Indeed, the play can, as so often, be thought of in terms of a collection of parts (the characters) of the whole (the drama). The action challenges and regroups the parts towards, or in the name of, a reasonably good outcome. But for some the cost is very high. In psychoanalytic terms it could be argued that the form of the play itself "contains" (in the sense of having the capacity to hold multiple, painful, heightened emotional states) a collective and symbolic representation of deep and enduringly conflictual and contradictory states of mind: those embodied by the various characters.

It could also be argued that the plot encompasses an extreme version of "splitting" between good and bad and the "projection" of that good or bad into cultural, religious, or personal representations. Yet it is, at the same time, about introjection—introjection of a specific kind: for example, that of the legacy of the older generation to the younger. What, in the end, *does* Portia's father bequeath to her—internally rather than externally? What *does* Antonio, in the end, bequeath to the lovers, to Jessica and Lorenzo, in such contrast to his original, unthinking, even compulsive and misguided generosity to Bassanio? Belmont takes him to his uttermost. When the text is perused with some care, the goodies-and-baddies divide collapses and something much subtler, in terms of the difficulty of coming to know oneself, slowly becomes established. This is precisely where the play begins. As we saw, the eponymous Merchant states that he neither knows nor understands himself. He is, simply, depressed.

> In sooth I know not why I am so sad,
> It wearies me, you say it wearies you;
> But how I caught, found it, or came by it,
> What stuff 'tis made of, whereof it is born,
> I am to learn:
> And such a want-wit sadness makes of me,
> That I have much ado to know myself.

There could be no more clear a statement of the main theme of the play—it is that of self-knowledge, of links in K of a kind that have to take account of the most infantile and destructive aspects of the personality in order to establish any basis for a social and political future which is founded upon principles and values rather than on outward show, in however subtle, but also crude, terms, legally, theologically, and deceitfully, that show is represented. A tale for modern times, indeed.

As Shakespeare so often makes clear, much rests, personally and socially, on the nature of the parental example, and of their legacy to the younger generation. The contrast may be between the authoritarian, repressive or target-driven, on the one hand, or, on the other, the authoritative and the growth-promoting. It may be between mindless indulgence and the necessity of keeping reasonable boundaries. Such dualities pervade *The Merchant of Venice*. To touch on but one: it could certainly be argued that the legacy of Portia's father does not necessarily represent the dead hand of tyrannical control beyond the grave, as initially seems to be the case. It represents, rather, some process whereby Portia slowly takes on, or takes in, values that, in terms of the play as a whole, would be those of genuine love, rather than of show; the struggle for truthfulness in the internal world rather than the taste for glitz in the external; of the humility of a recognition that the high moral ground is not her exclusive territory, by contrast with the phallic swagger of male arrogance. All these aspects suggest precisely what is epitomised, as already suggested, by the leaden casket. Lead is associated with death, that is, with the modesty and maturity to recognise the nature and meaning of the whole life cycle. Eventual death must be accepted, must be chosen even.

In *The Psychopathology of Everyday Life* (1901b), Freud approvingly quotes Otto Rank's description of how Portia is wracked in conflict by the fact that she wishes Bassanio to know that she loves him but is bound by her loyalty to her father to abide by his will in accepting whichever lover chooses the right casket. She inadvertently gives the game away. Despite herself, she *does* say which suitor it is whom she favours. That is, the "slip" both has meaning and is self-revealing.

> I pray you tarry, pause a day or two,
> Before you hazard, for in choosing wrong

> I lose your company; therefore, forbear awhile,—
> There's something tells me (but it is not love)
> I would not lose you …
> … I could teach you
> How to choose right, but then I am forsworn,
> So will I never be, so may you miss you,—
> But if you do, you'll make me wish a sin,
> That I had been forsworn. Beshrew your eyes,
> They have o'erlook'd me, and divided me,
> One half of me is yours, the other half, yours,
> Mine own, I would say: but if mine then yours,
> And so all yours. (III, ii, ll.1–17)

Rank comments (as quoted in Freud):

> The thing of which she wanted to give him only a very subtle
> hint, because she should have concealed it from him altogether,
> namely that even before he made his choice she was *wholly* his
> and loved him—it is precisely this that the poet, with a wonder-
> ful psychological sensitivity, causes to break through openly in
> her slip of the tongue; and by this artistic device he succeeds in
> relieving both the lover's unbearable uncertainty and the sus-
> pense of the sympathetic audience over the outcome of his choice.
> (1901b, p. 98)

To return, in conclusion, to "The Deserted Village" and the unspeakable current burden, though differently sourced, on the poor of a crushing fiscal legacy; the loss, for so many, of the wherewithal to support a
decent life. Goldsmith, towards the end of the poem, picks up a now
altered, even darker, note:

> Thus fares the land, by luxury betrayed …

The parental role of good government and governance has failed its
subjects. We need to return, too, to Judt's concluding words in this his
last book—a kind of rallying cry, so clearly articulating his objection to

what is going on in these modern times and urging all to look critically at our world and how we live. He quotes Tolstoy, so aptly expressing the passivity that characterises the status quo: "[T]here are no conditions of life to which a man cannot get accustomed, especially if he sees them accepted by everyone around him" (2010, p. 237). What a challenge to us all. As Judt, echoing that, so rightly stated, philosophers have hitherto only interpreted the world in various ways; the point is to change it. But the point is also the one that Upton Sinclair makes: that it is difficult to get a man to understand something when his salary depends on his not understanding it (2010, p. 168).

Most who are trying to combine thinking and doing will know about the hazards of the developmental path; about the uneven balance between progression and regression, whether personally or institutionally, between social and political advance or collapse. It is in this sense that *The Merchant of Venice* is a tale for all times and certainly for our own.

As Oliver Goldsmith knew, the power of poetry can reach the depths of what, propositionally, can be very hard to think about. So, the last words of this tangled tale must be Portia's. For it is she who delivers one of the most compelling speeches about human values and their betrayal ever uttered or penned. She is speaking of "just mercy", to draw on the title of B. Stevenson's (2015) story of justice and redemption. Portia stirringly draws the crucial distinction between law and justice, a distinction that must never be blurred or overlooked.

> The quality of mercy is not strain'd,
> It droppeth as the gentle rain from heaven
> Upon the place beneath: it is twice blest,
> It blesseth him that gives, and him that takes,
> 'Tis mightiest in the mightiest, it becomes
> The throned monarch better than his crown.
> …
> Though justice be thy plea, consider this,
> That in the course of justice, none of us
> Should see salvation: we do pray for mercy,
> And that same prayer, doth teach us all to render
> The *deeds* of mercy. (V, i, ll. 130–198)

References

Auden, W. H. (1963). *The Dyer's Hand and Other Essays*. London: Faber & Faber.

Bion, W. R. (1962). *Learning from Experience*. London: Heinemann.

Freud, S. (1901b). *The Psychopathology of Everyday Life. S. E., 6*. London: Hogarth.

Freud, S. (1916–17). *Introductory Lectures on Psycho-Analysis. S. E., 15–16*. London: Hogarth.

Goldsmith, O. (1770). The deserted village. Reprinted London: Simpson Low, Son & Co, 1861. A Note on Introjective Processes

Judt, T. (2010). *Ill Fares the Land. A Treatise on Our Present Discontents*. London: Allen Lane.

Keats, J. (1988). *John Keats. The Complete Poems*. London: Penguin Classics.

Meltzer, D. (1978). A note on introjective processes. In: A. Hahn (Ed.), *Sincerity and Other Works*. London: Karnac, 1994.

Meltzer, D. (1988). *The Apprehension of Beauty: the Role of Aesthetic Conflict in Development, Art and Violence*. Strathtay, UK: Clunie Press.

Shakespeare, W. (1605). *The Merchant of Venice*. The Arden Shakespeare. London: Routledge, 2000.

Stevenson, B. (2015). *Just Mercy: A Story of Justice and Redemption*. London: Scribe UK.

CHAPTER THREE

Psychoanalysis, colonialism, racism

Stephen Frosh

The ambiguities of psychoanalysis

Relationships between psychology and post-colonial theory are mediated in a variety of ways, most of them uncomfortable. This discomfort is produced by a mixture of criticism and what one might call a kind of studied blindness that produces a blank, uncomprehending hostility. The general direction of criticism has been from post-colonial theory to psychology; the converse, a psychological engagement with post-colonialism, is relatively rare, given the stance of apolitical naivety that academic psychology commonly adopts. "What has this to do with us?" is perhaps the most predictable response to questions about what psychology might have to say about, and how it might be implicated in, colonialist discourse. This is despite the existence of some contemporary writing from within psychology that shows exactly what it "has to do with us". This writing refers both to the damage psychology perpetrates and the strands within it that might fill out the post-colonial critique of power by articulating the contribution of mental states to the perpetuation of colonial culture and, conversely, the impact of such culture on the construction of the psychological—and hence social—subject (e.g., Hook, 2012). In this regard, it is ironic that one of the founding texts of post-colonial theory, Frantz Fanon's (1952) *Black Skin, White Masks*, is explicitly psychological in its interests, centring on how colonialism "enters the skin" of its subjects. Paralleling this, some of the most vituperative disputes in the history of psychology can be seen as struggles reflecting the emergence of post-colonial perspectives—notably the battles over "race and IQ" that split Western university campuses in the 1970s and always threaten to recur (e.g., Gould, 1996; Rose, Kamin, & Lewontin, 1984). At a more general level, it can perhaps be claimed that psychology and post-colonial theory need each other. Psychology needs post-colonialism quite patently, because without the challenge of post-colonial thinking it drifts into ahistorical and highly abstracted models of the mind that fail to theorise their temporal and spatial components. Post-colonialism needs psychology more subtly, because without some kind of effective psychological input it essentialises the socio-historical and is left grasping for a theory of the subject that attends to its complex affective and fantasmatic life. This means that the failures of connection between the disciplines impoverishes both; more to the point, it results in a theory of the subject that is either asocial, or that neglects the agentic possibilities for resistance and change.

When post-colonial studies and psychological theory have engaged with one another, it has most often been through psychoanalysis (e.g., Khanna, 2004). This is an especially complex situation, because of the controversial position psychoanalysis holds not only within post-colonial thought, but also in psychology. Denounced by most psychologists for the way it takes speculative licence with evidence and for its lack of scientific credentials, it has become attractive to some critical social psychologists and, especially, to those advancing the new "sub-discipline" or trans-disciplinary apparatus of psychosocial studies (Frosh & Baraitser, 2008). This is partly because of the status of psychoanalysis as an outsider to, and hence critic of, mainstream academic psychology; but it is also more substantively because in focusing on subjectivity and the agency of unconscious life, it creates an opportunity for considering how the human subject is not self-contained but is permeated by forces that it cannot necessarily understand or control. This means that although psychoanalysis has tended to concentrate on "internal" forces, it provides an opportunity to consider the social "saturation" of the subject;

or, put another way, it gives leverage to theories that deal with the formation of the human as a social subject. Psychoanalysis has been quite widely deployed in this way in some major social theories and has been advanced by international figures such as Judith Butler (2005) and Slavoj Žižek (2006)—the former drawing on Laplanchian ideas about the penetration of the subject by the other; the latter perhaps the prime proselytiser for certain forms (Žižekian ones, we might say) of Lacanianism. Whatever the reasons, the situation remains that psychoanalysis, aberrant relative of psychology that it might be, occupies a productive space in the current panoply of trans-disciplinary critical materials for intellectual study (Frosh, 2010) and that this is part of its appeal for post-colonial theorists.

This chapter explores the prospects for a psychological contribution to post-colonial thought through the mediation of psychoanalysis. It does not attempt to deconstruct or historicise post-colonialism itself, at least to any significant extent, further than to state the need for a post-colonial theory of the subject that incorporates an understanding of affective and "subjective" issues—precisely the area with which psychoanalysis is primarily concerned. The positioning of psychoanalysis as a progressive, critical approach is not, however, a particularly secure one. The central difficulty is the way psychoanalysis has frequently aligned itself with conformist and even "repressive" tendencies that reproduce colonial and at times racist tropes, often in the context of psychological individualism, but sometimes in an explicitly political manner (Frosh, 1999; Jacoby, 1983). This is despite the existence of a contrary urge in psychoanalysis, especially reflected in the "critical theory" tradition that made use of it in the 1950s and 1960s (e.g., Marcuse, 1955) but also in the work of several followers of Lacan (Stavrakakis, 2007) and some British social reformists (Rustin, 1991). The tendency of American ego psychology to give prominence to "adaptationist" perspectives has been widely noted and has been criticised both by political radicals (e.g., Jacoby, 1975, 1983) and by Lacanians (cf. Roudinesco, 1990, p. 175: "According to [Lacan] such a psychological science had been affected by the ideals of the society in which it was produced"). The adoption of a strong anti-homosexual bias by orthodox mid-twentieth-century psychoanalysts has had particularly damaging consequences for the practice and reputation of psychoanalysis as a whole, even though recent attempts to reconcile psychoanalysis and queer theory are beginning to bear fruit (Campbell, 2000; Frosh, 2006). Psychoanalytic assumptions about the nature of a civilised mind will be briefly discussed below; but overt forms of racism, notably anti-Semitism, have also on occasions been evident in its institutional practices (Frosh, 2005, 2012). Most relevantly, colonialism is a deeply problematic issue for psychoanalysis, because it is engrained in much psychoanalytic thinking and terminology, and this has effects on contemporary theory and practice in ways that are not always recognised. For example, as discussed further below, psychoanalysts often draw on the language of the "primitive" to refer to unreasoning elements of people's psychic lives. Thus, a notion that someone might be evincing a "primitive fantasy of destruction" is a very familiar one, but what is not acknowledged is that this terminology not only has its roots in a colonial opposition between primitive and civilised, but it also reproduces this division "unconsciously" when it is used. This is to say, the terminology is full of associations that position some ideas as civilised and some as primitive, reinforcing a developmental scheme that is heavily inflected by assumptions about the relationship between seemingly irrational and rational thought processes—and in particular who might "own" them.

The history of this stretches back to the beginnings of psychoanalysis, reflecting the colonial and racist (including anti-Semitic) assumptions prevalent in the Europe out of which psychoanalysis arose. Freud deployed the idea that the thinking of what he called "savages" was not only contrasted to "civilised" mentality, but also revealed the origins of mental life both for the culture as a whole (the contemporary savage being a throwback to the precursors of modern "man") and for the individual (the savage mind being like that of a child). For example, at the beginning of *Totem and Taboo*, subtitled "Some Points of Agreement between the Mental Lives of Savages and Neurotics", he wrote,

> There are men still living who, as we believe, stand very near to primitive man, far nearer than we do, and whom we therefore regard as his direct heirs and representatives. Such is our view of those whom we describe as savages or half-savages; and their mental life must have a peculiar interest for us if we are right in seeing in it a well-preserved picture of an early stage of our own development. (Freud, 1912–13, p. 1)

The repetitive first person plural pronoun is notable here: "we believe", "we do", "we regard", "our view", "we describe", "us", "our own development". The savage is the other, the not "us"; though as will be outlined briefly below, there is quite a degree of subtlety in what this might mean. Freud also was explicit about how "savages" share attributes with children, both in terms of how they think, and how they are thought about by "we adults". "It seems to me quite possible", he wrote (p. 99), "that the same may be true of our attitude toward the psychology of those races that have remained at the animistic level as is true of our attitude toward the mental life of children, which we adults no longer understand and whose fullness and delicacy of feeling we have in consequence so greatly underestimated."

The adoption of a binary between savage and civilised is not perhaps intrinsically racist and colonialist, but the assumption that the latter always displaces the former and, more importantly, that the terms can be applied to different people, is. In Freud's thought, savage societies hold to various types of irrational thinking (concreteness, mystical attitudes to death, etc.), processes reviewed throughout *Totem and Taboo* (Freud, 1912–13) and explicitly linked with children in more "civilised" societies. For instance, in writing of wish fulfilment (p. 84), Freud commented,

> If children and primitive men find play and imitative representation enough for them, that is not a sign of their being unassuming in our sense or of their resignedly accepting their actual impotence. It is the easily understandable result of the paramount virtue they ascribe to their wishes, of the will that is associated with those wishes and of the methods by which those wishes operate.

These ways of thinking make them "primitive" in the developmental sense that they should normatively be overcome by more advanced modes of being—a theme also taken up in the analysis of religion in *The Future of an Illusion* (Freud, 1927c). Although Freud himself does not press for political action that does this—he was interested rather in how science might overcome superstition—the general approach is consistent with the justification of colonialism and even slavery on the grounds of the inherent inferiority of the primitive. There is another subtle turn here, however, that is specific to Freud and the early history of psychoanalysis, relating to the intense anti-Semitism of Freud's time. Gilman (1993) showed how deeply rooted anti-Semitism was in the beliefs of many Europeans, markedly so in the Viennese among whom psychoanalysis grew up, and how widespread were ideas such as that Jews were castrated (hence, feminine), that they were "oriental" and maybe even "black", and that they were primitive not only in the religious sense (Christianity having displaced Judaism) but also psychologically, socially, and racially. Gilman suggested that Freud, consciously or unconsciously, constructed some of the most conspicuously radical elements of his theory in response to this. For instance, Gilman argued that the trope that Jewish men are castrated through circumcision is replaced in psychoanalysis by the idea that the castration complex is universal, so that all people—including the most gentile—follow a model set by the Jews. This Freudian impulse to disarm anti-Semitism by positioning the Jews as the truly civilised people (which was mirrored in the idea that as nationalism took hold in Europe at the end of the nineteenth century, the Jews might be the only "true Europeans" oriented towards a transnational comity) results in a shifting of the "other" of European society away from the Jew and towards the "savage", that is, the colonised, black "primitive" of slavery and the European imagination. This theoretical move attempts to relieve Jews from the opprobrium of primitivity (unsuccessfully, as was demonstrated unequivocally just a few years later) by passing it onto the colonised other.

There is always a danger with summary accounts such as this one, that the history it sketches simplistically reduces a tension-filled and ambiguous process to a linear narrative. It is certainly the case, for example, that psychoanalysis was from the start full of impulses that challenged and subverted the assumptions of the societies in which it found itself. Indeed, this is one reason for the mixture of explosive embrace and resistance that characterised the response to psychoanalysis: on the one hand, it fuelled enormous shifts in self-perception, artistic creativity, and even political and economic thought (not confined to outspoken radicals—see, for example, John Maynard Keynes' (1919, 1936) post-World War I use of Freudian ideas to argue for the importance of emotional factors in economics). In many respects, it is precisely in the tension between what Toril Moi (1989, p. 197) called, in relation to the attitude of psychoanalysis to femininity, Freud's "colonizing impulse"

and its contrary acceptance of "the logic of another scene"—the specific expressiveness of unconscious life—that the creativity of psychoanalysis inheres. Nevertheless, consideration of the rootedness of much
psychoanalytic thought in colonial assumptions is important not merely
to sweep away the ideological detritus, but also to identify where the
investments of psychoanalysis can provide leverage for understanding
the place of psychosocial theory in the post-colonial project.

A further example of the "detritus" might be found in some work by
Celia Brickman (2003), which offers an extensive account of how the
language of primitivity infects psychoanalysis. Like Gilman, she notes
how Freud's "universalizing reconfigurations" (p. 165) turn the despised
Jewish body into the model for humanity as a whole. From the perspective of post-colonialism, however, this move, which is subversive in relation to anti-Semitism, is "made at considerable expense", because "the
modalities of inferiority previously ascribed to the Jews did not simply disappear but were ambivalently displaced onto a series of abjected
others: primitives, women and homosexuals". Brickman elaborated on
how the assimilation of the Jewish other to Europeanism positions psychoanalysis as a colonialist discipline and incorporates racism into its
fabric of argumentation.

> Categorised as a member of a primitive race, Freud repudiated
> primitivity, locating himself and his work within European civili-
> sation, with both its scientific and colonising enterprises, and
> replacing the opposition of Aryan/Jew with the opposition of
> civilised/primitive. (p. 167)

In relation to psychoanalytic practice, primitive usually means either or
both of fundamental and irrational. A primitive impulse is never a rational one; it always arises unmediated from the unconscious and hence
has not been worked over by the secondary processes of thought. The
sleight of hand then is to link this kind of primitivity with the irrationality of the colonised other and then to make rationality itself the marker
of civilised human society—or even of what it means to be human at all.
After all, when one loses one's power of reason, one ceases to be able to
function as human at least to the degree that equal citizenship is at risk.
In the colonial context, this justifies colonisation: irrational primitives

cannot be trusted to run their own affairs; the civilised European is justifiably superior, for everyone's good. Commenting on Freud's anthropological speculation, Brickman (2003) noted how the psyche comes to be envisaged as a representation of colonialism and hence how Freud explicitly parallels the structure of the mind with that of (colonial) society:

> [By] correlating the progression of narcissism, the oedipal stage, and maturity with animism (savagery), religion (barbarianism), and science (civilisation), *Totem and Taboo* transposed the racial assumptions of the cultural evolutionary scale onto the modern psyche ... The psychoanalytically conceived norm of mature subjectivity was, by virtue of the correlation of libidinal development with the cultural evolutionary scale, a rationalism whose unstated colour was white, just as its unstated gender was male. (p. 72)

Even though these Freudian assumptions are mainly unstated, the terminology and the conceptual baggage of the "savage" and the barbarian remained with psychoanalysis for some time and is still lying only just-dormant in those references to "primitive feelings" that often can be found in clinical psychoanalytic discussions. A certain mode of rationality is given priority here, which is attached to masculine "reason" as it has developed over the period of industrial modernity (Frosh, 1994). That which falls short of it—the "unreason" attributed to women, children, and primitive cultures—is derogated and made subject to reason's imperialism. This is not, of course, to imply that one should fully affirm unreason as a simple alternative to colonial reason; it is rather to claim that the reason–unreason opposition is itself rooted in a colonial mentality that supports it and narrows the range of what is culturally validated. In a similar vein, Neil Altman (2000, p. 591) commented, "When Freud the ego psychologist said, 'Where id was, there ego shall be,' he defined the goals of psychoanalysis in terms reminiscent of the colonial mentality. In this sense, the structure of racism is built into structural psychoanalytic theory, particularly in its ego-psychological form." This claim is itself resonant of the critique of ego psychology mentioned earlier. The argument runs that because this form of psychoanalysis assumes reason to be superior to unreason, its concurrent assumption that unreason is characteristic of "primitives" means that it is promoting a colonising process (reason trumping unreason; civilised displacing primitive) that is embedded in a racist paradigm. As an instructive aside, it is perhaps worth noting that ego psychology itself has a complex set of origins, one of which regularly gets lost when its notions of adaptation are pronounced solely conformist and colonialist. The occlusion here is of the personal history of most of the post-Second World War American ego psychologists as migrants or refugees from Nazi Europe. Their concerns were indeed to find creative ways to adapt to a new society; in addition, they were exercised by the explosion of irrationality that had overwhelmed their lost homelands, and their impulse to find ways to fend this off and protect future societies from its recurrence was perhaps understandable.

The argument so far is that psychoanalysis has some of its roots in colonialist assumptions that continue to resonate in contemporary theory and clinical practice. Even though this is counterposed with a more complicated investment in a "seditious" mode of critique, the extent to which psychoanalysis is implicated in a colonialist frame makes it a problematic candidate for post-colonial and anti-racist adoption. Nevertheless, it is the case that psychoanalysis also influences contemporary post-colonial theory. This is mainly for two related reasons, one shared with many other disciplines (including psychology) and the other perhaps specific to psychoanalysis. First, the tortured history of psychoanalysis reveals how colonialism infects even disciplines that also have subversive possibilities. Psychoanalysis is a key instance of an attempt to speak "from the margins" about Western culture, and indeed to reveal explicitly how the claim of the West to progress and rationality is underpinned by violence and irrationality. In his theory of culture, Freud proposed that the murder of the primal father was the basis for all civilisation, including (in his 1939 text, *Moses and Monotheism*) monotheistic religion. In relation to individual psychology, the notion of the dynamic unconscious is such that it places the supposedly primitive at the core of even the most civilised subject. The unconscious is universal, no one is exempt from it; even the most refined person has lust and aggression within. Psychoanalysis reveals this and is consequently a radical opponent of the primitive/civilised distinction. Yet, psychoanalysis carries within it a history of racism and anti-Semitism that is still visible, not only in the fascination with the "primitive" mentioned above, but even in quite recent outbursts of anti-Semitism (Frosh, 2012). Psychoanalysis is thus an exemplary incidence of a disciplinary practice that both draws on colonialism and disrupts its categories at the same time, and exploring how this happens can teach us a great deal about the tentacles of colonialism and racism in intellectual life. Second, perhaps because it does speak from the heart of colonialism, psychoanalysis offers a route towards explicating the workings of the colonial mind and its legacy in the post-colonial world. Ranging from Fanon's (1952) seminal application of existentially inflected psychoanalytic ideas to the identity construction of the colonised mind (as well as to the explanation of racism), to more recent uses of Freudian theory in explorations of the "melancholic" aspects of the post-colonial state (Khanna, 2004), psychoanalysis has offered a vocabulary and set of conceptual tools for articulating the subtle manner in which sociocultural processes construct, and are in turn supported by, psychic configurations. Edward Said (2003) provided one summary of this in his presentation of Freud's late work, specifically *Moses and Monotheism* (1939a), as a critique of personal and national identity. This is constituted in "Freud's profound exemplification of the insight that even for the most definable, the most identifiable, the most stubborn communal identity—for him, this was the Jewish identity—there are inherent limits that prevent it from being fully incorporated into one, and only one, Identity" (Said, 2003, p. 53). Freud's proposition that Moses was an Egyptian emphasises how a nation is never homogeneous, either "genetically" (i.e. "racially") or culturally. The most important founding figure of Jewish culture is, according to Freud, an outsider, which is a specific instance of a general rule that can be applied everywhere—that identities are always heterogeneous and fractured. This emphasis on the "outsider" at the heart of the nation also undermines claims for the fixedness and superiority of European colonial culture, pointing to the reality that at its source is a hidden otherness. There is no single identity, it is always open to the other, and claims for its univocality depend on drowning out the voices of the others that have given it shape. The European is thus infected from the start with the disruptive presence of the colonised, and psychoanalysis shows how this occurs.

Effects of the colonial gaze

The second part of this chapter illustrates how psychoanalysis might act on this potential to fill out post-colonial theory. The adoption of psychoanalysis by post-colonial theory has a very specific origin in Fanon's (1952) *Black Skin, White Masks*. The central chapter's violent opening haunts Fanon's whole book and everything that has come since, and focuses attention on the impact of a certain kind of alienating gaze. Fanon saw himself observed:

> "Dirty nigger!" or simply, "Look, a Negro!"
> I came into the world imbued with the will to find a meaning in things, my spirit filled with the desire to attain to the source of the world, and then I found that I was an object in the midst of other objects. (p. 109)

And a few pages later, where the observer is explicitly a child:

> "Look, a Negro!" It was an external stimulus that flicked over me as I passed by. I made a tight smile.
> "Look, a Negro!" It was true, it amused me.
> "Look, a Negro!" The circle was drawing a bit tighter. I made no secret of my amusement.
> "Mama, see the Negro! I'm frightened." Frightened! Frightened! Now they were beginning to be afraid of me. I made up my mind to laugh myself to tears, but laughter had become impossible. (pp. 111–112)

This episode is commonly read in the light both of a Sartrean kind of alienation, in which the Black man is denied the reflection in the eyes of the other that would constitute him as a subject, and in terms of the Lacanian mirror phase (Lacan, 1949), which Fanon explicitly references later on (p. 161). In the latter, psychoanalytic, case, an important point is the difference between Fanon and Lacan, which is not marked by Fanon himself but is significant for comprehending psychoanalysis's limitations as well as its promise. Fundamentally, the difference is in terms of cultural relativity or specificity, as against the universalising tendency of psychoanalytic reductionism. The culturally undifferentiated Lacanian mirror phase attributes alienation to the adoption of the visual image as the "truth" of the subject, and sees all subjects as similarly constructed by this process. The Lacanian subject looks in the mirror and sees its image reflected back to it, and then appropriates that image as a source of comfort and a way of making meaning out of what was previously fragmented experience. In so doing, the subject adopts as "real" the image given back to it from the mirror; for Lacan, this is a description of how the ego functions to cover over the Real. Fanon, however, offers a specifically racialised version. The Black subject, subjected to the racist gaze, sees itself in the White mirror that removes the possibility of self-assertion and mastery and instead creates further fragmentation. The Black subject is positioned as an object ("I was an object in the midst of other objects") and does not appropriate the fantasy of integrated subjectivity. What has happened is that the Black subject has been fixed by an external gaze—the "mirror-as-camera" as Khanna (2004) put it. She went on:

> The psychoanalytic ambiguities of the mirror stage are, in a sense, then, the flip side of the colonial machinery that renders the colonized subject split, and visible only when refracting a certain form of light. The modern colonized subject has, then, a different ontological makeup than that of the colonizer rendered through the relationship of looking, and not seeing oneself as a mask, but rather, one's gestalt as a mask, and one's mask as a self. (p. 187)

Kelly Oliver summarises the way in which this marks out the Black subject as one who cannot share in the kind of alienation that Western theorists posit as essential to human subjecthood. "For Fanon," she wrote (2004, p. 24), "if man is alienated because he is thrown into a world not of his own making, the Black man is doubly alienated because he is thrown there as one incapable of making meaning … The privilege of autonomy and creative meaning making has been bought at a cost to those othered as inferior, dependent, and incapable of making meaning." Earlier, she made an important point about the romance of alienation in the West, and the reality of a different kind of alienation forced on the "other" by colonialism.

> What Fanon identified as the difference between the black man and man turns around this difference between originary alienation and its double, or underside, the alienation of colonisation and oppression. Fanon suggested that the black man is denied the form of alienation so precious to subjectivity according to various European philosophers. Rather, the black man is the dark, invisible underside of the privilege of subjectivity constituting alienation. (Oliver, 2004, p. 3)

Alienation of a certain kind—the "European notion of an alienation inherent in subjectivity" (ibid., p. 1)—is a luxury that allows certain people to deal with guilt and anxiety. Psychoanalysis recognises it, notably in Lacan's idea that separation of the subject from some little piece of reality—the "object a"—is essential for the constitution of subjectivity. When this separation collapses, for example when one comes face to face with a "double" in the form of an uncanny reminder of what one has become, the subject is deeply disturbed. Mladen Dolar (1996, p. 139) explained that it is here that the Lacanian account of anxiety is distinctive: rather than focusing on anxiety about loss (castration, birth anxiety, death): "[I]t is the anxiety of gaining something too much, of too close a presence of the object. What one loses with anxiety is precisely the loss—the loss that made it possible to deal with a coherent reality."

The kind of "alienation inherent in subjectivity" that is seen as necessary for the construction of the emancipated subject is blocked by the colonial relationship, which in the Fanonian example forces the Black subject to be constructed in the eyes of the White. The consequence is that the kinds of alienation that construct White and Black subjectivities are radically distinct from each other. The Lacanian frame again helps here. For the White subject, the mirror phase is characterised by a presentation of visual wholeness (the image in the mirror) that reassures the subject and leads to a sense of agency in the world. For the Black, colonised subject, the reflection is not of the image as seen by the subject her- or himself (and directed by the gaze of the mother);

it is a reflection of the coloniser's gaze, and as such is doubly alienating. Fanon, wrote Oliver (2004, p. 21) "describes the effects of the white mirror as undermining any sense of unification and control, and returning the black body and psyche to a state of fragmentation and lack of control." Put more broadly, the colonised subject is alienated from the possible space of meaning-making; what she or he sees is not a look of recognition coming from the other, but a look of disdain, fear, or blank incomprehension.

Colonial power is built on this capacity of the coloniser to remove the source of subjecthood from the colonised; and this power is reflected and institutionalised continuously by the gaze, resting on and marking the skin through the process that Fanon called epidermalisation. This particular kind of gaze projects the abjected elements of the White onto the skin of the Black. In particular, the Black is positioned as sexual, aggressive, and physical; and this legacy of slavery and colonialism continues to inhabit the dynamic of mastery that poisons the racialised subject. "For Fanon," claimed Oliver (p. 51), "values are secreted, injected, born of the blood, amputated, and haemorrhaging; they are analogous to bodily fluids. As such, they are dynamic and mobile; and more important, they move from body to body and can infect whole populations." Racism is made viral by this. Fanon himself commented (1952),

> When one has grasped the mechanism described by Lacan, one can have no further doubt that the real Other for the White man is and will continue to be the Black man. And conversely. Only for the White man the Other is perceived on the level of the body image, absolutely as the not-self—that is, the unidentifiable, the unassimilable. (p. 161)

The Black functions as a necessary repository for the White's disowned affects and fantasies—notably those of sexuality:

> The White man is convinced that the Negro is a beast; if it is not the length of the penis, then it is the sexual potency that impresses him. Face to face with the man who is "different from himself", he needs to defend himself. In other words, to personify the Other. The Other will become the mainstay of his preoccupation and his desires. (Fanon, 1952, p. 170)

Sexuality in the field of racism will be returned to below; but this kind of libidinally inflected racialised passion is a necessary component of an account one might try to give of why colonialism and racism are such inflamed, so personally felt, structures.

Derek Hook (2012) also drew attention to the way Fanon's notion of epidermalisation "prioritizes the visual register, providing an understanding not just of the stark visibility of race but of the effects of the 'racial gaze'" (p. 114). These authors and others emphasise how the White gaze constructs the Black subject from the outside, through the operations of bodily oppression and the kind of look that pins the denigrated other to the ground. The gaze is both destructive and admiring; or rather it is full both of hate and of desire, and as such is marked by envy and by a search for a mirror that will reflect difference. The White subject needs the Black to define itself; and it desires the Black as the repository of those necessary things—above all, sexuality—which it has repudiated out of anxiety and self-loathing.

The racist imaginary

A central contribution of psychoanalysis to post-colonial work is to provide a vocabulary that facilitates discussion of what might be called the excessive dimension of racist discourse. This does not mean that racism is ever not excessive—that it is ever purely rational in, for example, an economic sense (it is never rational in terms of its truth claims). But the intensity of the racist imaginary is always over and above anything that can be claimed to be in the interests of the oppressing group—whether colonialism itself, which works to subjugate the colonised society, often through terror, or whether it is the explicit violence of populist anti-Black, Islamophobic, and anti-Semitic racism. Characteristically, much of this theorising has been undertaken not by clinical psychoanalysts, but by sociologists and cultural critics deploying psychoanalytic ideas. For Adorno, Frenkel-Brunswik, Levinson, and Sandford (1950), in their classic post-war investigation of prejudice informed by social psychology, critical theory, and psychoanalysis, the source of this racist imaginary lay in a specific family scenario, in which an authoritarian father and the absence of affection produces a sadomasochistic personality structure unable to deal with the complexity of the world and insistent on the simplifying products of projection. This creates a persecutory environment full of hated beings, thus confirming the subject's vision of being ensnared in a dangerous situation in which the other has to be wiped out for the self to survive. In particular, difference cannot be tolerated because it always constitutes a threat.

> The extremely prejudiced person tends towards "psychological totalitarianism", something which seems to be almost a microcosmic image of the totalitarian state at which he aims. Nothing can be left untouched, as it were; everything must be made equal to the ego-ideal of a rigidly conceived and hypostatized ingroup. The out-group, the chosen foe, represents an eternal challenge. As long as anything different survives, the fascist character feels threatened, no matter how weak the other being may be. (pp. 324–325)

It is important to grasp the way the psychoanalytic component of Adorno and colleagues' work enables them to conceptualise the intensity of affect that racism of this kind involves. Racism is not a "simple belief" and its irrationality is not solely in the area of its truth claims (though of course it is irrational in that sphere). It is precisely the excessive affect added to the systematically prejudiced ideology that makes for a racist imaginary in the sense of an all-encompassing fantasy. Adorno and colleagues enunciated this in relation to the threat felt by the "fascist character" when faced with difference, and there is a lot of other psychoanalytic evidence for this, as in Theweleit's (1977) famous investigation of the proto-fascists of Weimar Germany. Indeed, the general theme that racism becomes constituted through a projective process whereby the subject disowns aspects of the self which she or he then finds in the outside world and feels persecuted by—and consequently directs violent hatred towards—is rife in the literature. It has its limitations, as all simplifying explanations will have; but it conveys well the way in which a racist subject will be both drawn to and repelled by the object of hatred, and in spite of all evidence to the contrary, will hold a genuine conviction that its very existence is threatening. In Fanon (1952), this racist passion is spearheaded by sexual repression: Whiteness, supported by an ideology of "purity" and a disavowal of sexuality, needs the Black "other" as a repository of its own discontent if it is to survive. The White man projects his repressed sexuality onto the Black, constructing him in fantasy as a sexual paragon and an object for his homosexual desire. The White's relationship to the Black is then mediated by this sexuality: the Black man, who contains the projected elements of the White's sexuality, is a constant threat to the potency of the White man, a stimulus to the desire of the White woman. Racist persecution of the Black is therefore fuelled by sexual hatred, something evidenced by lynchings throughout history.

The postulation that the racist imaginary is constituted not by "mistaken beliefs" of the kind hypothesised in psychological theories of prejudice, but rather by splitting and projection, draws together psychoanalysts from a wide variety of different positions. In previous work (Frosh, 2006), I have attended especially to the Kleinian analysis provided by the British sociologist Michael Rustin (1991), and the more classical ego psychological version outlined by the radical American psychoanalyst, Joel Kovel (1995). Summarising briefly here, it is the irrationality of mental structures organised around a fundamental "lie" that Rustin focuses upon, whereas Kovel is interested in the way in which American anti-Black racism uses the historical ground of slavery as a repository for White sexual fantasy—an account that has much in common with Fanon's earlier view. Rustin saw racism as deploying extreme defences against psychic fragmentation, defences that construct a paranoid world view that then reinforces the attack the racist psyche feels itself to be under. Beliefs about race, wrote Rustin,

> when they are suffused with intense feeling, are akin to psychotic states of mind … The mechanisms of psychotic thought find in racial categorisations an ideal container. These mechanisms include the paranoid splitting of objects into the loved and hated, the suffusion of thinking processes by intense, unrecognised emotion, confusion between self and object due to the splitting of the self and massive projective identification, and hatred of reality and truth. (p. 62)

Rustin emphasised the paranoid nature of racist thinking, something readily apparent in conspiracy theories and fantasies of being flooded by waves of immigration, or of being infected by immigrant-borne diseases, or poisoned by alien foods and culture. This is paranoid not simply because of its content ("everyone is against us; we are in a battle for survival") but because of the affective charge attached to the expulsion of intolerable fantasies into the other. The "election" of the racialised other as an object of hate is a way of closing down the thinking that would be necessary in order to deal properly with these unwanted fantasies, to integrate them properly into the subject's mind and hence make them survivable. Instead, these "unthought" impulses are evacuated into the other. Racial categories are particularly useful repositories for such anti- or pseudo-thinking not just because they are socially valorised for political purposes (such as colonialism and economic exploitation), but because they are fundamentally "empty" categories, with very little externally grounded, objective meaning. Rustin commented,

> virtually no differences are caught by "black" or "white" … This is paradoxically the source of racism's power. It is the fact that this category means nothing in itself that makes it able to bear so much meaning—mostly psychologically primitive in character—with so little innate resistance from the conscious mind. (p. 63)

The racist imaginary is thus constructed out of repudiated elements of the personality that are experienced as deeply threatening. Projecting them into the other means they no longer damage the subject from within, but it also creates a persecutory and threatening outside world which has to be defended against. Racialised others are especially selected as these hated external objects because they are made available to fulfil this role by the history and structure of racist and colonial societies, and also because, as a fantasy category, racial "otherness" can be used to mean virtually anything. The choice of these objects thus derives from the nature of racist societies, but is then perpetuated and accentuated by the way the personality gets distorted through its organisation around pseudo-thinking—that is, around what Rustin (1991) called a lie. This lie, which nominates the other as the cause of trouble as a way of covering over "internal" disturbance, becomes central to the preservation of the individual's personality and identity. The more strongly it is held, the more it is needed; the subject comes to be in love with the lie and fearful of anything that challenges it. "The 'lie' in this system of personality organization becomes positively valued, as carrying for the self an important aspect of its defence against weakness, loss or negative judgment" (Rustin, 1991, p. 69). Racism, socially structured though it may be, is consequently deeply invested in by the individual, distorting and disturbing her or his relations with reality and with truth.

It is useful to think of this not as an account of how social and psychological factors "interact", but rather as a psychosocial theory in which what are usually taken as inside and out are embedded in one another and are inseparable. Racism depends on the structures of racist and colonial societies to survive. The choice of the racialised other as the object to receive unwanted psychic projections is made possible by the fact that such others are already "nominated" as derogated and disempowered, yet also dangerous threats. The racist subject experiences her or his antagonism as belonging to the other and so holds to a rigid separation between internal and external. However, the point about projection is that it reveals precisely the permeability of subject boundaries: what is supposedly "inside" does not stay there but leaks out and finds its place among networks of identification and relationality that are organised socially. These are also part of the "self": racist ideation is intense precisely because it is felt. The meaning of a "social subject" is located here: each subject is constructed in and by the demands of (colonial) society, of course acting upon it in its own way, but nevertheless riven by it and inconceivable without it.

Kovel (1995) provided some more leverage on the way in which racism bleeds into the historical structures of the social in a way that leads back to colonialism, here in the context of slavery. The contrast he used is between a monolithic and rigid mode of thinking and what he termed a "polycentric" mind (which he linked with a now valorised "primitivity") that is open to otherness and difference, "associated with an openness of the psyche to the world and, in primitive society at least, an openness of society to otherness" (p. 221). In Kovel's account of history, capitalism suppressed such openness in favour of the rationalist concept of the singular self, the unified personality. Western modernity is built on the renunciation of alternative possibilities of being; the drive for profit swamps the impulses for pleasure and enjoyment. Noting the need for a specific, socially located explanation of how this renunciation turns into racism as what he called the "peculiarly modern form of repressive exclusionism", Kovel asked the following question: "Could it be that as the western mentality began to regard itself as homogeneous and purified—a cogito—it was also led to assign the negativity inherent in human existence to other peoples, thereby enmeshing them in the web of racism?" (p. 212).

The vitality and polymorphism of the world becomes flattened and narrowed into a rigid mode of reasoning and a single narrative of experience; this means that much that is real is excluded, and returns to haunt the subject as a frightening, because potentially uncontrollable, irrationality. Racism enters into the equation because this irrationality is located in the other—the one who, through exclusion and election as the "alien", comes to embody the supposedly non-human. The following passage, redolent of Fanon's description of the sensuality-denying, sexually repressed foundations of "Whiteness", powerfully conveys this point of view:

> A persistent shadow had dogged puritanism, the dominant cultural type of the early capitalist order—a spectre of renunciation and rationalisation, of the loss of sensuousness and the deadening of existence. In this context the animality projected onto the black by virtue of his or her role in slavery became suitable to represent the vitality split away from the world in Puritan capitalist asceticism. Sensuousness that had been filtered out of the universe in capitalist exchange was to reappear in those who had been denied human status by the emergent capitalist order. Blacks, who had been treated as animals when enslaved, became animals in their essence, while the darkness of their skin became suitable to represent the dark side of the body, embodying the excremental vision that has played so central a role in the development of western consciousness. In this way Blacks were seen as beneath Whites in reasoning power and above Whites in sexuality and the capacity for violence. (Kovel, 1995, p. 217)

Kovel is arguing here that the development of Western modernity, built on slavery and capitalist accumulation, produced a psychological imperative to disown multiplicity and sensuality and to project it into the Black other. The power of this psychosocial organisation is so great that it can "enter into the evolution of the psyche" (ibid.) denying the possibility of openness to any new experience which is not in the interests of accumulation. Instead, the repressed sensuousness, preserved unconsciously because otherwise the psyche dries up completely and is deadened, is experienced as threatening and subversive, as well as exciting. It is bestial, animal, fit for projection onto those slaves who are designated by the complex social drive of capitalist imperialism as not fully human. Their physical Blackness, marking them as distinct, is merged together with already-existing psychic defences against what Norman Brown (1959) has called the excremental vision to create the ideal object of repudiation. We are back to the idea of the "primitive" here, as the object into which everything messy and "unsophisticated" is projected; Kovel's addition is to show how this is linked with the specific history of slavery to make the Black other its representative.

There are numerous potential difficulties with the kind of psychoanalytic explanation of racism outlined here. Although I have been emphasising the status of psychoanalysis as a psychosocial theory that breaks down the usual individual–social (and psychology–sociology) binary, there remains a strong temptation when using psychoanalytic concepts to work from the inside out. The social world then becomes populated by projections that emanate from within, without always maintaining consideration of how the opposite effect occurs too—how the apparently "inner world" of the subject is built around the incorporation of messages from the social other—a perspective adopted by some psychoanalysts very strongly (e.g., Laplanche, 1999), but nevertheless one that is not routine in psychoanalytic thinking. Even progressive approaches such as those described here tend to assume the presence of some fundamental psychic urges that will unavoidably create problems should they fail to be expressed. In Kovel's account, sexuality has this status: because colonialist culture suppresses and narrows it, it leaks out and has to be projected into the body of the Black other. But sexuality itself takes many forms, even within modernity, and although it is a useful shorthand to think of it as something that always seeks to make itself known, this is too mechanistic to do justice to the complexity of constructive processes that produce sexuality in the first place.

The detailed exposition proposed by Kovel places the racist imaginary in a clear and specific social context—the rise of bourgeois modernity built on the slave trade and the colonialist election (and derogation) of the Black body as recipient of the excluded and feared elements of the White psyche. This alerts us to the energy of the racist "unconscious", its "excremental vision" and also its elaborate enjoyment, again in the sense of something that goes over-and-above what might be expected, and explicable, on the basis of sociopolitical and economic interests. Perhaps the clearest exponent of this in recent times has been Slavoj Žižek, whose elaborations of the racist dynamic occur within a powerful system constituted in part by Lacanian concepts. Žižek (2006) commented generally that, "The ultimate lesson of psychoanalysis is that human life is never 'just life': humans are not simply alive, they are possessed by the strange drive to enjoy life in excess, passionately attached to a surplus which sticks out and derails the ordinary run of things" (p. 62). In the context of racism, this kind of enjoyment does not mean "having fun"; it means that there is something surplus and unnecessary to which humans are nevertheless passionately attached. Jodi Dean (2007) summarised Žižek's approach here, referring specifically to his 1993 text, *Tarrying with the Negative.*

> Since a community's enjoyment consists in no positive attribute, it comes to the fore in myths and fantasies, myths that generally explain the ways our enjoyment is threatened by others who want to steal it, who want to ruin our way of life by corrupting it with their own peculiar enjoyment. In turn, we find enjoyment in fantasising about their enjoyment, in positing an enjoyment beyond what we imagine for ourselves. So, we don't like the excess of others' ways of life (their music, the way they smell, their relation to their bodies). Their way of life seems immediately intrusive, an assault, like they are flaunting it, daring us, blatantly refusing to sacrifice their enjoyment and come under a common symbolic order. Why do their lives seem so authentic, so real? Why are they so much more in tune with their sexuality, able to eat and drink and live while I am hard at work? The very excessiveness of their enjoyment makes them "them", other, foreign. (p. 22)

Yet, as Žižek (1993) noted, it is precisely this excessive element in the other that attracts us, that makes us feel the other has something we do not have—a fuller life, more energy, more intelligence, more passionate sexuality. The field of fantasy is obviously what is in operation here. Moreover, once one possesses the idea of the other's enjoyment as being more than that which is available to the subject, one opens oneself to the logic that proposes that if this is the case, then one's enjoyment must have been stolen. The Jew has stolen the money, the Black has stolen sexuality: this is what drives much racist fantasy, and it is hard to theorise the excesses of racism without recourse to such an idea about how it is fantasised. For Žižek (1993), in full Lacanian mode, such an imaginary is premised on the repression of a different awareness, that what has been "lost" or stolen in this way was never part of the subject at all: "What we conceal by imputing to the Other the theft of enjoyment is the traumatic fact that we never possessed what was allegedly stolen from us: the lack ('castration') is originary, enjoyment constitutes itself as 'stolen'" (p. 203). This is part of a larger debate on how fantasies of loss can obscure realities of lack—how the incompleteness of the subject can always be laid at someone else's door. The key point here, however, is how the theorisation of excess in this way can say something about the perpetuation of racist ideology and imaginary states: The other is not only denigrated and hated; the other also has what we want, and this causes a rage that has nothing to do with the real situation.

Hook (2008) draws together some of these disparate threads by aligning Fanon and Žižek in their accounts of how racism gets "under the skin". Fanon's (1952) line of analysis emphasises the projection of the White's sexuality onto the Black man, only for the White man to find it returning as envied aspects of his own disavowed sexual embodiment. Hook reads this in relation to the Lacanian idea of the surplus of enjoyment that is both needed and yet is feared, because it locates the psychic life of the subject in the body and hence in what is "bestial" and mortal. The consequence of this, as noted above, is that the racist subject is obsessed by a lack which she or he translates into a "loss"—implying that it has been stolen by someone else, who now possesses it. Hook (2008) elaborates:

> One might thus speak of the racist envy of a given "regime of enjoyments", that is an experience of lack in which the racist subject wishes to take back those surplus enjoyments that they perceive in various "racial others". The enjoyments in question are properties that the racist subject feels themselves singularly entitled to, but is lacking; these are properties that have as such

been stolen away by others, whose possession thereof therefore qualifies these "racial others" as radically blameworthy. In such moments the "enjoying other" becomes curiously important to the racist, certainly so inasmuch as they might be said to represent a repository of enjoyments that need be taken back. We return thus to a familiar lesson in the psychoanalysis of racism: the "racial other" is needed, envied, desired far more than the racist subject can ever admit. (p. 146)

For Hook, the rendering of Fanon into Lacanian territory draws attention to the ways in which racialising embodiment acts within a regime of colonial and racist thought that means that the body, as well as being "a vessel of physical experience and affectivity", is also subjected to "the ideological imposition of particular frames of value and meaning" (p. 149). The consequence is a kind of eternal tension between the affective and embodied experience of the subject, and its writing over by a symbolic and ideological structure that is intrinsically linked to the colonial. In this tension or "antagonism of the real" lie both the persistent power of colonialist ideology and perhaps the route to its unpicking.

Conclusion

This chapter has been concerned with the utility of psychoanalysis for post-colonial thought. Post-colonial theory has been ambivalent towards psychoanalysis, for good reasons. Part of this is the general suspicion of psychological approaches, with their individualistic focus and general history of neglect of socio-historical concerns. In addition, there are specific elements of psychoanalysis's conceptual framework that draw upon, and advance, colonialist ideology. Freud's postulation of the primitive or savage mind, which still infects psychoanalytic thinking, is a prime example here. On the other hand, psychoanalysis's assertion that all human subjects are inhabited by such primitivity goes some way to trouble such normative assumptions. In addition, psychoanalysis offers a number of tools that grant leverage on post-colonial issues—most notably, the damage done by colonialist and racist thought. Two specific contributions to post-colonial psychology made by psychoanalysis are described: the "colonising gaze" and the "racist imaginary".

Post-colonial studies offer a strong challenge to assumptions that are rife in psychology and not absent in psychoanalysis either. Primary among these is the view, still prevalent despite years of critique, that it is possible to theorise individual human subjects as if they stand outside the specific cultures in which they are embedded, and to use concepts that are free from social and historical freight. Post-colonialism asserts that psychology is itself constructed as part of the regime of power of colonialism, a point that has been discussed here in relation to the origins and investments of psychoanalysis. It also invigorates the search for ways of investigating the "social subject" that are genuinely psychosocial, in the sense that they work at the point of articulation of what has historically been separated out into the ideological realms of sociology and psychology. I have tried in this chapter to identify some ways in which psychoanalysis responds to this challenge. This is not to claim that psychoanalysis is unequivocally and unproblematically aligned with post-colonialism. It has too many embedded convictions that stem from colonial practices, in particular a pronounced individualism that often makes social structure secondary. Nevertheless, psychoanalysis can be used both to trouble colonial and racist assumptions, and as a stepping stone to some subversive theory.

References

Adorno, T. W., Frenkel-Brunswik, E., Levinson, D., & Sanford, R. N. (1950). *The Authoritarian Personality*. New York: W. W. Norton.

Altman, N. (2002). Black and white thinking. *Psychoanalytic Dialogues, 10*: 589–605. doi: 10.1080/10481881009348569.

Brickman, C. (2003). *Aboriginal Populations in the Mind: Race and Primitivity in Psychoanalysis*. New York: Columbia University Press.

Brown, N. O. (1959). *Life Against Death: Psychoanalytical Meaning of History*. Middletown, CT: Wesleyan University Press.

Butler, J. (2005). *Giving an Account of Oneself*. New York: Fordham University Press. doi: 10.5422/fso/9780823225033.001.0001

Campbell, J. (2000). *Arguing with the Phallus: Feminist, Queer and Postcolonial Theory: A Psychoanalytic Contribution*. London: Zed.

Dean, J. (2007). Why Žižek for political theory? *International Journal of Žižek Studies, 1*: 18–32.

Dolar, M. (1996). At first sight. In: R. Salecl & S. Žižek (Eds.), *Gaze and Voice as Love Objects* (pp. 129–153). London: Duke.

Fanon, F. (1952). *Black Skin, White Masks*. London: Pluto.

Freud, S. (1912–13). *Totem and Taboo. S. E., 13*: vii–162. London: Hogarth.

Freud, S. (1927c). *The Future of an Illusion. S. E., 21*: 1–56. London: Hogarth.

Freud, S. (1939a). *Moses and Monotheism. S. E., 23*: 1–138. London: Hogarth.

Frosh, S. (1994). *Sexual Difference: Masculinity and Psychoanalysis*. London: Routledge. doi:10.4324/9780203313732

Frosh, S. (1999). *The Politics of Psychoanalysis: An Introduction to Freudian and Post-Freudian Theory*. London: Macmillan.

Frosh, S. (2005). *Hate and the 'Jewish Science': Anti-Semitism, Nazism and Psychoanalysis*. London: Palgrave. doi:10.1057/9780230510074

Frosh, S. (2006). *For and Against Psychoanalysis*. London: Routledge.

Frosh, S. (2010). *Psychoanalysis Outside the Clinic: Interventions in Psychosocial Studies*. London: Palgrave.

Frosh, S. (2012). The re-enactment of denial. In: A. Gülerce (Ed.), *Re(con)figuring Psychoanalysis: Critical Juxtapositions of the Philosophical, the Socio-historical and the Political* (pp. 60–75). London: Palgrave.

Frosh, S., & Baraitser, L. (2008). Psychoanalysis and psychosocial studies. *Psychoanalysis, Culture & Society, 13*: 346–365. doi:10.1057/pcs.2008.8

Gilman, S. L. (1993). *Freud, Race and Gender*. Princeton, NJ: Princeton University Press.

Gould, S. J. (1996). *The Mismeasure of Man*. New York: W. W. Norton.

Hook, D. (2008). The "real" of racializing embodiment. *Journal of Community & Applied Social Psychology, 18*: 140–152. doi:10.1002/casp.963

Hook, D. (2012). *A Critical Psychology of the Postcolonial: The Mind of Apartheid*. London: Routledge.

Jacoby, R. (1975). *Social Amnesia: A Critique of Conformist Psychology from Adler to Laing*. Brighton, UK: Harvester.

Jacoby, R. (1983). *The Repression of Psychoanalysis: Otto Fenichel and the Freudians*. New York: Basic Books.

Keynes, J. M. (1919). *The Economic Consequences of the Peace*. London: Penguin.

Keynes, J. M. (1936). *The General Theory of Employment, Interest and Money*. New York: Classic House.

Khanna, R. (2004). *Dark Continents: Psychoanalysis and Colonialism*. Durham, NC: Duke University Press.

Kovel, J. (1995). On racism and psychoanalysis. In: A. Elliott & S. Frosh (Eds.), *Psychoanalysis in Context: Paths between Theory and Modern Culture* (pp. 205–222). London: Routledge.

Lacan, J. (1949). The mirror stage as formative of the function on the I as revealed in the psychoanalytic experience. In: J. Lacan, *Écrits: A Selection* (pp. 1–7). London: Tavistock.

Laplanche, J. (1999). The unfinished Copernican revolution. In: J. Laplanche, *Essays on Otherness* (pp. 52–83). London: Routledge.

Lewontin, R. C., Rose, S., & Kamin, L. J. (1984). *Not in Our Genes: Biology, Ideology and Human Nature*. London: Penguin.

Marcuse, H. (1955). *Eros and Civilization: A Philosophical Inquiry into Freud*. Boston, MA: Beacon.

Moi, T. (1989). Patriarchal thought and the drive for knowledge. In: T. Brennan (Ed.), *Between Feminism and Psychoanalysis*. London: Routledge.

Oliver, K. (2004). *The Colonization of Psychic Space: A Psychoanalytic Social Theory of Oppression* (pp. 189–205). Minneapolis, MN: University of Minnesota Press.

Roudinesco, E. (1990). *Jacques Lacan & Co.: A History of Psychoanalysis in France, 1925–1985*. London: Free Association.

Rustin, M. (1991). *The Good Society and the Inner World: Psychoanalysis, Politics and Culture*. London: Verso.

Said, E. W. (2003). *Freud and the Non-European*. London: Verso.

Stavrakakis, Y. (2007). *The Lacanian Left: Essays on Psychoanalysis and Politics*. Albany, NY: SUNY Press.

Theweleit, K. (1977). *Male Fantasies: Women, Floods, Bodies, History*. Cambridge: Polity.

Žižek, S. (1993). *Tarrying with the Negative: Kant, Hegel, and the Critique of Ideology*. Durham, NC: Duke University Press.

Žižek, S. (2006). *The Parallax View*. Cambridge, MA: MIT Press.

CHAPTER FOUR

Consultancy on deregistration to a care home for the long-stay mentally ill: you can take Stig out of the dump, but can you take the dump out of Stig?

Liz Greenway

Introduction

Stig of the Dump is a modern classic children's novel by Clive King, published in 1963. It is an adventure story about a secure, adventurous boy, Barney, befriending a dislocated primitive caveman, Stig, who, deprived of his own people, language, community, and orientation of time and place, has made a creative adaptation of a rubbish dump. From the outset, there is mutual respect, creativity, and a non-verbal dialogue between the two, but the power imbalance changes as Barney finally enters Stig's world and feels like the outsider to a whole other universe with its own vigour and sophistication.

I present this story as a metaphor to explore the policies and provision for mentally ill patients in the UK National Health Service (NHS). The story was published during the 1960s at the same time as the then minister for health, Enoch Powell, made his "Water Tower" speech, conveying his intention of "nothing less than the elimination of by far the greater part of this country's mental hospitals as they stand today" (studymore. org.uk/xpowell.htm). The problem is, it seems likely that there may have been a fantasy of the abolition of mental illness accompanying the intention to eliminate mental hospitals. This may be manifested either through turning a "blind eye" in care homes themselves, or through a "gap in services". This potentially leaves Stig with no place to go, with his only option to make the best of being dumped.

This chapter will consider the front-line experience of not just "care in the community" ("the policy of transferring responsibility for people in need from large, often isolated, state institutions to their relatives and local welfare agencies", www.dictionary.reference.com/browse/community+care), but give consideration to the wholesale shipment of the mental asylum back into society. A brief consultation was undertaken in an inner-city registered housing association, Horizon, that provides care to those who would in times past have found themselves in asylums; that is to say, the chronically mentally unwell, in this case, those who often have a history of both homelessness and mental illness.

This consultancy was undertaken on a pro bono basis as part of a postgraduate project. It was suggested by the manager of a community mental health team who was aware both of the availability of the consultant and a need in Horizon for a reflective space for staff, and the consultancy was then agreed to by the manager at Horizon. I will start by outlining the sociopolitical context and then describe the consultancy. Thereafter, I will reflect and consider my understanding theoretically from systemic, psychoanalytic, and group perspectives. This understanding will be informed by my own emotional antennae from experiencing countertransference phenomena and from associations I made to the projections and provocations I encountered. I will then conclude by linking the impact of political rhetoric to my experience of the distress and dysfunction at local level, and reflect on the possible societal impact of contemptuous decision-making.

Historical and ideological background

Lifelong housing in asylums of those deemed sufficiently disturbed/disturbing to be locked up and kept out of sight, originally described as "pauper lunatics", became the norm following the County Asylums Act in 1808 and Lunacy Act of 1845 (www.mind.org.uk). In 1990, there was a radical overhaul of socio-psychological provision, under the new NHS and Community Care Act of Margaret Thatcher's government. However, in parallel, Thatcher herself had said in 1987, "I think we have gone through a period when too many children and people have been given to understand, 'I am homeless, the Government must house me!' and so they are casting their problems on society and who is society? There is no such thing!" (www.margaretthatcher.org/document/106689).

The political landscape that expressed "society? There's no such thing!" decided that, nevertheless, community was a phenomenon real enough to bear the relocation and care of the institutionalised or mentally unwell. Since this radical rethink, there has been plenty of planning concerning the objectives that care staff should implement for their customers, a term which seemed at odds with the needs of these individuals, who were mostly in no position to choose and purchase their own care. More than two decades later, this now translates into policies describing personalisation for patients and the movement towards deregistration for most currently registered housing provision. This is a philosophical continuation of Thatcher's stance that "there is no such thing as an entitlement unless someone has first met an obligation". She expressed concern about impoverished, abused, or neglected children, but without an idea that they actually grow into adults who may have no concept of "obligation" other than feeling owed for their lack (www.margaretthatcher.org/document/106689).

But who must remedy this lack? From as far back as the Thatcher era, governments have imposed targets as if the "problems of human nature" were somehow forgotten. I am reminded of Charles Dickens's *Hard Times* (1854) which tells the tale of fact vs. fancy: "Facts alone are wanted in life. Plant nothing else, and root out everything else. You can only form the minds of reasoning animals upon Facts: nothing else will ever be of service to them" (p. 9). The link I am making in organisations is the wish not to look beneath the surface and to know about the unconscious (fancy) in residents and in the staff group too, whose evident struggle is their attempt to offer containment simply by keeping the focus on objectives (facts). The danger is that this then leads to staff burnout and either physical abandonment, with constant turnover of staff, or emotional absence and indifference. Deregistration means that issues of medication, money, and self-care will no longer be dealt with by those who are employed to provide supported housing, and so residents must be independent in these areas or be moved on. Somewhere else, there will continue, albeit an ever-shrinking, possibly contracted-out, registered care provision, most likely out of central London. This could result in an underhand return of invisible asylums. The difficulty is that customers who were taken originally from the Victorian mental institutions and placed in currently registered care homes think of this "last-chance saloon" as their lifelong home. Staff and residents alike have been living with this sense of an eternal "organisation in the mind" (Armstrong, 2005), and this is currently under threat.

The idea that commissioners can simply instruct managers of housing associations to foster independence in residents who are often institutionalised is the real madness in the system. It is as if these long-stay patients suddenly are seen as customers with the ability to make choices in accordance with personalisation. In this chapter, I will describe the impact of this shift in policy and the way it leaves not just residents in a stupor but staff demoralised, burnt out, and heading for the pub.

The dilemma for the consultant, in parallel with the conflict in staff when "keyworking" customers, is which defences to leave unchallenged. "Keyworking is a system for providing individualised social care through named persons. A keyworker is the person who has responsibility and accountability for the care of the service user and for decisions relating to their situation" (www.socialcareassociation.co.uk/Portals/0/Public%20 Docs/Keyworking%20in%20Social%20 Care.pdf). Evaluating whether defences had been erected by staff in order to enable them to cope was an important component of the consultancy, as overly exposing them to the impossible nature of their task could have been destructive.

Another area of difficulty integral to this work is touching the pockets of madness in oneself; which is likely to be both the underlying motivation for working with others who have been affected by breakdown, and concurrently the dread and fear of it. Bion (1970) writes of "nameless dread", and Winnicott (1989) writes of "unthinkable agonies". Eigen (1999) coined the phrase "toxic nourishment", and explains that:

> Winnicott suggests … the breakdown feared already happened …
> The infant's environment cannot protect it from overstrain, and the person carries the imprint of being broken in infancy … while the personality was beginning to form, a time too early to organize, hold and experience, what was or was not happening.

As one grows, defences organize around this point of madness which one sometimes glimpses in disorganizing moments. (Eigen, 1999, pp. 171–172)

The nature of the work with severely mentally unwell residents is potentially full of "disorganising moments". Organisations tasked with accommodating "unhoused minds" (Scanlon & Adlam, 2008, p. 529) often have their own ghosts, which can include drug misuse and deaths resulting from overdoses, which can traumatise employees and leave them with professional scars.

Organisational consultancy may at least offer a way to consider the systemic problems that culminate from a toxic mixture of political rhetoric, lack of investment, simplistic and dangerous misunderstanding of mental ill health, and a system-wide contemptuous attitude towards those who do not contribute to glowing statistics. The work of consultancy may be to make contact with this mess, and tolerate the fear that one could become subsumed by it. To really make contact with the reality of community care, it is necessary to get close enough to the experience of staff and residents at registered care homes without over-identifying with their visceral life-and-death struggle in a last-ditch attempt to enable functionality, or to stay too far away by attempting to be invincible by arrogant attempts at rescue.

There can be a feeling that the life has been sucked out of care homes, and sometimes there is an acknowledged wish to develop potential; for example, setting up horticulture in a disused garden. Metaphors may abound with regard to a wish for a nurturing, enabling environment rather than warehousing (Miller & Gwynne, 1972). Nevertheless, management, after all, have to speak the commissioners' language and play their game, while managing staff at the front line doing what is possible, and all the while living with the tension this creates. Commissioners are funded by a government divorced from the experience "on the street" (Cooper, 2010).

The consultation

The manager of the local community mental health team oversaw the mental health treatment of the residents and knew that there was a high rate of staff turnover and a new manager in place at Horizon. Aware of the possibility of a pro bono brief consultation, she informed Horizon's manager and he agreed to meet with the consultant. He decided to go ahead with the consultancy "because we need it and it's free", and invited the consultant to a team meeting with staff at which were agreed the times and dates of eight regular, reflective staff group one-and-a-half-hour weekly sessions.

To maintain confidentiality and yet to give a flavour sufficiently close to the experience, I will attempt to give some generalised details from the setting, with the identity of the organisation and individuals changed. In this chapter, I will refer to the story *Stig of the Dump* and give one of the residents the name "Stig". I did not use this metaphor during the consultation sessions with staff; it was an idea that evolved through my own reflections afterwards. This not only maintains confidentiality but adds a societal metaphor for those who are seen as "down and out" and living on the edge of community life. I use this as a mechanism to consider the assumptions that are made about those who live in this way, as if it is they who are unsophisticated, inept individuals when, in fact, they provide a social commentary on the housed, the secure, and on those who have made apparently sophisticated decisions about registered care. This metaphor is therefore a challenge to the assumptions of normality and a reminder of the danger of treating inappropriately people with such needs.

The main thrust of this consultancy initially was to consider the impact that pending deregistration was having on staff and residents. Staff explained that the idea of those residents who are institutionalised becoming completely responsible for their own medication, toileting and hygiene, and rent just did not seem feasible. Staff confirmed that many of the long-stay residents behave as if in hospital and describe staff as "nurse", even though no staff are medically trained. In parallel, a few staff themselves seemed somewhat institutionalised and resistant, while others were responsive to the consultation.

In the sections that follow, I will describe the events and conversations that took place at the meetings at Horizon, and my reactions and thoughts about these, as they occurred.

First impressions

As I was leaving a setting-up session, one of the residents arrived back from a shopping trip dragging bags behind her. Looking up to reveal smeared red lipstick, she called out to some younger male residents for help. They ignored her. This patient, whose name was Maggie, would reappear from time to time on my visits to Horizon, and I considered the metaphor that she represented; was I to be ignored, helped, seen as useless? In contrast, Ann, with her shaven head, simply sat staring in reception and barely seemed to move. I wondered about the impenetrability and intransigent nature of organisational difficulties.

A week later, I attended a staff meeting and met the team. I felt fearful of making a mess, perhaps like clients who soil themselves with anxiety. I could sense the powerful projections ripe for being identified with! Maggie was leaving as I arrived and, although she did look dishevelled and eccentric with her vivid, garish lips, she was nevertheless braving the outside world. I discovered there were many temporary and agency staff; it was the residents who were mostly "stable" in their immovability. That is, until now, when moving them on suddenly became a political imperative. The danger seems to be that complex decisions that should be based on human need are instead based on misconstrued financial restraint and political rhetoric, and are urgently imposed.

Meeting the team

In stark contrast with reception, where the resident Ann seemed in catatonic stillness, there was high energy inside the staff room. I explained to the staff that I am an organisational consultant and that I had agreed with management to offer eight sessions with a cross-section of changing staff to consider the impact of deregistration. Management interjected support and suggested that a core group of regular attendees would be useful. I then explained that I would not be offering clinical supervision; in other words, that I would not be focusing on individual patients' diagnoses, medication, or clinical presentations, but rather on staff dynamics in the team and what it is like to work here in the face of deregistration and change.

A support worker replied, "like some kind of horror movie where it hangs over you somewhere in the distance." He gestured a threatening, gripping hand in my direction. There was laughter among the team and a murmur of agreement. I offered an interpretation that this was perhaps an indication that they would be showing me how violent the struggle is and letting me know how threatening and horrific it can feel, but also that there is a feeling of being in the grip of something.

Session 1

I wondered how working in a modern-day community asylum might impact on staff. The struggle of "getting in" continued throughout the consultancy: somehow there was an obstreperous gatekeeper both to the physical building, but also the organisational psyche. There were painstaking efforts in evidence to help a resident with her payment of expenses in pounds and pence; a way of training residents to be ready for deregistration.

I wondered what the residents made of my presence. Somehow, even if unconsciously, they nominated one of their group as their visitor to the staff consultancy. In this written description, I will refer to him as Stig, and he will represent the resident group in the account that follows. Stig is at real risk of being rubbished or ending up in the rubbish dump—but there is more to be considered about what he represents than assuming he is simply a passive individual recipient of services. The Stig in the story is more than just a caveman living in a dump—he shows his morality, integrity, and complexity when he has the chance and helps save society from its thieves.

I introduced myself to the ten attendees at the meeting and described my function, "to provide a reflective space to bring thoughts and feelings about organisational changes, for example, deregistration".

A hope was conveyed that deregistration would become an activating force which would motivate staff as well as residents. However, this was countered by despair, as it was perceived that there were many more residents who were long-stay inpatients, institutionalised, and of retirement age, unable to become independent, than had been suggested. To account for this difference in attitudes, I suggested of this long-stay group, "Perhaps they seem to occupy a large space in your minds, and perhaps at times they look older due to such tough lives."

Anxiety was expressed by staff about being responsible for such vulnerable adults and a fear of being held accountable if something went wrong. However, this brought memories of residents being badly affected by the idea of deregistration and the panic that had been felt by staff, relatives, and residents about the prospect of residents losing their home, in some cases after seventeen years there. A letter had been provided by senior management that staff were instructed to send out to all residents and their relatives conveying the idea of deregistration taking place at the end of the same month. Staff described worried relatives phoning up for hours and how awful it was. Staff appeared to feel let down and angry that they had had to carry this trauma and threat—and then it had not even happened! There was also a sense in which they felt they had managed without a manager or a consultant then, and so the timing of the sessions now was wrong; too little, too late, perhaps.

Fears were then voiced about job security, and others bemoaned about poor pay and dispensability. Management responded that, in theory, in the current era, although unlikely, another organisation could make a bid and take over provision, but funding should continue for up to a year. At this point, I was aware of my responsibility not to offer an "alarming letter" that would threaten their professional homes; in other words, to be respectful of their social defences (Menzies, 1960)—which may mean being mostly in denial about short-termist political planning for long-term patient needs!

The splits in the group were already becoming apparent—anxiety vs. nonchalance; abandonment vs. stickability; fear vs. high hopes of deregistration. One support worker dared to say how boring she found the work, and she hoped deregistration would change this.

Session 2

A support worker would say during this session that one of the residents would tell her he did not like her culture, rather than the colour of her black skin, and would often look past her. I asked what it felt like to have that kind of experience, and she said she does not let it bother her: "If you let things like that bother you, you're in the wrong job." I thought about Winnicott's (1958) "Hate in the Countertransference". Most staff keep moving on, and I had a stream of new faces attending the sessions throughout, even the final one. There were eight attendees in this session.

At a strategic level, the most shocking idea was communicated—that three out of five registered care homes in the locality were being deregistered, not including Horizon. Residents judged to have high support needs that could not be accommodated after deregistration in Horizon would probably be moved out of the borough into care that would be more like a locked ward, with even less scope for independence.

Concern about management of medication was raised, in particular the risk arising in some cases because it was such a challenge to keep track of all residents when they each had different needs and levels of responsibility for their prescriptions and medication. Throughout the consultancy, there was a huge emphasis on the onerous nature of medication, and a hope of freedom following deregistration when they would no longer have responsibility for it as an organisation.

There was a theme of "difference" among the attendees in this session, both in terms of medication and also breakfast options, which could be chosen by residents and to a greater or lesser extent facilitated by staff. Some staff spoke proudly of their ability to foster independence in residents. Collective meals were described as the most stark reminder that they are in an institution, as nobody really spoke and there was nothing much for staff to do apart from clearing up at the end. I asked whether they could feel a bit redundant. I offered an interpretation that, "Perhaps your function as staff on these occasions is to show residents that indeed this is an institution—it offers containment and perhaps, in some ways, it's important both for residents to develop independence if that's possible and maybe at times for there to be a social situation such as a shared meal."

Following the previous session, full of descriptions of agitated staff and residents struggling with deregistration, the general attitude to this sea change was different today. There was agreement that the idea of moving towards deregistration now, before it was even implemented, was motivating staff to empower residents towards independence. It sounded as though they felt guilty for their previous complaints, and so today compensated with rhetoric or positive clichés, which in fantasy might satisfy commissioners. However, it was recognised that residents who had been institutionalised for seventeen years, "are going to need time and it's baby steps". A new member of staff proudly used the term "customer". Others retorted that they were rebels here at this particular project and say "residents". The rest of the staff chuckled.

There was a regular theme: having a party or going to the pub—perhaps to stimulate life, communicating a sense of celebration or connection, but also drowning sorrows, or breaking down boundaries, something that could feel exciting or dangerous.

Session 3

Continuing this theme, allusions were made in this next session to raucous behaviour by staff when off duty, for example in the pub, by the nine attendees. The main thrust seemed to be that most of the liveliness was somewhere other than in work with the residents, which seemed deflating. Armstrong (2005, p. 81) proposes that, "Every organisation contains a pathological version of itself (a shadow side) … to serve as a psychic retreat when the internal or external situation of the organisation threatens the limits of its capacity." Perhaps, to manage the assaults directed to the organisation by government directives and to cope with the persecutory demands from residents, "mobilisation of the pathological version, as a latent system within the organisation" had become chronic and, although it did "not prevent working from getting done … it interfered … through robbing it of vitality and meaning" (Armstrong, 2005, pp. 81–82).

There was an organisational myth emerging towards deregistration: it would be a cure for ills not only in residents, but would remedy staff complaints of stress and boredom too. The shortcomings of personal care were described, along with complaints about the old-fashioned attitude of psychiatry. There was the idea that residents are unwilling/unable to achieve imposed, apparently meaningless objectives, based on government directives, which were perceived by the staff as irrelevant and possibly causing them to leave, go absent, or feel undermined.

Suddenly, there issued forth an outburst describing a feeling of boredom with discussing deregistration. After which, concerns about staff turnaround and low pay were disclosed. One redeeming comment: "I think the way to keep the job interesting is to focus on individuals because they are endlessly interesting. Although personally, I think that's where personalisation might clash with what somebody actually needs due to their mental health capacity … commissioners come and go … focus on the residents."

Session 4: naming Stig

The eight attendees to this session raised questions about how to manage the routine demands of the work and daily rituals, the possibilities of difference among staff and residents, and at the same time managing risk. At times, we had gallows humour, and other times, more of a party mood. Then the tick-box issues of health and safety were bemoaned.

However, it seemed almost impossible to pause and get hold of concern. I thought it was important to acknowledge our weekly visitor, as he seemed significant, and I wondered what he was bringing to the group to think about:

> Consultant: Is it Stug who comes and does his check on us every week?
>
> Chorus: No, Stig.
>
> Support worker: Well, there aren't so many staff downstairs so he's come to check where we are. Then he'll feel OK.
>
> Consultant: So the health and safety of the place is very important to particularly anxious or paranoid residents?

The level of institutionalisation and difficulty taking in any nutrition from human interaction became apparent: "Small, round tables with table cloths and plastic plants have been trialled, but the residents didn't like it at all, so old, long, impersonal tables were brought back," said one key worker sadly.

However, in facing these challenges of boredom, risk, and institutionalisation, perhaps the group of attendees was beginning to think together, and I noticed a "chorus voice" and wondered whether this was a sign of a working group emerging. Aggression was openly expressed by one of the two team leaders; a request was made for a punchbag for staff; initiatives being thwarted among staff were discussed; and a wish expressed for there to be more competitiveness.

Session 5

There were two pairs in this session in the staff group—a nonchalant pair, and a couple concerned about risk of violence. The manager showed commitment through attendance, as usual. I wondered if perhaps the team were in a permanent state of fear of resident madness and/or violence, staff burnout or resignation, and/or commissioner expectation. I felt superfluous and disconnected, as if staff simply go through the motions of duty, and consultancy was another empty task that they had to drag their bodies through. I wondered about the reduction in attendees to five, and whether my previous confrontation of staff with their own boredom had felt to them like an attack.

Nevertheless, a crucial issue of risk started to become manifest from this session onwards, as if there had been a turning point in the consultancy. Perhaps sufficient trust had been established to enable a real exchange. The issue of risk posed by customers and whether female workers should be accompanied at times was raised. Some discussion followed about residents signing, or refusing to sign, their risk assessment, which may be an indication, suggested the manager, of "how much or not they concur and engage with the reality or the way it's perceived"; or "may indicate their relationship to the institution," I added. A description of recent resident violence to staff and the lack of safety bleepers or walkie-talkies and staff resorting to using their personal mobiles at work was mentioned, and I raised the possibility that, "Staff can become institutionalised and switch off to their own sensitivity which might alert them to concern, which is actually worth paying attention to. Managing anxiety is also necessary, or else the system may provoke a denial through turning a blind eye to risk."

However, when I tried to link the strain of managing anxiety with people leaving their posts, this was denied, and a suggestion made that people mostly leave as a result of promotion, not burnout at all! It seemed to me that as soon as we got hold of something as a group, it was too slippery and difficult to focus; as if by talking about concerns, all staff would leave. The strain of weekend shifts and lack of weekend staff was also stressed.

Progress in terms of the work with residents was described as making arrangements for them to go on a trip to the seaside and to hold a sports day.

Session 6

This time, instead of Stig visiting the session in person, he was thought about and considered by the group of six attendees. The session started with more fantasies of greater freedom and flexibility and less responsibility, and time being taken up with medication post-deregistration. The session continued along the lines of the arduous nature of the work: from trying to teach resistant residents how to use the washing machine, to managing others who decline the psychiatrist's suggestion of managing their own medication, to lack of take-up of a visiting optician. A disappointing turnout for the seaside was described, with only three residents taking up the trip, but there was immense pride and satisfaction, and evident emotion, about how Ann, who rarely goes out, made the effort worthwhile as she was excited and loved their outing. This perhaps suggested mobilisation of "stuckness" in the organisation.

The crux of the consultancy: Stig of the dump

Almost an hour had passed when two support workers entered; they gave the impression of having a deliberate plan. Finally, the crux of the consultancy manifested.

Support worker 1:   But what about Stig? I mean his flat is really dirty and he's got two fridges full of newspapers and things he's picked up from the street. He used to be street homeless, didn't he? Why has he got two fridges?

Support worker 2:   Yes, he lived on the streets. But he doesn't like you cleaning his flat, he's not comfortable when it's clean. But I think, what if an inspector came and saw the state of it.

Support worker 1:   But it was cleaned last week. Well, then it's dirty again.

Support worker 2:   But no, you can't accumulate thick dust like that on the skirting board and the TV in a few days. Perhaps we need to think more about cleaning. That flat needs a really deep clean.

Consultant: But what you're saying is that it's the dirt and the smell of it that makes him feel at home and he's living like that, here in registered care with an idea of making him more independent. He's showing the state of his mind and he's not very well. That's the reality you're faced with in terms of some of these residents who have been here since before 1995.

Support worker 1:   That's what's so difficult. Mmm, it is.

There was a feeling of a full session, and not wanting to end. There was a poignant, heartfelt moment when the reality of the work was powerfully communicated. The perpetual question seemed to be, "You can take Stig, and those like him, out of the dump, but can you take the dump, his disturbance and others' projections, out of Stig?" I was left preoccupied with issues of neglect of duty of care, from the organisation towards staff and from staff to the residents. I was also in a quandary about person-alisation: "choice and control to those who receive services" (Cooper, 2010). If taken too far, this can lead to Stig recreating his dump and being left to it, which is a perpetual health hazard. When concern was raised about an inspector seeing the filth, at that moment I was being seen like the outside observer bearing witness to the shame.

Session 7

Staff described this session as organisational therapy, as opposed to "supervision", which had been the inaccurate descriptor at the outset. There was a theme of viruses, treatments for them, and whether antibiot-ics are effective. I felt that this was a dialogue among the seven attendees about what kind of "medication" could help them with the "infections" in their work; perhaps something ongoing would help rather than one dramatic gesture. Some difficulty was expressed about trying to enforce progress in preparation for deregistration, thereby making residents worse, for example, inducing panic attacks.

The attendees were thoughtful and pointed out the painful reality for some residents, and how, if this becomes intolerable, retreat or regres-sion can follow, and then there's the grey area between what commis-sioners expect and demand, and what people can actually manage.

Session 8: last session and review

Unusually easy access into the building caused me to note the contrast from trying to enter a fortress on my early visits to almost an open house now. There were four attendees to this last consultancy session. They started discussing success stories and celebratory parties and creative, progressive residents in some of the other projects. Management was on leave and therefore absent from the consultancy for the last two weeks, "felt not only to be contemptuous of the group, but also to be expressing that contempt in action" (Bion, 1961, p. 49).

However, there was a willingness to have a meaningful dialogue and consider residents and staff interactions in a reflective way. I was particularly encouraged as there was a willingness to think, and also an acknowledgement of the possibility of professional burnout resulting from a mismanagement of boundaries in a wish to be overly helpful. This enabled a frank dialogue about successes and difficulties, satisfaction and frustration. I had hopes that the attendees to this final consultancy session could form a creative core to support the larger system. There was also an acknowledgement of the loss of the consultancy: "I'm disappointed it's coming to an end, really. It's the only project I've worked in where there's been this kind of space, and I think it's valuable."

Disappointment was conveyed about the lack of investment in staff, frustration about lack of development, and dismay at the lack of recognition of the stress of the job. They all expressed as a joke the fear of ending up in the currently empty flat at the home and becoming a resident themselves, which was a significant recognition. Some satisfaction was expressed about the progress of some clients, who could now have a civil conversation.

Then came the final word from Stig, who defiantly put his head around the door and blew cigarette smoke into the consultancy session. As I left, stubborn Stig was sitting in reception looking self-satisfied and triumphant, as if he was blowing in the face of authority: "You can take Stig out of the dump, but you can't take the dump out of Stig."

Afterthoughts and reflections

I came to realise the primitive, visceral needs of residents and the taxing nature of the work. Swinburne (2000, p. 223) describes in his paper "Home Is Where the Hate Is":

> borderline and schizophrenic individuals … tend to make up
> the bulk of residents within community mental homes [and]

function in a manner akin to that of the early infant prior to the development of internal space via the interjected experience of a containing maternal object relationship ... as a consequence of this the challenge facing staff working in such environments becomes one of replicating maternal containment as the prerequisite to therapeutic aspirations or notions of meaningful change within their client group.

In retrospect, I can see that the consultancy sessions may at times have felt like the weekend work that staff were wishing to get out of and management had the worry of trying to staff. In this way, it's possible to see that the transference directed towards me as the consultant is of a bad, demanding object that expects thinking, making links, and communicating. But actually, when thinking did take place, some very violent thoughts and images were brought to mind, and so there was an avoidance, "a taking leave" from the mind. There was a risk of becoming indifferent, lapsing on the duty of care, or even losing "being human" and becoming robotic.

This led me to consider the following hypothesis: because the reality of the challenges in the work are overwhelming, there is a way of turning a "blind eye" to difficulty/complexity/suffering and a wish not to think or feel. This may lead to an apparent nonchalant/robotic attitude, with a lack of safety devices in place to manage risk; a wish not to see danger and tokenistic records, on one side, and at other times a feeling of being flooded by overwhelming demands that may lead to despondency and a feeling that there is little possibility of making an impact or having efforts recognised. This is likely to lead to "asylum annexes" in which individual residents and staff feel in a mad world and left alone to confront their isolation, anxiety, and decline in a macho culture.

This is the risk of "asylum in the community": that there is an illusion that rather than being an institution providing care to the most chronically mentally unwell, there is a fantasy of a rehabilitation centre to empower independence and enable moving on. This can cause a "dump" into those members of staff who allow themselves to see the primitive functioning of the long-stay residents, the "Stig", but who then themselves are pathologised for what they draw attention to. Eventually, this "dump" gets re-projected into Stig, who recreates a physical "dump" and becomes the receptacle for "rubbish" in the organisation.

The issue of re-parenting

The general difficulty with many residents is lack of self-awareness in order to differentiate their individuality, so that becoming more "independent" is a far-off milestone. To help clarify this from a theoretical perspective, we can consider Mahler, Pine, and Bergman's (1975) and Winnicott's understandings of infant development. "His majesty the baby" (Freud, 1914c) is at the "autistic phase" (Mahler, Pine, & Bergman, 1975), which is the auto-erotic stage in life during which self-absorption is so intense as to disallow recognition of the mother as a separate being. He matures through "the psychological birth of the human infant" (ibid.), an accomplishment enabled some months later following attuned nurture, if the skin and mind boundaries of the caregiver and baby can be recognised by both as separate. Winnicott (1965) draws our attention to "there is no such thing as a mother without a baby" and vice versa, and in the end "good-enough parenting" is desirable—overindulgence or neglect both result in difficulties, hence his book title, *The Maturational Processes and the Facilitating Environment*.

Similarly, key workers and their resident clients have a reciprocal relationship. Some of the residents, it would seem from the descriptions given and appearances made, have not re-emerged as identifiable individuals with their own body/mind boundary. This may be exacerbated by staff needs for closeness and merger—needing to be needed—or conversely, a fear of getting too close to the madness in their charges and therefore keeping distant and becoming neglectful. This leads to the split of warehousing vs. horticultural (Miller & Gwynne, 1972) attitudes in staff, who on the one side may feel overwhelmed and therefore emotionally absent from their roles, or, on the other, struggle to regulate the closeness. Research exploring the social model of disability has produced substantial evidence that social attitudes to disability have a serious and damaging effect on the quality of services and resources made available to disabled people and their families. Cooke (2000) highlighted how the endemic marginalisation of disabled people promotes the acceptance of a lower standard of care for them, and is one of many researchers promoting the "social model" of disability, referring not to impairments but to social barriers (Paul & Cawson, 2002, pp. 262–281).

Thinking systemically, this is encapsulated succinctly by Foster's description (1992, p. 1), "To give a person the care that they need can be institutionalising in the manner that it is done … [after all] … it is not bricks and mortar that define an institution but the manner in which an organisation behaves towards the bodies in its care." Miller and Gwynne (1972) describe a concept for good community care which seems eternally applicable in a multitude of settings. They define it as a system that is able to meet the needs for both psycho-physical dependence and independence concurrently, and crucially a support system to monitor the two in terms of how they operate together and how the balance needs to be dynamic in response to client/resident ability. However, in considering the unconscious motivation for social barriers, or indeed team dysfunction, Bion (1961, p. 39) explains that, "The group … is charged with emotions which exert a powerful, and frequently unobserved, influence on the individual. As a result, his emotions are stirred to the detriment of his judgement." If basic assumption oneness is operational, then:

> Through this defence, team members avoid struggling with differences by behaving as if everyone in the team were the same. This is a flight from true multi-disciplinary working resulting in staff functioning at the lowest common denominator of sameness, giving up the satisfaction which comes from professional expertise in favour of team cosiness. This defence obscures the value of difference and drastically reduces the options available to the client. (Foster, 2010, p. 3)

However, the further danger is that if staff are unable to appreciate and use difference within their team, they may also turn a "blind eye" (Steiner, 1993) to differences in the client group and treat them with a panacea of "same treatment" no matter their level of functioning. It follows that this then further induces dependency and institutionalisation within residents, and a vicious circle is set up between the two groups: a staff group impaired by basic assumption oneness (Turquet, 1974, p. 360) treating with indifference and lack of creativity a resident group in basic assumption dependency, expecting to be looked after. Through this deconstruction, we start to get a systemic picture of despair. Bion (1961, p. 48) acknowledges, "A group whose members cannot attend regularly must be apathetic and indifferent to the sufferings of the individual patient." However, this is not the full picture, as there are also signs that basic assumption "me-ness" was in operation: "a case of everybody does their own thing with residents as if they were all the boss whereas what they need to do is to wait for the actual key worker, who knows the resident best, to share their view first and then make a decision together not on his own. But we don't always do that around here." Hatcher Cano (1998, p. 84) captures this theoretically: "Me-ness group members defensively collude with the assumption that there is no group at all—just unaffiliated individuals, whose only joint purpose will be to thwart the formation of a group out of fear that they might be submerged in it or persecuted by it if it did form."

In this case, the staff often acted in a disparate manner akin to parents who are not a united couple and can be individually drawn in to favouritism towards the uncontained, paranoid resident "children". It is possible that their mental health will deteriorate in a chaotic system which does not hold individual residents in a reliable, consistent organisational mind. I thought about the need for some mothers to emphasise their ability to care due to their own infantile needs, and the parallel with staff who may feel insecure and demonstrate their effectiveness in a misguided way by automatically doing things for residents without assessing whether this is appropriate. This may foster dependency and cause deterioration of function, and the cumulative effect over time is institutionalisation. At the other end of the spectrum, premature demands for independence do not enable a secure base within individuals, and the threat of losing one's "home" can cause destabilisation, decline, and a desperate clinging. Subtle attunement to physical capability and emotional readiness are key in this work in rehabilitating residents, just as with "rapprochement" (Mahler, Pine, & Bergman, 1975) with toddlers finding their first steps, exploring the world, and then returning to the secure base, and with adolescents/young adults leaving home and coming back metaphorically or literally with dirty linen. In some ways, whenever we are confronted with change, we revisit, emotionally, these early formative stages, and if they have been traumatic, we will find navigation through relationships, job changes, different life stages such as mid-life and ageing, much more traumatic. For some residents, this is the cycle they are stuck in, and from which they may never emerge due to the extent of their historical and present difficulties; it is as if they are still weaning, or refusing to become weaned.

However, the nature of the residents' mental illness not only "leads to the dynamics of institutionalisation … [whereby] … home is constantly under attack from the unconscious process of the resident group" (Swinburne, 2000, p. 224), but, in my experience, also to "asylums in the mind" in staff who withdraw and vegetate or flee from a capacity to think individually or collectively. This may happen through the mechanism of projective identification whereby the physically and mentally broken-down state of individual residents gets not just under the skin of the organisational body and assaults the physical integrity of the "care home", but additionally, perhaps, penetrates the nervous and digestive systems of staff, leading ultimately to burnout or abandonment.

My second hypothesis is that shame can get a grip of the staff as a result of identifying with the governmental expectation of transforming the residents from needing the kind of care provided by a registered home into more functional people who can have their needs met in a deregistered care home. Residents such as Stig who do not manage this represent for the staff the evidence of having failed in the task so defined.

Stig was the only resident to come to visit the consultancy, and for all but one session. He was central and showed me the living essence of organisational difficulties, and perhaps challenged the consultancy not to forget him. However, like a troubled child displaying familial strife, holding Stig in mind seemed too painful, and so he had been left like a "Stig of the dump" to rot in his own filth. After this revelation, there was a clear demonstration, by management particularly, of a need to "forget" about him and the work with me, by avoiding the subsequent consultancy sessions, as thinking and linking meant being confronted with a failure too difficult or painful to face. In their minds, as an authority figure, I may have been partially identified with the persecuting policymaker, while Stig may have been seen as a saboteur to meeting their targets. I made an attempt to help free them of their shame by helping them see that it is the expectation that is unrealistic—you can take "Stig out of the dump, but you can't take the dump out of Stig". However, staff do nonetheless have to work within a system that requires in one sense that they have to play the game of appearing to enable people to "get better" and yet be confronted by each resident's pathology, resistance, and insistence on finding their own level—which may include filling a fridge with dirt and newspapers from the street.

In being challenged with Stig, staff, and anyone who cares to observe closely enough, are confronted with an aspect of human nature that is destructive and despairing by which the death drive triumphs (Freud, 1901b) in a purgatorial perpetuity. For staff whose internal motivation for doing the work is likely to be to make internal reparation (Klein, 1959) for unconscious infantile destructive phantasies, they are thwarted by the impossibility of the task and confronted with a double dose of shame. The shame comprises the original trauma to their own psyche and then again in the breakdown in attempts at reparation by a failure of the primary task. The staff's own needs for containment mostly go unmet, and just like a mother who tries to apply a baby manual for care but is unavailable to spontaneously attune to different expressions in her infant, due either to aspects of her own mental health being impaired or to her current environment lacking support, so staff may become indifferent to, or at worst neglectful of, residents who cannot perform the required milestones that cause them, in turn, to fail the latest standards of housing and care. This may conveniently deposit feelings of failure and shame into staff, and these are then defended against through turning a "blind eye" or manic activity. This may evoke retaliation, withdrawal, breakdown, despondency, or manic defence, and/or an attempt to dump this multitude of disturbing feelings, including feeling useless, back into residents or into a visiting consultant.

I wondered many times whether I could make a difference and compensated by perhaps over-linking and thinking. Misplaced overemphasis or apathy seemed to be a general feature in this work, and we could see this in relation to risk, which Foster (1998, p. 84) describes succinctly:

> Paternalism and over-protectiveness are characteristics of the risk minimization position evident in policies … which if we are not careful may lead to unnecessary restrictions being placed on the liberty of those identified as being a risk to others and to themselves. This in turn limits the possibility of integrating the mentally ill in their communities. We have to find a middle road

between being over-cautious by unnecessarily limiting our own and our clients' experiences, and being cavalier by putting ourselves and others in too much danger.

Barney's grandmother in *Stig of the Dump* seemed to enable just the balance—sufficient nurture and protection, and yet space for adventure and imagination. It is this combination of "fact and fancy" (King, 1963) that is so qualitatively different from the "fact versus fancy" of *Hard Times* (Dickens, 1854).

Conclusion

In this consultation, staff members were able to bring fears and concerns that seemed to have been festering and sapping creativity from the staff group. Whether this was sufficient an experience for it to have been internalised by the organisation for its healthier functioning remains to be seen. Foster (1998, p. 85) summarises the core issue:

> An unspoken but powerful expectation is placed on professionals whose job it is to care for the mentally ill in the community: that they will make mental illness disappear, either by curing the clients or by making them invisible.... the real task of professionals in mental health work is to do what highly anxious and disturbed people, communities or systems cannot do: that is, to think while keeping in mind the disturbing and conflicting aspects of the situation.

As consultant, I am left, as so often are staff working with those with mental illness, not knowing whether I have made a difference. While my own narcissism certainly was not indulged, as there was no recognition of my input by management, it seems that important reflections were brought to consciousness and shared, and some necessary understanding and realisations developed. With the final four attending the last consultancy session, the two team leaders and two committed support workers, I was left hopeful that a reflective core might continue. It seems that the team present for the last session could acknowledge the value in having a reasonably undistorted mirror that reflected back.

This means that they were demonstrating a capacity to emerge from the organisational psychotic "hall of mirrors". My hope is that there will be less avoidance of clients, less hiding in the staff office, and that some of the vitality that staff members currently access in manic defence via the pub and the staff room can become more widely available. Ideally, more effective systems of care need to be engendered by communicating staff concerns with a thinking organisational mind, contained in a reflective team within a building that provides a home for minds as well as bodies. I am aware of the challenge this presents due to the "fear of break-down", as conceptualised by Winnicott, and the use of social defences, as described by Menzies (1960), to defend the work group against the anxiety emoted by madness, not only in residents, but in the political climate. We can usefully consider Winnicott's conceptualisation of the personal from an organisational perspective: in the simplest possible case there was therefore a split second in which the threat of madness was experienced, but anxiety at this level is unthinkable. Its intensity is beyond description and new defences are organised immediately so that in fact madness was not experienced (Eigen, 1999, p. 172), who quotes (Winnicott, 1989, p. 127).

The question would be what structural containment can there possibly be in a political climate in which professional survival is insecure and the validity and necessity of the work is being attacked. Foster (1992, p. 6) hypothesises that:

> Workers in the field of community care need to feel adequately contained themselves in order to provide effective containment for their clients .... Can we as workers in community care provide adequate containment for the projections of our clients and of other workers in the field and struggle to think about our own tendencies to project and enact before acting or are we, given the extreme anxieties that the demands of the job can stir up in us, liable to respond like the uncontaining mother?

There is a risk that dysfunctional silos will develop within the organisation, and the asylum, an actual building before 1990, then retreats as a virtual pocket in staff minds, leaving organisational, group, and individual madness uncontained beneath the radar. For some staff, this will be reminiscent of Winnicott's "breakdown", described earlier in this chapter, hence high staff turnover. Perhaps we can all try to avoid either metaphorically joining in with Stig by getting down in the dumps or fleeing in an attempt to abandon what he represents inside ourselves.

I would like to end by turning back to the sociopolitical and wider implications. Foster (1998, p. 85) poignantly describes how primitive responses towards those with mental illness demonstrated "mental disturbance within our society". Ultimately, residents pay the price. Foster (1992, p. 7) describes the risk: without adequate containment creative thought becomes impossible and madness or disturbance is put out of mind. We can project all of this into those labelled mentally ill but we can no longer conveniently put them out of sight. Instead we see the casualties of this process on our streets.

So while the Olympic Games is a test of stamina, fitness, and agility, the well-being of services is under threat with a danger of a growing split in society between the fit and the unwell; an undesirable outcome for all. The risk is that the Stigs of our communities will create their dirty dumps either in care homes through neglect or on the streets as they are deliberately or inadvertently dumped back outside as undesirable. However, society has demonstrated its outrage towards wealth imbalance through summer riots in 2011 in England and anti-capitalist demonstrations internationally, and so perhaps some of the projections into Stig and his dump can, over time, be reabsorbed. However, as a cautionary note, in one of their adventures, Barney and Stig manage to prevent thieves masquerading as TV repairmen from making off with Barney's granny's silver when Stig "let out a sound that was something between a growl and a howl and dashed at the man, raising his horrible club" (King, 1963, p. 88). We should be wary of stealing resources and imagining there will be no price to pay.

References

Armstrong, D. (2005). *Organization in the Mind: Psychoanalysis, Group Relations, and Organisational Consultancy*. London: Karnac.

Bion, W. R. (1961). *Experiences in Groups and Other Papers*. Hove, UK: Routledge, 2010.

Bion, W. R. (1970). *Attention and Interpretation*. London: Tavistock.

Cano, D. H. (1998). Oneness and Me-ness in the baG. In: P. Bion Talamo, F. Borgogno, & S. A. Merciai (Eds.), *Bion's Legacy to Groups* (pp. 83–94). London: Karnac.

Cooke, P. (2000). *Final Report on Disabled Children and Abuse*. Nottingham, UK: Ann Craft Trust.

Cooper, M. (2010). Better use of resources. *Housing, Care and Support, 13*(4): 2–4.

Dickens, C. (1854). *Hard Times*. London: Penguin, 1995.

Eigen, M. (1999). *Toxic Nourishment*. London: Karnac. forum.ukqcs.co.uk/home/forum/topic/36/8/1/17/ (last accessed July 30, 2012).

Foster, A. (1992). *Institutional Consultation in the Community*. London: Tavistock Clinic, Paper no. 140.

Foster, A. (1998). Thinking about risk. In: A. Foster & V. Z. Roberts (Eds.), *Managing Mental Health in the Community: Chaos and Containment*. New York: Routledge.

Foster, A. (2010). Notes from Angela Foster's theory session on November 30, 2010: D10 Basic Assumptions Revisited—One-ness & Me-ness in Organisations.

Freud, S. (1901b). *The Psychopathology of Everyday Life. S. E., 6*. London: Hogarth.

Freud, S. (1914c). On narcissism: an introduction. *S. E., 14*: 67–102. London: Hogarth.

King, C. (1963). *Stig of the Dump*. London: Puffin, 1971.

Klein, M. (1959). Our adult world and its roots in infancy. In: *Envy and Gratitude, and Other Works, 1946–1963* (pp. 247–263). London: Hogarth, 1975.

Mahler, M., Pine, F., & Bergman, A. (1975). *The Psychological Birth of the Human Infant: Symbiosis and Individuation*. London: Karnac.

Menzies Lyth, I. (1960). A case-study in the functioning of social systems as a defence against anxiety: a report on a study of the nursing service of a general hospital. *Human Relations, 13*: 95.

Miller, E. J., & Gwynne, G. V. (1972). *A Life Apart: A Pilot Study of Residential Institutions for the Physically Handicapped and the Young Chronic Sick*. London: Tavistock.

Paul, A., & Cawson, P. (2002). Safeguarding disabled children in residential settings: what we know and what we don't know. *Child Abuse Review, 11*: 262–281.

Scanlon, C., & Adlam, J. (2008). Refusal, social exclusion and the cycle of rejection: a cynical analysis? *Critical Social Policy*, *28*: 529.

Steiner, J. (1993). *Psychic Retreats: Pathological Organizations in Psychotic, Neurotic and Borderline Patients*. London: Routledge.

studymore.org.uk/xpowell.htm (last accessed July 31, 2012).

Swinburne, M. (2000). 'Home is where the hate is': analytic perspectives on the modern mental home. *Psychoanalytic Psychotherapy*, *14*(3): 223–238.

Turquet, P. M. (1974). Leadership: the individual and the group. In: G. S. Gibbard, J. J. Hartman, & R. D. Mann (Eds.), *Analysis of Groups: Contributions to Theory, Research, and Practice*. San Francisco and London: Jossey-Bass.

Winnicott, D. W. (1958). Hate in the counter-transference. In: *Through Paediatrics to Psychoanalysis: Collected Papers* (pp. 194–203). London: Tavistock.

Winnicott, D. W. (1965). *The Maturational Processes and the Facilitating Environment: Studies in the Theory of Emotional Development*. London: Karnac, 1990.

Winnicott, D. W. (1989). *Psycho-Analytic Explorations*. C. Winnicott, R. Shepherd, & M. Davis (Eds.). Cambridge, MA: Harvard University Press.

www.caremanagementmatters.co.uk/documents/PeterGrose.pdf (last accessed July 30, 2012).

www.dictionary.reference.com/browse/community+care (last accessed November 12, 2011).

www.margaretthatcher.org/document/106689 (last accessed October 8, 2011).

www.mind.org.uk/help/research_and_policy/the_history_of_mental_health_and_community_care-key_dates (last accessed August 18, 2011).

www.socialcareassociation.co.uk/Portals/0/Public%20Docs/Keyworking%20in%20Social%20Care.pdf (last accessed September 14, 2011).

CHAPTER FIVE

Power and the manipulation of the masses: Third World perspectives*

Edgard Sanchez Bernal

W e have long believed there to be a divide between the world of the mind and the reality we witness and construct. Division between the internal and external permeates every sphere of our reality. Our constructions of self, and our construction of the world outside have ushered in eras of self-perceived human magnificence— through culture, society, and the like—and have been epitomised by our modern religions' anthropocentricity. While we strive to meet the falling angel, often we forget our humble origins as the rising ape (Pratchett, 1996). A primitiveness that pierces all our sophisticated ideals and structures is lying in wait just beside the fall of order. One only has to imagine the fallout of a nuclear conflict for the law of the jungle to supersede all other constructs, ideals, and truths.

How can someone murder a loved one and attempt to kill another, then feel the full support of his community and resultant impunity?

---

* This chapter is a modified version of a paper read at the Institute of Psychoanalysis Clinical/Theoretical Seminar: The Political Mind Seminars, "The role of the unconscious in political and social life" (2015).

How does our collective behaviour morph in different environments and what effect does this have on our laws and notions of justice?

While sociology and external world focused theories have provided answers regarding the what and the how of the workings of our complex external structures, exploring our internal world—what makes us who we are—can shed a light on the why.

The internal world

While still raising controversy in matters of the mind, the founding father of psychoanalysis—Sigmund Freud (1856–1939)—laid crucial foundations in the colossal challenge of understanding the human mind. By focusing his medical expertise on those suffering from mental illnesses, he gleaned many striking insights into the "healthy" mind and the delicate relationship between the world without and the world within. This relationship, as Freud highlights (1915e), is often dissonant due to external factors (including neurophysiology) obscuring the world of internal motivations. It is these motivations that play a very important role in making us feel and behave as we do.

The discussion of the differences between mind, brain, and environment has been ongoing since the dawn of time and is beyond the aim of this chapter. However, Freud's medical education followed the premise that like every organ in our body, true understanding requires knowledge of its development from inception. Thus, for the mind, it started by laying attention not only on the symptoms his patients came with, but by laying attention upon the narratives that came along with them. This was gradually extended to comprehending the minds of babies, toddlers, adolescents, and adults, noting the progressive stages of development while also perceiving the ever-present nature of early narratives throughout each stage (1905d).

If it is in our minds where we perceive all the ideas by which we understand the world, it is possible to hypothesise that looking into such an inner screen may help us understand the world. The reverse can also hold true. To further illustrate this, we shall now discuss a clinical scenario that has stuck with me for years.

Ms P

A single woman in her early thirties (Ms P) came to me seeking treatment for PTSD (post-traumatic stress disorder). She was one of four children and recalled the iron law set by her father throughout their upbringing. She described her father as a despot and authoritarian, who often resorted to physical and emotional abuse to impose his authority upon his wife and children.

Ms P and her siblings travelled to the First World for higher education. In this period, one of her sisters fell in love with someone who was not of their ethnicity. Ms P became aware of this, and so did her mother. Her mother was described as being more flexible than her father, thus, when her sister ended up getting married, Ms P and her mother attended the "secret" wedding. Her father and the rest of her siblings were left in the dark as such an act was clearly against the principles with which they had all been brought up.

A few years later, through some unforeseen circumstances, Ms P's father was made aware of the fact that his daughter had been secretly married, and that his wife and Ms P had attended the wedding. Ms P told me that when her father was informed, in a fit of rage, he stormed into their home and beat his wife to death in front of Ms P.

After this brutal deed, Ms P was chased by her father and managed to evade the bullets shot after her. She escaped in a state of utter terror and horror. As the local authorities got involved, it was Ms P that was arrested rather than her father. The political sway her father held within the community diverted the interest and punitive measures away from him. Thanks to some outside help, Ms P was allowed out of police custody and promptly fled from her native country, arriving to the First World as a refugee on humanitarian protection grounds.

Hierarchies, power, and family

A very powerful parental figure appears to have the quality of a god-like entity—one that decides what is right and what is wrong, decides who lives and who dies. This may be linked to the fact that we humans are born in a state of total physical and emotional dependence and remain in such a state for longer than any other mammal (Freud, 1926d). We would not be able to survive without the active positive care of our parents or primary caregivers during such a long period of time. Our survival, in the first stages of life, is not in our hands. This situation leaves an indelible trace in our psychical system. One of the first developments of this power asymmetry occurs when it shifts its life–death dependency stage towards a new symbolic representation—being loved or not being loved (1926d, p. 81). Being loved becomes life, and not, death. This is evidenced by the common presentation of young patients suffering from the painful feelings of a broken heart and resultant suicidal ideation.

If Ms P's father appeared in front of our eyes, he would not be perceived anywhere near as powerful as Ms P sees him. It is the biological and emotional past, of her experience with her father having been a central figure of authority and love ever since she was born, that made him so powerful. However, in front of our eyes, it would be difficult for us not to see the authoritarian, the coward, and the murderer.

Alongside the biologically and emotionally determined power, Ms P's father also held power within his community, which reinforced in Ms P her sense of weakness compared to her father-god. What is to be regarded as right or wrong is a task given to parents, a lesson that is internalised by children as well as projected onto the community's justice system. The latter has historically taken the flavour of an authority, often symbolised by law, which imposes its mode of action in a brutal or delicate balance between force and love, between imposing and convincing.

Bertrand Russell emphasises a key aspect in the conception of law, noting that "The degree of feeling in favour of Law is one of the most important characteristics of a community … [and that] the law is almost powerless when it is not supported by public sentiment" (1938, p. 38). Thus, Russell highlights that the true power of law lies not in the hands of its enforcers, but more within the community who directly or indirectly back it up.

The community and the collective

As a community develops, some of the roles of the powerful primitive father figure are passed on from parents to community, in the form of schoolteachers, community leaders, and so on. This marks a gradual transition of power towards the community establishment. The crisis of adolescence could be seen, under this perspective, as one manifestation of the decreased power of the parents in the transition of power from the home to the community.

We will now look at an example of individuals that live in a complex society, in communities that Dario Maestripieri (2007) has studied for more than twenty years, writing extensively on their behaviour. These groups enact "strong dominance hierarchies and long-lasting social bonds between roughly half their members". Individuals compete for "high social status, and the power that comes with it, using ruthless aggression, nepotism, and complex political alliances. Sex, too, can be used for political purposes." The leaders of said collective often use "threats and violence" to retain the best land, resources, and potential partners. Dominant leaders use "frequent and unpredictable aggression as an effective form of intimidation". Less capable members of the society are marginalised and forced to live on the periphery of the group's land, where they are vulnerable to external forces. They must wait for the others to eat first and then scrounge for the leftovers.

I have purposely left out that the author quoted above is referring to a rhesus macaque primate community. The creeping discomfort that such a comparison brings is worth noting, as if we were not that different from mere animals. For millennia, humans have distanced themselves from the term animal as if we were exceptional. We have historically sympathised with the idea that we humans are at the top of the pyramid of living beings. Aristotle thought that among living beings, there was a preordained hierarchy: "That plants are created for the sake of animals, and animals for the sake of men; the tame for our use and provision; the wild, at least the greater part, for our provision also, or for some other advantageous purpose, as furnishing us with clothes, and the like."

According to Aristotle (384–322 BCE), humans were the "masters" due to their power to reason. Nowadays, we have realised that we are clearly no "masters" and that our survival is unavoidably dependent on fauna and plants, not by solely eating them, but by living alongside them sustainably. I suggest that we have elevated our condition as *Homo sapiens* too far, as if we were an exceptional difference, blinding ourselves to the similarities we share with animals, particularly regarding our behaviour in and as communities.

In these rhesus macaque societies, we see that behaviours are either encouraged or repressed whether by rewards, like sexual fulfilment, or punishment, like physical beating or being forced out of the community. In Ms P's case, a sexual infringement of the law, within her family, was punished by a death by proxy and she was consequently forced to live away from her group in order to survive.

Although there is no doubt that some aspects of our behaviour have developed in many positive ways from our primitive and primal reactions, it is always worth being aware of how close we still are to falling back to less developed and civilised ways of being. History has taught us how communities that appear to be at the height of civilisation can collapse and enact the cruellest of behaviours, as demonstrated by both World Wars. Highly sophisticated thoughts do not spare us from primitive behaviours. We have deluded ourselves into thinking that once we achieve some kind of sophisticated education, we have exorcised our irrational self. Irrational thoughts and consequent behaviours occur much more than we suspect, making up a large part of our most natural self. Glimmers of such irrationality frequently appear in our dreams, daydreams, and fantasies. In our waking moments, fears and bias often lie as the foundation of such irrationality, and part of our everyday lives consists of the filtered and irregular metamorphosis of our unconscious irrationality into our conscious awareness. However, much of the unconscious irrationality subtly influencing our behaviour stays put.

How subliminal and unconscious representations dictate and influence collective behaviour has been a continuous personal source of intrigue.

First and Third World

Despite the First and Third World being questionable terms, I will use them for two reasons: first, to highlight the still existing the continuing chasm that divides our external worlds; and as a psychoanalyst, to lay attention upon the importance of our internal and often divided worlds.

When images of a Third World urban centre appear, let's say a busy road, often what is perceived or commented on is the apparent chaos and disorganisation in which the traffic seems to flow—how there appears to be no regulation whatsoever and how often minor or major traffic accidents occur.

Those of us who have been born in such places have a tendency to feel awe and admiration when first travelling to iconic places in the First World—be it North America or Europe, and more recently some Asian nations. The contrast between the aforementioned image with the First World is striking, from chaos to order—an organised flow of people walking, driving, going up and down stairs, etc. I remember as a child in my country how when such scenes were described, the comment that would often follow was along the lines of how the Americans or Europeans were so civilised, not like us, who did not behave in an orderly manner.

This same view was held by most of the European "Conquistadores" of the New World—the inhabitants of the New World were not civilised, so, were they even human? This question became so widely disseminated that a petition was sent to the highest Roman Catholic authority of the time, questioning whether the aboriginals, whose behaviour was most uncivilised, merited having any of the rights accorded to human beings. The Conquistadores were unable to answer this question, and the issue was only partially put to rest after a lengthy debate in Spain, *The Valladolid Debate* (1550–1551), in which two religious authorities advocated opposite sides: Fray Bartolomé de las Casas defending the aborigines as "rational beings"; while Juan Ginés de Sepúlveda (1941, p. 155) argued that human sacrifice of innocents, cannibalism, and other "such crimes against nature" were unacceptable and should be suppressed by any means possible, including war. A papal encyclical, *Sublimis Deus*, under Pope Paul III, in 1537, took the side of the aborigines, stating that the indigenous people were entitled to have human rights ... at least on paper. (They were technically humans, but it became the duty of the Conquistadores to make them Christian, as then these aborigines would become the right kind of pious human ...)

Exploring this First versus Third World phenomenon, it is worth noting that when displaced people from the Third World come to the First, their behaviour seems to shift subtly to that of wherever they are, becoming almost unnoticeable; they would appear not to be alien to the regulated flow of people going up or down electric escalators; or if driving, would follow the local traffic regulations. This apparent immersion indicates that, by their behaviour, we would not be able to recognise most of them among groups of others walking in Paris, London, or Washington, DC.

We are aware that in Third World locations, the gap between extreme poverty and affluence has been and is significantly more visible than in the First World. The experience of dining at a restaurant anywhere in the Third World, and being surround by beggars, is not uncommon. But the gap that divides these two worlds is narrowing. In the past few decades, a number of so-called Third World countries seem to be in the good books of world economy experts, while homelessness and extreme poverty are growing in many First World countries.

When I speak of Third World populations behaving in the "civilised" manner of First World inhabitants, I am of course not referring to the well-educated elite of such Third World countries, as it is likely that they have been educated either by European or American standards. I refer more to the displaced Third World population that for all sorts of reasons end up in the First World, and how they mould to the behaviour of whatever place they end up living in.

It appears that something in the environment where we live seems to determine our behaviour in ways that go beyond our awareness, as these people that I am referring to behave differently, but by no means think that something in them has changed—the modification of behaviour happens in an automatic manner, and most frequently reverts to usual once back in their home countries. These interchangeable ways of being seem to challenge the notion that behaving in a "civilised manner" has to do with learning and knowledge, but more with behaviour outside our conscious awareness.

Within these different manners of being, are we referring to ideology? Are we referring to defensive mechanisms? Regardless, something very powerful seems to silently mould the behaviour of groups in our society, where such behaviours disguise themselves under the invisibility cloak of the "normal".

Internal motivations

Ms P's predicament is initially conceptualised as suffering from PTSD. She lives in fear of her father appearing at any street corner with the aim of killing her. Any noise startles her, she fears walking in crowded places, noisy places, and tells me how she often has nightmares of the scene where she was witness to her mother's murder.

Ms P became, by defying her father's belief system, an enemy, as did her mother, but not only her father's enemy. Due to matters of culture, where her community disapprove of their kith and kin marrying outside their own, she became an enemy of her native group. Her father hides his criminal act beneath the cover created by this cultural fog. We are aware of how for centuries, masses have been manipulated by all sorts of indoctrinations. This patient confirms her perception of her father's omnipotent power upon witnessing her mother being beaten to death, but, notably, it is further entrenched by the experience of the surrounding community backing-up her father.

Ms P struggled to accept the possibility that beneath the horror and terror of what she had witnessed and experienced, feelings of rage and thirst for revenge reverberated. The fact that her father was the object of such feelings was by no means new; nor her manner of defending herself against them. Ms P throughout her lifetime was witness to her father being the personification of tyrannical justice. Nonetheless, she was able to accept and acknowledge this as being wrong, in an intellectual manner, probably due to her academic education; she was aware her father was wrong and had been wrong for years. This was exemplified by Ms P allowing me to know that she had secretly had some boyfriends in the past who were not of her ethnicity.

Ms P's aggressive drive had been so curtailed through the years that it was not a surprise to perceive something in her demeanour, a person in her early thirties, that elicited an impression and image of a young girl. Despite her mature physical appearance, a girlish voice and manner permeated her being. This regression allowed us to infer that for years it had been Ms P's defensive mechanism to quash her natural aggression through its opposite—submissiveness and passivity.

At various times during the initial sessions, Ms P made slips of the tongue. When telling me about her nightmares, she would describe dreaming a scene where her father was killing not only her mother but her also. However, the way the words came out her mouth were how she (Ms P) was killing him. This allowed me to infer a repressed thought in her mind, a wish to kill her father. Upon bringing to her attention this line of thought, she initially resisted to acknowledge such a wish. The submissiveness that can be induced into us by years of unjust passivity will not just be erased or emotionally acknowledged within a few months of therapy sessions.

Ms P was clearly more in touch with the fear of being killed than of committing parricide. She spoke of being frightened and startled when hearing any noise, as somewhere in her internal world there was the fear of her father plotting to kill her. The feelings such an image brought to the surface flooded her with fear, that although understandable, also elicited in her an enormous ambivalence … that she appeared only to resolve by an awkward internal compromise—a third option, in the form of an intrusive thought to kill herself.

Freud (1912–13) suggests that in the earliest human horde, the group of expelled males—brothers who have been expelled by the father who has seen them as potential rivals—return together to the horde and kill their brother/father/ruler/god. He suggests that this event may have been one of the seeds for the creation of religions as it generated a need for a whole set of rules to manage the guilt triggered by such a crime: sin, which Christians, for example, think they are born with.

Thus, some religions' ethos seems to promote help to others who are weaker, playing on such feelings of guilt, promoting acts of charity, trying to be good to others, and so on. Recently, I was listening to a young man telling me that he had not really been taught his religious creed as well as he should have been. He had been brought up in a non-affluent area, and he argued that this meant his religious education was not done by well-educated leaders. He told me of having been shown, while he was in sixth form, videos portraying extreme injustice and the persecution of kindred souls, and then being repeatedly told that these things were happening only because they—the ones who were watching the video—had not been behaving in a good-enough manner; the way that their God would want them to behave. They were told that all of their religious peers are like brothers, and the bad behaviour of one makes all other brothers of the same creed suffer more.

Listening to this made me reflect that not all religions seem to work only on one aspect of guilt, as the account relayed to me by this young person imparted much more a sense of responsibility: "I will help others by becoming more orthodox, and by doing so, my brothers' suffering decreases." Improving one's behaviour would balance out the rewards of God to all brethren. Yet this responsibility, at its core, masks a repurposed and embellished form of guilt. A fear appears to be suggested that were he not to behave in the most orthodox manner, others of his religious persuasion would have their suffering increased. "And so, I will help others by becoming stricter within my own religious duties." This exemplifies how guilt has been used for centuries as a tool to manipulate others.

Psychoanalysis has realised that guilt is a feeling that roots itself very deep in our unconscious mind. Ms P's refusal to accept her parricidal wishes stemmed from the guilt these wishes produced in her. Thus, guilt's role in distorting and manipulating truth and behaviour cannot be understated.

I am fully aware that in the name of all gods, history has witnessed too much bloodshed, probably more than for any other reason. I am also aware how when the leaders of communities exercise power with tyranny, tyranny becomes the normal currency of our interactions.

In the description of the rhesus macaques given earlier, the research of that community also found something that I think is worth keeping in mind. When the alpha male, the leader of the pack, behaved in a bullying, authoritarian manner, there appeared to be enough evidence to suggest a tendency in the pack to behave similarly. An increase, within the primate community, of bullying and aggressive behaviour peaked at such times. Fortunately, there is also evidence in the opposite direction, when another alpha male arrives as leader, who shows less tyrannical behaviour, there is a tendency for the pack to mirror this (Maestripieri, 2007).

We can easily be tempted to think that within different human communities at present, there have been situations where a certain type of leader tends to generate a trend, as if the political leader of an elite country can end up facilitating in other countries the rise of a similar type of character. It could be helpful to think that such a parallel rise might be explained by the concept of mirror neurons. Mirror neurons are premotor neurons in the prefrontal cortex of our brains that tend to mimic behaviours observed in others. They function akin to a testing ground for enacting the behaviours ourselves (Rizzolatti & Craighero, 2004). In psychoanalytic language, it may well have to do with what we have thought of as one of the earliest defensive mechanisms—identification. In a community, such a concept can be observed strikingly when a behaviour goes viral (e.g., the "Gangnam Style" and Fortnite dances). In less extreme scenarios, the trendy and popular provoke widespread imitation in every sphere of our social lives (such as the hairstyle of a professional footballer or a new tech app or device). I posit that communities can also become the mirror neurons of other communities. In the previous century, examples of this are the rise of Hitler, followed by Mussolini and Stalin, and in present times, the rise of Trump, followed by Bolsonaro and others. This perspective may contradict the notion of a conspiracy theory, where evil figures in high places pull the strings of the global marionette, and solidifies the argument that communities nowadays see each other as role models. Just as a dance can spread like wildfire globally, ideology and protests can spark into life from seemingly disjointed sources, while influencing each other nevertheless. This hints at an irrepressible contagion of behaviour that is beyond our awareness.

Manipulation of the masses

As mentioned earlier, the boundaries between what has been called the First and Third Worlds have become even more malleable and mobile in the last few decades than ever before. In the same way that Third World countries see their elite achieve similar status as First World aristocracies, the First World has also become prey to what has been for years common in the Third World—extremist ideologies. The recent events in Europe, Asia, the United States, South America, Russia, and China could be seen as examples of how the mainstream ideologies are having trouble preserving their boundaries or their territory. It looks as if the definition of ideology is being challenged by other ideologies, within these long-held territories, that communicate a completely different set of principles. In most of the Judaeo-Christian world, we are well aware of the moral code such ideologies impose upon us, and in the last hundred years, it is clear how much territory the religious authorities have lost.

Ideology has been defined mainly by Marxist theoreticians as some sort of false consciousness that leads people to hold a belief system that by itself has as its aim to keep a ruling group/class in power. How interesting it would be for this belief system not only to be a way of thinking, that is taught and learnt, but more importantly, for it to be a subliminal (unconscious) communication that leads to a way of behaving.

Ms P had something in her that made her different from her community that reacted in the way it did to her father's crime. Her father was cruel with all his children, but some of her siblings never placed blame on him. What made her different? Is it that unconsciously she hated her father so much due to how unjust and unfair he was in his behaviour towards her mother and them? Is it that she sees the wrong of acting in such a way? Is it that her love for her mother makes her father her natural rival? Is it because she has a different ethos?

Psychoanalysis offers a chance for someone like Ms P to explore, within her own self, the many questions that her predicament puts forward. It relies on the capacity we have to voice experiences, internal and external, and to become aware of the many meanings and feelings these link to. It does not suggest a direction. It clearly believes there is a reason for everything, but only the one who is willing to put all their thoughts on the table of analytic enquiry may get closer to those individual meanings. It is possible that the more we allow ourselves to look at our internal world and make some sense of it, the more we facilitate an understanding of all the projections that we have made into the external world—society, religion, culture, and the like. It is not so much the external world that we do not understand, it is more our internal one.

So, what is the difference between the so-called First and Third World? I find there is some value in Bertrand Russell's (1938) description of law: "Law, as an effective force, depends upon opinion and sentiment even more than upon the powers of the police."

This description emphasises opinion and sentiment, which I think has to be linked to a sense of democracy, meaning that a community feels that their voices are heard, that justice happens, disregarding social class, race, or any other type of power. In the Third World, often police on the street carry sophisticated weapons and guns, but there is barely any justice. In the Third World, law is still very rudimentary, and quite unjust. In my work as a psychoanalyst, I have become aware that there are also First and Third *Internal* Worlds, that depend less on the geographical or financial conditions of one's country, and depend much more upon the parents' capacity to provide a sense of safety and joy to the next generation. This, in turn, will make them much more able to be just with themselves and to elect and demand fairness, justice, and a more egalitarian society.

References

Aristotle. *A Treatise on Government*. Book I, Chapter VIII. London: J. M. Dent & Sons, 1928.

Freud, S. (1905d). *Three Essays on the Theory of Sexuality*. S. E., *7*: 125–171. London: Hogarth.

Freud, S. (1912–13). *Totem and Taboo*. S. E., *13*. London: Hogarth.

Freud, S. (1915e). The unconscious. S. E., *14*: 159–215. London: Hogarth.

Freud, S. (1926d). *Inhibitions, Symptoms and Anxiety*. S. E., *20*. London: Hogarth.

Ginés de Sepúlveda, J. (1941). *Tratado sobre las Justas Causas de la Guerra contra los Indios*. M. Menéndez y Pelayo & M. García-Pelayo (Trans.). Mexico City: Fondo de Cultura Económica.

Maestripieri, D. (2007). *Macachiavellian Intelligence: How Rhesus Macaques and Humans Have Conquered the World. Chicago, IL: University of Chicago Press.* http://news.uchicago.edu/releases/07/071025.monkeys.shtml

Pratchett, T. (1996). *Hogfather*. London: Corgi, 2013.

Rizzolatti, G., & Craighero, L. (2004). The mirror-neuron system. *Annual Review of Neuroscience, 27*(1): 169–192.

Russell, B. (1938). *Power: A New Social Analysis*. London: George Allen & Unwin, 1938.

CHAPTER SIX

Whistle-blowers—moral good or self-interest? The psychological dimensions of defying a perverse or corrupt authority*

David Morgan

"First they came …" is a famous statement and provocative poem attributed to pastor Martin Niemöller (1892–1984) about the sloth of German intellectuals following the Nazis' rise to power and the subsequent purging of their targets, group after group.

> First they came for the communists,
> and I didn't speak out because I wasn't a communist.
>
> Then they came for the socialists,
> and I didn't speak out because I wasn't a socialist.
>
> Then they came for the trade unionists,
> and I didn't speak out because I wasn't a trade unionist.
>
> Then they came for the Jews,
> and I didn't speak out because I wasn't a Jew.

---

* An earlier version of this chapter originally appeared on the website http://www.publicinterestpsychology.co.uk.

> Then they came for the Catholics,
> and I didn't speak out because I wasn't a Catholic.
>
> Then they came for me,
> and there was no one left to speak for me.

For many people the miasma of fame that surrounds Julian Assange and Edward Snowden is seen to be rooted in their narcissism and however much they dress it up, their one day in the sun is seen, quite possibly erroneously as I will be discussing later, as driven by self-interest. Films are made about famous whistle-blowers and their place as A-list celebrities seems assured to us gawping onlookers. Through their disclosing acts they, rather than governments and leaders, seem to become the important ones. But for most of the people I have seen since becoming a consultant for WhistleblowersUK (WBUK), it is a very different story.

Everyday whistle-blowers, those whose names do not become a public entity, experience loss, not gain, through their decision to disclose. And whatever it is that they disclose, in the many fields these people emerge from, the whistle-blowers I have met are waiting to have, or already have had, their pension rights, mortgages, and jobs rescinded, their comfortable places of esteem in their communities dismantled, and, equally importantly from a psychological point of view, they have lost their peace of mind and quite often their faith in their own value and motives.

I am here to discuss what motivates a whistle-blower and to look at the psychological profile of people who risk, or gain—depending on where we stand—so much.

Let's face it, "whistle-blowing" as a term sounds vaguely pejorative, like a "snitch", so I favour the term "social disclosure" because it gives the clue to what altruistically motivated disclosure is really about. In Germany there is no word for whistle-blower at all; instead, they use a word that translates as "traitor", which shows us how suspicious we are of the people who break the rules. Traitor or discloser, narcissist or idealist, these are the poles of our discussion.

We expect in countries such as Nazi Germany, Pinochet's Chile, or North Korea for there to be hideous consequences for any perceived betrayal. We know that terrorist states do all they can to stamp out any dissent. And we like the idea that different mores apply in our own countries, that we live in a land of freedom and protection for human rights. In comparison with the totalitarian states I have mentioned, we in the West do of course enjoy significant freedom. But what I have discovered is how tough and suspicious our societal attitudes are to people we perceive as different, not only those who break free from our public laws and standards but also who undermine all our cosy assumptions about the safety of our world. When a whistle is blown we all listen, and we have to decide each and every one of us how we react to the people who tell us things we may not want to know.

In Britain, criticism or threat to the social order is muted, or seen as anti-authoritarian, naive, an attack on the parental authority, the status quo. Compliance, playing the game, and loyalty to one's organisation is often seen as a sign of psychological health. In my own professional institution, a criticism of the authority of some senior people is usually construed as trying to see into the parents' bedroom. Most of us are well over fifty!

What countless, less famous whistle-blowers discover is that the same blocks to speaking about problems, betrayals, failures, and exploitation apply in Britain just as in any totalitarian state, albeit more subtly. Powerful pressures are brought to bear on those who risk speaking out.

I am thinking of the people I have spoken to in the last year, including:

> The vehicle manufacturer who discovers that his factory has been using seriously substandard materials, is in a position to create unemployment for himself and everyone he knows. The economic impact of a scandal to his company, already on the brink of economic collapse, would be disastrous. But he is also aware that the lives of the product's users are at risk. He goes to and is shunned by his union and bosses. But still he speaks out. He receives death threats in the post and loses his job. His health begins to deteriorate. He is accused of having mental health problems, which of course he now does and probably did before in a pre-morbid personality everyday sort of way. He goes to his MP and is told that there is no evidence. The MP and local newspapers are funded by interested parties.

The judicial person who discovers the conglomeration of Freemasons in her chosen profession and believes that they have operated a cover-up over a certain case. And she decides to tell the story.

The banker who discovers that in the House of Mammon all that matters is profit (why the surprise?) and, as a consequence of dodgy auditing, that his mother's pension company is eaten up by sharp practice.

In the field of state provision, in hospitals and social services, even today when people speak out over damaging cuts, or mis-management or the appalling culture of un-care at Stafford Hospital or neglect in social care teams, they are liable to be disbelieved, humiliated, and dismissed. As I sit and listen to the many stories of painful internal conflict, fear, anger, and sometimes bitterness and regret, I think to myself would I, an NHS worker for twenty-five years, without a financial cushion to fall back on in my private life, have stood up and been counted, risked my mortgage and my children's futures, would or did I put my own self-interest and survival above the altruism of revealing neglect and incompetence? If I had been at the Bristol Children's or Haringey Social Services, would I have said anything in the interest of saving lives? I hope so, but I'm not sure.

In terms of thinking about the psychological precursors and sequelae of the disclosers I have met, as a psychoanalyst and clinical psychologist, I ask myself, does idealism exist? Is disclosure a narcissistic or an altruistic act? Does it matter?

Since I volunteered to work for WBUK I have worked in person or on the phone with more than 100 disclosers or potential disclosers and it's a fascinating but paranoia-inducing job. The first comment from my first-ever psychological assessment with an established and successful discloser was, "Is this place [my consulting room] bugged?"

I am used to working with psychosis and I normally see this sort of fantasy as a projected form of aggression, externalised onto the outside world, where it then persecutes the originator, from outside in the minds of others or through delusions and hallucinations. Through externalisation, the internal aggressive impulses are thus reduced and put out to tender. But with this group, the feeling has remained for weeks and the question, "Is your room bugged?" no longer seems so delusional. I tell myself that I'm not that important, but the stories I hear are compelling and mostly feel genuine.

Undoubtedly, many of the people I see do exist in paranoid states of mind and some must surely have had traces of these states before they disclosed. Afterwards they feel watched, their level of trust is low, and it is easy to write them all off as vexatious litigants and troublemakers. A small minority may indeed be less than idealistically motivated, but even they may have something important to say; like victims of abuse it is essential that we find ways to hear it. Traumatising as it is to hear and seductive as it is to turn a blind eye or just pathologise, the ultimate defence of the cushioned psychoanalyst, I have become convinced that the psychological profile of the whistle-blower is no different from that of anyone else.

Of course, not all whistle-blowing is benign or altruistically motivated. HMRC has an anonymous phone line for people to report tax evasion which is consistently used to denounce neighbours, work colleagues, and family members (Holder, 2018). While disclosure can be an altruistic act, it can all too easily be used for revenge and humiliation. At times, some whistle-blowers are clearly eager to attack authorities through resentment. Stalled careers, failed love affairs, and no pay rise can see increases in some individuals' willingness to shame or punish their communities, employers, or families.

The organisation as an institution seems to appear at times dedicated to the destruction of the moral individualist. Frequently the organisation succeeds. Which means that whistle-blowers are broken, unable to reconcile their actions and beliefs with the responses they receive from others. Understandably, many people who disclose expect some reward, praise, respect. Almost always they have to face disappointment. We don't very often want to know.

In order to make sense of their stories, some whistle-blowers must set aside the things they have always believed: that truth is larger than the herd instinct, that someone in charge will do the right thing, that the family is a haven from a heartless world. Any psychoanalyst can tell you that we project onto external authorities our internal versions of parental figures. When those parental figures are benign and fair-minded, the failure of external authorities to live up to the projection can be devastating. Many whistle-blowers recover from their experience but even then they live in a world very different from the one they knew before their confrontation with the organisation. Some people have to leave the country and start anew. One aspect of social disclosure that is underestimated is the emotional fall-out that is occasioned by revealing truths that other people prefer to keep hidden. In other words, shooting the messenger. Disclosers of uncomfortable truths can become the recipients of a great deal of hostility from a variety of quarters. Like the psychoanalyst, disclosers threaten to make something conscious and known that has either been hidden or brushed under the carpet through a range of people turning a blind eye.

There will be powerful forces ranged against the discloser in order to maintain the status quo. Disclosers threaten whatever defences and belief systems institutions have developed to permit the behaviour that is being exposed. Revelations can be experienced by the institution and colleagues as humiliating and attacking. Others will see themselves as justified in retaliating against a whistle-blower, so there may be a concerted effort to discredit or pathologise them.

Having an understanding of group hostility to revelations that are threatening to cohesion can be of considerable use to an individual who needs to find a way to maintain their self-belief at times of personal stress and marginalisation. Part of this, in my experience, is getting help to understand the unconscious reasons for putting themselves in this situation in the first place. And that takes us to the heart of individual psychology, personal experience, and unconscious motivation. Any previous emotional and psychological difficulties will be exacerbated or, if not evident before, brought to the surface. Motives and personal integrity will be publicly questioned so that through reversal and projection, the institution that is being questioned can evade any sense of responsibility for wrongdoing. The discloser is therefore made to feel the wrongdoer, arousing serious self-doubt and depression.

The group

I was asked to provide a consultation to the whistle-blower group due to the following crisis. There was a threat of division which was very disturbing to some of the new members who had already suffered a lot at the hands of their respective organisations and saw the new group as a fresh hopeful start.

My intervention was along the lines of:

> We are losing the common cause that united the group. It's break-ing down into the single causes that brought you all together in the first place: the armed forces, banking, health care, social services. We were managing together in one group, avoiding the splits in our society that we are now in danger of mirroring.
>
> Maybe a divorce is inevitable, the male bankers and armed forces separating from the health and social care services, but try not to forget the personal victimisation and the trauma that every-one, regardless of which sector they belong to, has experienced.
>
> It is this that united us and falling back into your individual sectors means that this common cause is lost. It does weaken our strength.

This seemed to stabilise the group and prevented an immediate break-down between superficially right- and left-wing elements.

My intervention continued further:

> I am wanting to offer a potential understanding of the current state of play with a whistle-blower.
>
> As we all know, any group has to address what their core inter-ests are, what they have in common. It is important at the moment for us to address what these core interests are and whether a divorce would be harmful to those core interests that we all hold dear.
>
> Can we create a space to examine with an open mind what our differences are? Sometimes, as we know, a divorce can be the best approach to differences. However, by opening our minds to so-called irreparable differences, conflict of interest, personali-ties, and politics with a small p, and recognising these tensions are normal in all organisations, something other than divorce may be achieved.
>
> If there are real reasons to work together they need to be addressed and to sustain the group, there has to be some discipline

about it, there is a need for a work group to avoid the splits into factions and parental-like quarrels. Everyone has a reason to feel abused or hurt because this is the way of human nature and organisations.

I would like to suggest in this meeting we attempt to discover if there really is a different interest and a best way forward.

To discuss whether it's best to stay together for our common interests and goals, or have an amicable divorce, which as we know is sometimes better for the children. If it's the latter, people can then choose to be in one or the other or both groups.

Question that we all need to ask? Can we identify these common interests and avoid the small 'p' politics?

The conclusion being we might stay together or divorce into two separate organisations which nevertheless support each other, as in divorce.

I would ask that to allow this to happen all hostilities come to a halt.

As you can see, conflict otherwise just escalates, especially with dreaded email exchanges.

There has to be a generosity towards each other, a gentleman's agreement rather than various accusations which are the small 'p' politics I am talking about.

We remain one organisation in the interest of us all or we become two organisations that come together for certain things, which allows people to join with either.

As you all know, voluntary organisations are often full of resentments as they can feel there is no reward for hard work and they can become dysfunctional. Can we sort out these differences before we divorce? Is the common interest we all share worth staying together for?

Crowdsourcing is a form of whistle-blowing where one uses the people inside the organisation to provide information to maximise the objective. This technology of crowdsourcing is always at the cost of command and control. See how happy people working at Waitrose are!

Whistle-blowers are a version of crowdsourcing, albeit a conflict version. The information from these crowdsourcing initiatives could be used to strengthen our organisation, bring about an amicable staying together or separation where we still work towards a common goal.

I would suggest that we have a conciliation meeting to discuss the issues and see what transpires. I am objective and would offer to chair it.

Meanwhile, there are new people wanting help.

I hope that you do not mind me writing to you as I found your contact. I am an ex-whistle-blower who was/is involved in a very large corporate lawsuit.

I have been unable to secure any employment since a damaging article was published. I am now suing my former attorney and a bunch of others involved.

I am finding life very hard to deal with. I am willing to spend every penny of my savings to see my case go to trial (and hopefully win). The problem I am having is that although many recruiters have said on the phone that the press article is indeed very damaging to my career (as companies do not want to take the risk of hiring me as a director or in a managerial role, because I may do the same to their company), the recruiters do not want to tell me this in writing. My lawyer is telling me that we really could do with recruiters or experts to come forward and help support my case here. It has been very damaging to my professional career.

I'm hoping that through your organisation I may be able to find such help. I and my family have been through years of absolute hell since all this started. What makes this so incredibly bad is that the people I placed my trust in were the ones that deliberately went out of their way to make my name public, knowing fine well the dire consequences this would have on me.

Mr G

Or

I am a consultant in a surgical unit and have just been sacked and offered a gagging clause because of my concerns about the way medical care is failing in my hospital.

Mr S

As Fred Alford (2001) talks of Orwell who used the term "double-think" in his book *Nineteen Eighty-Four*, the psychological phenomenon behind this is called doubling. For example, you are a middle-level functionary in a bureaucracy or corporation and you possess some truth you know does not conform to your institution or boss's agenda. Doubling, splitting as I would call it as a psychoanalyst, means you can hold true to your personal morality while maintaining a separate public or institutional morality. At home you may never behave this way but at work, telling the truth may hurt not only your boss but your institution, your livelihood, and the health and safety of your family. In such situations it is helpful to be able to hold contradictory positions to separate out your different selves and different loyalty structures (Alford, 2001).

Why do whistle-blowers do it? First of all, as Alford states, they aren't able to double or split themselves. The inherent contradiction would be too great and too painful. They may fit in with Hannah Arendt's idea of the heroic men and women, people who talk seriously with themselves about what they are doing, people who cannot double, or do double-speak. They feel a compulsion to "do the right thing". As one patient said, "I had to do it, I couldn't live with myself if I didn't speak up." They can't not choose to abide by their conscience.

The trouble is, blowing the whistle separates whistle-blowers from their former lives. Organisations constrained by law not to fire or retaliate against whistle-blowers find a way to do so. For example, Julian Assange was resident in a small office in the Ecuadorian embassy in London for many years. Edward Snowden remains in Russia after seven years. A nuclear scientist, after whistle-blowing about security risks, finds herself assigned to making copies or emptying waste paper baskets. For the first time, her reports are negative and she is passed over for her long-awaited promotion.

Global capitalism does create problems and it's one that affects us all in different ways. It unites a lot of protest going on in the world and I would include whistle-blowing as one of those protests. They are all reactions against different facets of globalisation, with the idea that there might be something more important than financial expansionism.

This was brought home to me recently when I saw a head of a global bank was able to pay millions of pounds to get his mother the best medical treatment in the world, whilst a relative of mine with the same illness was treated at a good but underfunded NHS hospital. The former patient extended her life by several years due to the groundbreaking treatment she was able to purchase. Let's face it, who hasn't lost a bit of social conscience in the name of self-interest in the years of total market economy.

We are currently confronted by further expansion of the market, the creeping enclosure of public space, the reduction of public services, health care, education, culture, and increasing authoritarian power led by the buck (Žižek, 2013).

All whistle-blowers are dealing with a specific combination of factors, one economic (from corruption to inefficiency in the market itself), the other a demand that individual morality can make a stand against organisational might. How else can we fight the excesses of the market place?

> A market economy thrives on inequality so self interest will always triumph over the moral good. Think of the violent reaction to Obama's universal health care plans. (Žižek, 2013)

Any whistle-blower attempting to throw light on these atrocities has to be vilified lest they expose the rottenness we accept to maintain our lifestyles which are quite often based on the suffering of others. We saw this repeated with the Covid-19 pandemic and lack of safety equipment: those that whistle-blew this appalling situation were often sacked or heavily criticised.

We all want to believe in a rational world of logic but the excavations of the whistle-blower are so disturbing to our nicely structured lives that we prefer not to know. By its very nature, whistle-blowing is about unveiling deceit, and our theories of life can be so comfortable that we can all find ourselves not wanting to know. The lone voice of the whistle-blower fulfils a role in society that most of us are too afraid to do. We often want to kill the messenger because the message makes us uncomfortably aware of our own compliance.

David Bell in his important paper "Primitive mind of state" (1996) says,

> The introduction of the Market into the National Health Service, could be seen within the perspective of the destruction of the Welfare consensus.

> The ideology of the Market and the attack on welfare-ism derives considerable support from their appeal to primitive parts of the personality that view dependency or vulnerability as weakness, the process originally described by Rosenfeld who termed it "destructive narcissism".
>
> NHS reforms create fragmentation and alienation. This has led to primitive survivalism, such as competition between clinics, modalities, medical directors doing MBA's which, although a natural outcome of the process described, is proving very costly in terms of its effects on staff morale, an essential component of adequate health-care delivery. (p. 49)

Very few of us in the NHS have said much in the face of these changes. In fact, I think to protect our jobs we have colluded quite often with the process, to the extent that I attended a meeting towards the end of my time, where the patient had become a product. I felt like I was in *Animal Farm*, and again bowing to Orwell, it was becoming difficult to perceive any difference between the businessman and the health worker. They had become the same.

The scandals of mid-Staffordshire were so ably disclosed by the courageous Kay Sheldon who was described as a paranoid schizophrenic by her enemies. The terrible tragedy of Baby P was brought to light by the equally courageous Dr Kim Holt. Margy Haywood, a nurse, who covertly filmed the abuse and neglect of elderly patients in an NHS hospital for BBC's *Panorama*, lost her nursing registration for "breaching confidentiality", while the staff who were abusing patients were allowed to carry on working. These are the symptoms of this "mind of state", where the individual is sacrificed to market forces and the welfare state suffers (Bell, 1996). This is clearly not just in the field of medicine but also many other fields, such as the destruction of the legal aid service.

Case study

A consultant I see for depression, who has no office, has to hot desk with four other consultants, and is having to meet a patient appointment target that compensates for the fact that he is now the only consultant in a department that has been decimated by cuts and is reliant on cheaper locum doctors who do not have the same commitment. The depression does represent an aspect of his early experience as a child where achievement mattered more than emotional involvement.

The health authority he works for expects him to do the impossible, recreating his early experience. My helping him to separate his own issues, disappointment with authority from the disappointing parental authority, and his fear that I will let him down has been important, as has been his exploration that maybe this time he should stand up for himself and for his patients. He brings two dreams to a session. In one, he can't find a lavatory anywhere to get relief. This is a common nightmare. In another, he sees three white-haired analysts who have not done the homework they should have prepared, which is reading the paper that he is trying to read to them. To add insult to injury, they are blaming him for his poor presentation. The multilayered aspect of these dreams demonstrates his dilemma: he both has to deal with his evacuations and the failings of others who might blame him to avoid their own faults.

Session 1

The background to this sessions is that the patient felt better after the last session but since then has lost another supporter and feels like one after another is going, and is feeling quite alone.

The therapist's thoughts are given alongside the patient's words in the following dialogue.

> [*Long silence*]

Therapist: *He is terribly worried that the system he has created inside himself is collapsing and he fears he is losing control. Can he get the support that he needs for something more authentic both from me and inside himself?*

Patient: Yeah, I am tired of being a whistle-blower! I guess you're right, it's true—more people are bailing out. I feel no one is interested in my story anymore. Without it what do I have left?

Therapist: *The story isn't working anymore, but I think he is also saying he is not convinced by it, the single narrative, that he listens to. His investment in it is declining but what else can take its place?*

[*He tells me a dream*]

Patient: I am playing a game. The opposing team bring on a sub. I'm the only one who sees how small it is: it's like a spider and it crawls onto a piece of flooring where people are playing.

Therapist: *He realises this spider is going to push the balls out of the way: humans vs. spiders football teams. (He says he was watching Brazil's humiliating defeat on TV last night.) Spiders have lots of legs, sticky webs, the humans getting all caught up in them.*

He is trying to come back to what hasn't been got straight, not just out there in others who he feels have been guilty of much, but there is a game going on between human and spiders. He is aware it's his internal team; like everyone he has multiple ideas and a problem with integrating these aspects.

Patient: I am aware of this, my own powerful destructive forces. I can't deny I have those violent feelings. I have been reading something, resisting the reality and ploughing through forces that are ranging within me, I do have this side of my personality.

Therapist: *He was very aware of this when he was on the telephone to J in America, this awareness of his own ability to hurt. Then he loses touch with who he is speaking to and begins to feel persecuted and disorientated.*

He is aware that he is no longer sure who he is talking to or what is going on. There is a major feeling of something destructive that he is becoming aware of, this is something he needs to look at both in himself, and others, but there is a sticky web he is spinning to distract him, a complicated web of thoughts to avoid his fear and understanding.

Patient: I am a loner, someone said, who is always playing a game of football on my own whilst the main game goes on all around me.

Therapist: *I think he begins to see the web he weaves, that prevents him from seeing his predicament, by creating an enemy or a football match. (Brazil's defeat last night a humiliation, but he is trying to get rid of all this stuff, trying to get me to be the enemy trying to defeat him.) He is capturing his humanity.*

Patient: I am very worried about a documentary and being exposed all over again.

Therapist: *This is a worry but I think he is also worried by what he is saying or documenting and realising about himself that he wants to hide from, because of his fear of being punished.*

Session 2

Patient: [Tells of a dream where he is lost in the back passages of Finsbury Park (associated with anality).]

Therapist: *He can get out or stay in his back passage.*

We are never going to be able to decipher in full the unconscious and conscious motives of those who disclose. I am not sure we need to. We can argue for as long as we like about the personal stories and pathologies of our most famous whistle-blowers like Edward Snowden and Julian Assange. I could write case histories filled with the early experiences that motivate later acts of brave or foolhardy or vicious disclosures. But perhaps the most important thing we have to keep in mind is that societies who cannot tolerate disclosure and transparency are on their way to being the totalitarian states that most of us abhor. Whistle-blowers therefore act as the conscience for us all.

> We never know how high we are
> Till we are asked to rise
> And then if we are true to plan
> Our statures touch the skies.
> —Emily Dickinson

References

Alford, C. F. (2001). *Whistleblowers: Broken Lives and Organizational Power.* Ithaca, NY: Cornell University Press.

Bell, D. (1996). Primitive mind of state. *Psychoanalytic Psychotherapy, 10*(1): 45–57.

Holder, R. (2018, September 10). 40,000 Whistleblowers Tip Off HMRC Tax Dodger Hotline. *Money International.* https://www.moneyinternational.com/tax/40000-whistleblowers-tip-off-hmrc-tax-dodger-hotline/ (last accessed June 1, 2020).

Žižek, S. (2013). The global protest. *London Review of Books, 35*(14).

CHAPTER SEVEN

Alice Miller on family, power, and truth

Luisa Passalacqua and Marco Puricelli

Alice Miller (1923–2010) was an eminent Swiss psychoanalyst of Polish origin. She studied for her doctorate in psychology, sociology, and philosophy at the University of Basel in Switzerland, and then completed her psychoanalytic training in Zurich. For two decades she was involved in teaching psychoanalysis, but her career later took a dramatic turn: she quit both the Swiss Psychoanalytic Society and the International Psychoanalytical Association to embark on an in-depth study of the factors causing and affecting child abuse. This resulted in the publication of several books, each one approaching this topic from a different angle. The most noteworthy are *The Drama of the Gifted Child* (formerly *Prisoners of Childhood*) and *Thou Shalt Not Be Aware: Society's Betrayal of the Child*. The latter won her the Janusz Korczak literary award in 1986.

Even before Miller undertook her lonely crusade to restore a sense of respect for childhood, another pioneer, Polish doctor Janusz Korczak, a paediatrician and educator, and the director of a Jewish orphanage, had lived for thirty years with children from the humblest walks of life, coming to him in a disturbing condition of abandonment, often with signs of severe abuse (quoted by Miller, 1984). In his writings we find a denunciation of the ongoing structural violence inflicted on many children, a cause he cared about just as strongly as Miller did a few years later. In a world where only what the adults decide matters, little ones are forced into a predicament of true slavery, humiliated and subjugated, constantly controlled, often threatened and beaten. That was in the early twentieth century.

It is indisputable that ours is a planet where only eighteen countries out of the 192 members of the United Nations prohibit physical abuse of children, a recent prohibition to which Alice Miller herself actively contributed while she was still alive.

Even in a democracy, we all take for granted that an adult's will is overtly or covertly imposed on their children. This condition isn't different to the condition of citizens in a totalitarian state: children are adults' property, just like the citizens of a totalitarian regime are property of the State (Miller & Ward, 1981). The adult exerts a form of absolute power on the child, and that is considered normal in society. Many children aren't beaten or otherwise physically or sexually abused, but more and more of today's children are manipulated, spoiled, and smothered, and thus suffer comparable—if not worse—mental damage.

In academic circles Alice Miller was criticised for having noticed that the traumas of children were real, arising from actual experiences of violence, not from fantasies or imaginations—similarly and according to the first theory of seduction by Sigmund Freud. Maybe in Miller's early works it is possible to find some sort of reductionism in considering sexual or physical violence to be the only forms of childhood abuse. Nevertheless this concept has been gradually extended to incorporate less evident forms of emotional abuse, where by "abuse" she means the use of a person for the purpose of fulfilling one's needs or desires, irrespective of the used person's permission and with no respect for their consent, interest, and will (Miller, 2007). Even less blatant variations of abuse generate unconscious anger and resentment that will be turned into violence later in adulthood. This concept of abuse is critical in order to understand why childhood is marked by real trauma rather than fantasies, drives, or "shameful" desires of the child.

There are many forms of cruelty that have not yet been explored enough, because the wounds inflicted on the child and their consequences are poorly understood, as well as many other forms of resulting traumas that are not sexual or physical in nature that equally lead to repression, and therefore mental disorders. So much attention has been given to toilet training in psychoanalytic literature. But from the moment babies are born there are endless ways in which adults can exert their willpower on them: adults can impose on the baby when to eat, when to sleep, when to be cleaned, only to accommodate a mother's or father's demands. This gross variation of authoritarianism is taught very early on in child development, long before toilet training. More than that, it is contrary to any common sense (which we all take for granted) that one eats, sleeps, and has a shower mostly when one pleases: that doesn't apply to infancy, precisely the age where a greater flexibility is needed—and expected—from a mother.

On a more complex level, an apparently "devout" new mother can be very needy and sensitive to rejection due to a series of conflicts from her own childhood. She can be convinced that her baby doesn't love her because he isn't smiling at her or perhaps she may feel rejected when her baby begins to be interested in the world around him, or when he expresses his aggressiveness and vitality, in situations like biting, scratching, hair pulling, kicking, and screaming. In these critical moments she could turn into a cruel and vindictive human being who acts out retaliation through resentment and withdrawal of affection (Winnicott, 1986). All of those moments are not so easy "to see", in so far as such an unconscious mechanism is based mainly on passive aggression. But for a child, being ignored is terrible: it means not to exist and to experience intense anguish. For him to feel deprived of affection is definitely unsustainable. When children are very young, they do not know and cannot be sure that the attitude of their parents is temporary; then if this situation is prolonged, the moment comes when they have a true experience of death.

As a society, we are so accustomed to witnessing emotional abuse that we stop paying it any attention. Most abuse takes place behind closed doors and there is no one to witness or validate the experience of the abused. Usually, the abuser will deny the abusing behaviour.

Even today, whatever happened to children in their infancy is of little interest, no children's organisation defends them as a class, and metapsychology seems to have no model for the discrimination of children (Miller, 1979).

Yet we are puzzled when we discover neurological differences in the brain of offenders or otherwise "disturbed" individuals. It is now clear that *trauma forges the brain*: the findings presented by Bowlby and Spitz decades ago have been corroborated by the most recent neurobiological research. The studies in question suggest that not only active battering but also the absence of loving physical contact between child and parent will cause certain areas of the brain, notably those responsible for the emotions, to remain underdeveloped. Repeated traumatisation leads to an increased release of stress hormones that attack the sensitive tissue of the brain and destroy existing neurons (for example, Sapolsky, 1994). Nowadays computer scans can reveal the brain injuries that occur in children who have suffered beatings or who have been abandoned. Such scans are referred to in numerous articles by researchers on PTSD in neurobiology, particularly Bruce D. Perry, who is also a child psychiatrist (1994). Other studies of mistreated children have revealed that the areas of the brain responsible for the management of emotion are twenty to thirty per cent smaller than in normal persons (Miller, 1998).

With today's knowledge, Miller's clear-cut stance against the drive theories of psychoanalysis is much more understandable to many current practitioners, who have more or less blatantly reintegrated Miller's theory into their practices. So it is no longer a heresy to say that drive theories belong to the same mentality that has always helped parents and educators in justifying the physical, emotional, and sexual abuse of children.

Miller reports that Freud had discovered the seduction of children carried out by their parents, but this truth was unacceptable in his time. If Freud had insisted on seduction theory, he would have faced the complete opposition of and ostracism by the bourgeoisie. The theory of the Oedipus complex made it possible for him to safeguard the image of the parents (Miller, 1984): despite the undoubtedly innovative and questioning nature of Freud's research, he remains in essence a representative of bourgeois and patriarchal society.

Miller's dissociation from psychoanalysis grew through her essays published in the eighties (*Pictures of a Childhood, Banished Knowledge, The Untouched Key, Breaking Down the Wall of Silence*) and reached its culmination in *Thou Shalt Not Be Aware*, whose very title evokes the notion of the repression of child abuse, a taboo that psychoanalysis itself was unable to discard. Her critique of psychoanalysis was later extended to all psychotherapeutic approaches, with rare exceptions for individual therapists.

Child trauma as source of violence

Psychohistory, the science of historical motivations, combines the insights of psychotherapy with the research methodology of the social sciences to understand the emotional origin of the social and political behaviour of groups and nations, past and present.

The way in which Miller contributes to psychohistory is through the examination of the biographies of well-known people and the analysis of their childhood histories. Her work is mainly focused on disturbed personalities, bloodthirsty dictators, serial killers, as well as individuals who turned their destructiveness against themselves. But it also extends to those who, thanks to art, were able to liberate themselves from a violent past, and those who gave in to self-destruction despite art.

In her work *The Untouched Key* (1988) Alice Miller explores the clues to the connections between childhood traumas and adult creativity and destructiveness. This has clear political implications for the understanding of that human destructiveness on a mass scale that we know all too well. The individuals from art and politics whose early life she studied and compared in various books include Dostoyevsky, Chekhov, Schiller, Rimbaud, Mishima, Proust, Joyce, Kafka, Nietzsche, Picasso, Kollwitz, Buster Keaton, Hitler, Stalin, Ceaușescu—the list goes on. From *The Untouched Key* we learn that the upbringing of artists and that of dictators are shockingly similar (1988).

Miller's biographical quest to understand why, given the same upbringing, one becomes a dictator and another an artist, culminated in the realisation that what makes a difference for a mistreated child is having a *helping witness* around the house, someone the child can turn to for validation. It doesn't necessarily have to be the mother, it could be a sister, as in the case of Kafka and Dostoyevsky, or a nanny, or even a nurse, as in the case of Balzac. Moreover, it doesn't matter whether the witness is aware of this fundamental role he or she is playing, which is exerted through empathy and compassion towards the child.

According to Miller, having or not having a helping witness around in childhood determines whether a mistreated child will become a despot who displaces his repressed helplessness against others or an artist who will tell about such suffering.

The crux of Miller's theory is that individuals who fail to recall the mistreatment, violence, and humiliations inflicted on them during their childhood, and therefore cannot live through the resulting unpleasant feelings towards their parents, are bound to displace their repressed rage onto weaker subjects. This is a dynamic that resists every rational argument, because it has its roots in the unconscious.

Although biographies offer an abundant material containing precious information, hardly ever can one find anything relevant to the childhood of well-known figures. When there is anything at all, their parents are often idealised in historians' descriptions. Miller explains that any deeper approach to such biographies would hardly be appreciated by those who have themselves a tendency to idealise their own parents (Miller, 2007).

Hatred and destructiveness can be expressed in many different ways, and if they become appealing it is only by the support of several ideologies; in any case they all have the same root in the family, with no exception.

Writing about Saddam Hussein, Miller notices that every unscrupulous tyrant "mobilizes the suppressed fears and anxieties of those who were beaten as children but have never been able to accuse their own fathers of doing so, thus keeping faith with them despite the torments suffered at their hands … Beaten, tormented, and humiliated children who have never received support from a helping witness later develop a high degree of tolerance for the cruelties inflicted by parent figures and a striking indifference to the sufferings borne by children exposed to cruel treatment" (Miller, 2004).

Adolf Hitler had perfectly internalised his father's sadistic attitude, so that when he raised his voice and had outbursts of rage, whoever was listening to him shook like a frightened child. The same sadism was later found in those millions of people who granted him legitimacy as well as the brutal efficiency we know from history books (Miller, 2007).

Miller went in search of the true motives of many other dictators. In all of them she identified "the effects of hatred of a parent that remained unconscious not only because hating one's father was strictly prohibited but also because it was in the interests of the child's self-preservation to maintain the illusion of having a good father. Only in the form of a deflection onto others was hatred permitted, and then it could flow freely" (Miller, 1998).

Children are too fragile to be aware of the anguish deriving from the subtraction of affection. They have to suppress this anguish to survive. Suppression in childhood is life-saving. Besides, children's condition of dependence makes them completely loyal, naive, and hopeful: they are bound to idealise their parents in order to entertain the illusion they are receiving love. They have to trust their parents to love them, just to survive psychologically. Therefore, psychological abuse wouldn't have such devastating effects on children if it wasn't for the associated absolute trust that accompanies it, and for the belief that parents never make mistakes. In addition, it is easy for children to mistake love for its many surrogates. Unlike the prisoner of a concentration camp who faces a hated tormentor and knows it, *the child faces as his persecutor his most beloved parent, and this tragic complication is what will affect his future life for the worst* (Miller, 1983). *A child who grows up in a (most likely nuclear) family does not have a helping witness*; this child's *parents represent his whole universe*. In such a dramatic situation, it is inevitable that this child will develop a destructive drive (Miller, 2007).

When a child is subjected to an oppressive upbringing, he represses his feelings of pain, rage, suffering, sadness, and disappointment. That in turn causes a reduction in vitality and produces a sense of alienation from the self and his own authentic needs and wishes (Miller, 1983). As adults, many would rather die, or symbolically die by neutralising their own feelings, than keep that sense of powerlessness alive, in the face of parents who used the child to meet their own needs, or as a target for their pent-up hatred, or even as a source of love they needed themselves at the time. As long as the anger directed at a parent or other first caregiver remains unconscious or disavowed, it cannot be dissipated (Miller, 1998).

Feelings of anger, helplessness, despair, longing, fear, and pain—split from what had motivated them—continue to express themselves in destructive acts against others: a dramatic alternative to turning on oneself. Other ways to defend against the cruelty the subjects suffered is to deflect it on others by means of a wide variety of manipulative and antisocial practices such as blackmailing, prostitution, perversions, sexual abuse, crime, and war. In less extreme but more common forms, hatred is poured on "weak" substitutes (children, partners, patients, believers, employees, etc.). Even more typically, the victims of those acts will be one's own children, treated as scapegoats, and these attacks will always be legitimated as part of their so-called "education". The tragedy is that people mistreat their children precisely to escape the awareness of what their own parents did to them.

In Erich Fromm's *Anatomy of Human Destructiveness* (1973), in which he also examines Adolf Hitler, destructiveness is seen as a consequence of the denial of trauma. Hitler's followers were victims of the same pedagogical mentality, as well as the same character structure. This is the concept of "social character" as defined by Fromm (1941): through the family, society creates in children precisely the character structure suitable for the reproduction of society itself, the kind of character traits that are bound to reproduce abuse at the expense of the next generation.

It may be the case of a growing trait in our society: lack of empathy. The complete denial of suffering causes an inner emptying, and very often blocks the unfolding of our innate ability to feel compassion for others. In fact one of the many forms of cruelty that we inflict on children consists in not allowing them to express their anger and their grief (a sort of empathy for oneself) without them running the risk of losing the love and affection of their parents.

Instrumental forgiveness

Among the monotheistic religions, Christianity is theoretically the one that is most compatible with a vision of the human being that gives due import to childhood. No other religion seems to respect children to such an extent. In fact, Miller writes: "No religious tradition remembers anything like a couple like Mary and Joseph, able to leave their home country to save their children. The fact that Jesus grew up with parents whose only concern was to show them love and attention cannot be disputed" (Miller, 1984, p. 103). Too often, however, the actual pedagogical practices were inconsistent with the Christian gospels, which are unanimous in highlighting the importance of Jesus' childhood and the fundamental role of Mary and Joseph. Many religious institutions that raise children and adolescents do so in a way that promotes "poisonous pedagogy".

This is an expression Miller took from Katharina Rutschky, *Schwarze Pädagogik* (Miller, 1983); by that she means a repressive educational approach based on punishments and rigid rules, and more generally on a detached stance and restricted loving, often rationalised through the traditional claim that it is enacted "for the child's own good". Today such pedagogy appears under more subtle forms of "love" (so-called smothering) where the parents' destructiveness is disguised in the form of love, and thus more difficult to identify (Miller, 1983).

In Morton Schatzman's essay *Soul Murder: Persecution in the Family* (1973), the author re-examines the famous "Schreber case" in Freudian literature, as well as many other psychoanalysts. Dr Daniel Gottlieb Moritz Schreber was never a patient of any of them, never a patient of Freud. He was analysed indirectly through his diaries, which showed the delusions dominating the psychotic phases of his life. Schreber was an Austrian judge who complained of being persecuted by God, who knew everything about him and was highly judgemental. Schatzman discovered that Schreber's father was an orthopaedic doctor and self-styled "pedagogue" who wrote books on the topic of repressive upbringing which were read and studied by the teachers, who in turn taught the generations that led to Nazism. The basic principle was that children are born with inherently evil inclinations and therefore they must be reshaped by infusing them with good principles. Schreber's father was proud of having brought up all of his children according to such principles. Needless to say, each one of them faced a dark fate: suicide, disappearance, mental hospital. Schatzman connects Schreber's father's pedagogy to Lutheran Protestantism, in which the utmost sin is disobedience.

Who was Martin Luther, the man who reformed the Church that indoctrinated the country which ultimately perpetrated the genocide of the Jews? What was wrong in Germany at that time? The answer is not in history books about the Third Reich as one would expect, but in a little article written by an ex-psychoanalyst (Alice Miller), published in an unknown journal of psychohistory, and mainly ignored by mainstream literature thereafter:

> Martin Luther … was an intelligent and educated man, but he hated all Jews and he encouraged parents to beat their children. He was no perverted sadist like Hitler's executioners. But

400 years before Hitler he was disseminating this kind of destructive counsel. (Miller, 1998)

And about Martin Luther's childhood:

> His mother beat him severely before he was treated this way by his father and his teacher. He believed this punishment had "done him good" and was therefore justified. The conviction stored in his body that if parents do it then it must be right to torment someone weaker than yourself left a much more lasting impression on him than the divine commandments and the Christian exhortations to love your neighbour and be compassionate toward the weak. (Miller, 1998)

The fourth commandment, usually taught in abbreviated form as "Honour your father and your mother" has served to trigger a sense of guilt in billions of adolescents and adults over the centuries, due to their ambivalent feelings towards their parents (Miller, 1990). To all appearances, this commandment sounds like an obligation to unconditionally accept one's parents through submitting to them. Actually, in its original form, this commandment had a different meaning: it encouraged you to give the right weight to your father and your mother, so that your days may be long upon the Earth. In other words: understand who your parents really are, consider carefully the influence that they have had on you, otherwise your days will never be truly yours. Only if we begin to understand this—instead of simply "pay respect"—do we become masters of our own mind (Sibaldi, 2012). In fact this interpretation is compatible with other parts of the Bible: in Genesis, in Exodus, and even in the Gospels themselves there are criticisms of the family as an institution. For instance, forty days in the desert had helped Jesus to keep a distance from his parents, hence his statement, "If anyone comes to me and does not hate his father and mother (…) he cannot be my disciple" (Luke 14.26).

The convenient reinterpretation of the fourth commandment in terms of submission to parents paid lip service to parents with narcissistic disturbances. Unlike most scholars, Miller said it clearly: many patients as children were the narcissistically cathected objects of their mothers. If so, *the culture of indiscriminate forgiveness favoured precisely not only violence but also the sense of guilt of what some call "co-narcissists" (for example, Rappoport, 2005). This is systematically overlooked in psychotherapeutic practice, where the focus is on the patients, and theoretical abstractions place them within constructs which imply that their pathology developed in a relational void where the parents were behaving normally—and yet something went mysteriously wrong.*

The reason why it was so hard for Miller to find like-minded colleagues was that most traditional psychotherapists had not fully felt their own childhood pain, and never acknowledged how their own parents had hurt them; as a consequence, they were unable to be of real help to their clients. If therapists have never "lived through" this despair and the resulting narcissistic rage, they will automatically transfer this situation onto their patients. Until work on their own past engenders in them a sacrosanct indignation, what they have endured in their childhood will still feel like a normal situation, and they will have no empathy to offer to anyone. If the adult patient suspects that his real source of suffering lies in his childhood experiences, the obtuse therapist reassures him that it is certainly not the case—and even if it was the case, the patient would have to learn to forgive, because it is precisely his resentment that makes him sick. Such conventional therapists, laden with pedagogical agendas, are unable to truly help their patients, and offer them their morality instead. The patient is convinced that the therapist speaks out of a sound experience, and defers to her authority. He doesn't know, and has no way to find out, that such assertions actually express a deep-seated fear of her own parents (Miller, 1984).

To the best of our knowledge, the hidden influence of the early religious upbringing of therapists on their later therapeutic relationships with their clients has never been researched. It may have been acknowledged in pastoral counselling, by definition religious in nature, but in every other practice the secular aspect of psychotherapy is taken for granted far too easily. What is rarely understood is that having become an atheist does not free a therapist from the unconscious conditioning that took place in the early years. What is left of such conditioning will inevitably affect the therapeutic performance.

Psychotherapists often minimise their patients' childhood wounds, fear their repressed anger, or try to "integrate the good with the bad" prematurely. Having to locate all the "good" in the parents (and in oneself) and all the "bad" elsewhere is in itself a source of confusion. The ambivalence experienced as adults in relationships is a form of disorientation that reflects the ambivalence of the original relationship with parents who combine good and evil all too easily, first enhancing their own image and then behaving in ways incompatible with that image.

Miller believed that forgiveness does not resolve hatred; it covers it in a dangerous way in the grown adult, who often comes to rely on displacement on some scapegoat. This is precisely what makes it possible to pass on trauma from one generation to the next. Trauma specialist Katharina Drexler, in an article on transgenerational traumas, writes that most unresolved traumas are passed on to future generations through the introjection of the traumatised parent (Drexler, 2013).

Therefore, putting even the slightest pressure on a patient to forgive his parents is not only useless, it is counterproductive and is one more missed chance to leverage the true original cause of patients' disturbances, especially when the most natural emotional responses to mistreatment have been denied. At the very least, the concept itself of forgiveness should be reformulated to incorporate the acknowledgement of such feelings; it cannot be called "forgiveness" unless it coexists with an awareness of the damage and with the anger that came as a response.

Psychotherapists' knowledge about the origin of mental suffering forces them to take a stance as regards the social environment surrounding patients. In Miller's opinion, the psychotherapeutic process necessarily implies a process of identification in which there are only two opposite possibilities: the therapist can identify with the patient as a child or she can identify with his parents. The therapist will be able to identify with only one at a time, at different stages of therapy. But in the latter case, the therapist will not have access to the childhood truth of the patient, and neither will the patient. The patient, who was traumatised by his parents as a child, is now facing a new parent, the analyst herself, who will do anything to cover parental responsibility, and will do that by giving an oedipal reading that blames the patient himself and denies the reality of traumatic experiences that emerge during the therapy (Miller, 1984). This is for Miller a true therapeutic abuse, resulting from several variations of that original fear of hurting their own parents that therapists retain.

Psychotherapy is one of many discourses that attempts to make sense of human suffering, beside medicine, art, and religion. A kind of moral fortitude is required to bear and process mental pain, and to make a good therapist. Neville Symington in *The Making of a Psychotherapist*:

> An individual can bear mental pain only if there is someone there able to bear it with him. Fundamentally, it is not a question of saying the right thing, but of being conscious of the pain in the other person, and not saying anything that will save us and the patient from experiencing it. (Symington, 1996, pp. 53–54)

The political therapist

If the psychotherapist enters the role of the enlightened witness without hesitation, she will stand on the child's side. This position will make it possible to take into account all of the possible factors that lead to the inevitability of the adult child's mental condition.

As Miller repeatedly points out, in the theories of Melanie Klein, the emotional life of the infant indirectly expresses a rejection by the adult of her own emotional life, now embodied by the infant. Klein, with her "cruel infant" concept, as well as Kernberg, with his theory of the child's innate pathological narcissism, both disregard the reactive nature of child development and fail to take into account that it is the unmet needs of parents and their attitude towards the child that generate in the latter forms of aggressiveness, sexuality, and narcissism (Miller, 1984).

In Miller's time there was already some consideration for environmental factors, which could be readily found in Kohut, Mahler, Masterson, Winnicott, Khan, Bowlby, and others. But Miller disagrees when their theoretical ambition is to discover, behind the development of the child, the universal goals and factors that may play a role in pathogenesis. For example: for Kohut, the lack of emotional closeness; for Mahler, difficulties at the stage of separation and reconciliation; for Masterson, being devoured or subtraction of affection in the child's attempts to become autonomous; for Winnicott, the lack of maternal holding; for Kahn, the lack of maternal protection in the face of stimuli; and so on. *In Miller's opinion, all of these factors mean something traumatic, but perhaps do not lead inevitably to neurosis, if they can be articulated as painful injuries.* This does not happen with parents who are feared, or whom the child must "respect". In such cases the history of the trauma will be overwritten by alienating narratives and the trauma will have to be repressed: this very event produces neuroses.

Clearly grasping the context in which a mental condition is formed is the necessary prerequisite for the articulation of trauma as trauma. This, in itself, is therapeutic. Miller's suggested analytic approach is the search for a patient's early childhood reality while avoiding any attempt to spare their parents. It is paramount to focus attention not only on what happens to the child, but also on the parent in the very moment of the mistreatment, and in the same terms we use for the child: drives, defence mechanisms, denial, rationalisation, displacement, and so on.

With a more complete account of what happened comes the recovery of one or more feelings associated with it, both in the patient and the therapist. The "Millerian" psychotherapist cannot really remain neutral in the face of the historical account of the patient, as long as her empathic capacity is intact. When the trauma is restored to its original context, clarity is gained and things are called by their real names, and as a result the most uncomfortable feelings may arise: indignation, even horror.

Horror is precisely the feeling that narcissistically abused children forget as they become abusing adults in turn. Horror is the healthiest emotional reaction to abuse, whether to oneself or to others. The psychotherapist's capacity—or incapacity—to experience horror raises questions about the role of psychotherapy in society, and the stance of the psychotherapist not as a *professional*, but rather as a *citizen*, in regard to the things which produce mental illness in such a society—and the politics that accompany it all.

As early as the sixties, Esther Bick warned the analyst against the risk of accusing or blaming the parents. Nothing of what is done in the therapeutic setting has to turn into a confrontation with the patient's mother and father—as if blame were the only option of an ex-patient who has become aware of the damage that his environment has caused to his mental health. But the examples are endless. The world of psychotherapies seems to be completely cut off from politics, in that therapists act as if what happens in their consulting rooms had—and should have—little or no political impact on the external world and culture as a whole. The positing of political discourses and agendas stemming from the therapeutic setting is actively discouraged even in the most "confrontational" approaches where patients are encouraged to express their truths to substitutes instead of their real recipients: their parents and "significant others" (i.e. psychodrama, Gestalt therapy, and family constellations). Invariably, more "adaptive" behaviours are encouraged: either patients make new choices in their environment, or they will have a new approach to the same old situations and contexts. But we don't know any therapeutic protocol that encompasses how a patient brings her new awareness out of the consulting room and into relational, familial, occupational, or social contexts. Such an agenda would be seen as a pathological product of an incomplete process. With the only exception of family therapy (systemic in nature), no such guidance is provided as part of the setting.

This is partly explained by the imperative of confidentiality: very few individuals would ever declare that their new approach to old situations is the result of them being in therapy, even when such a "shameful" admission wouldn't be necessary for the purpose. Another explanation is a widespread belief among practitioners that activism is to be seen as a symptom. Once more, Miller disagrees. In *For Your Own Good* (1980), taking Nazi Germany and the war in Vietnam as examples, she compared the childhoods of the professional American soldiers who served in Vietnam on a voluntary basis. Miller found that the most vindictive war criminals had been raised brutally in their childhoods. An empirical study (Oliner & Oliner, 1988; also quoted by Miller, 1998) has concluded that

> the only factor distinguishing the rescuers from the persecutors and hangers-on was the way they had been brought up by their parents. People given early affection and support are quick to emulate the sympathetic and autonomous natures of their parents. Common to all the rescuers were self-confidence, the ability to take immediate decisions and the capacity for empathy and compassion with others. Seventy percent of them said that it only took them a matter of minutes to decide they wanted to intervene. Eighty percent said they did not consult anyone else.

In activism, anger is at the service of the ego, so it is partly unconscious energy but it is more integrated within the personality and channelled into something constructive; it doesn't derive from rejection, abandonment, or other severe unconscious traumas. So it is energy stemming from a relationship with "good enough" parents or a therapeutic processing of the above traumas, which has resulted in a more integrated personality. As Winnicott puts it, beyond the good enough mother lays the foundation not only of mental health, but also the child's strength of character and the richness of his personality, as well as the ability to be happy and to rebel and make a revolution (1986).

Psychopathy as a systemic condition

In *For Your Own Good* Miller speaks of the "narcissistic dyad" and symbiotic relationship between Hitler and his supporters (1980), something that develops on a dyadic, familial, or group level and that philosopher Dr Sam Vaknin called "pathological narcissistic space" (1999). Thus it is not simply a dyadic phenomenon, it may be a group one and involve more than two subjects, one or more of them being full-blown narcissists.

There is nothing new in the idea that, given the importance of interpersonal and social context, neurosis isn't just a subjective individual phenomenon, and may show in broad layers of society (Innamorati, 2010). In the same way, pathological narcissism is a systemic phenomenon and it is of little use to study so-called narcissistic personality disorder as the epiphenomenon of a larger dynamics, unless we also look at the practices that somehow reproduce its mechanisms everywhere. Often, the same person displays both narcissistic and co-narcissistic behaviours, depending on the circumstances (Rappoport, 2005). So, for instance, many show the "entitlement pattern" without necessarily meeting the criteria of the most commonly used diagnostic manuals for narcissistic personality disorder (Ronningstam, 2005).

Another point for a more group-related approach is the more recent knowledge we have of psychopathy, the so-called *dark triad*, which includes narcissism, together with "machiavellianism" and "psychopathy" proper. Not only is there no validated, specific treatment to cure narcissistic personality disorder, there is also no body of scientifically sound research on the treatment of psychopathic offenders in general (Hemphill & Hart, 2002) for a number of reasons, among them inconsistent concepts and measures of psychopathy (D'Silva, Duggan, & McCarthy, 2004).

Indeed, a fresh outlook is needed on psychopathy, one which takes into account the phenomena that can be observed around individuals showing psychopathic traits, involving what would be clinically considered non-psychopathic individuals.

One only needs to look at the prolific visual culture on psychopathy, about which there are numerous publications on psychiatric journals (for example, Hesse, 2009). Psychopathic characters are very popular: in nearly every movie there is a male or female psychopath. Shadd Maruna of Queen's University Belfast suggests that people need psychopaths, since they are nothing but "a screen upon which we project our guilt as well as our anxieties" (Garland, 2001). In other words, the viewers of psychopathic characters seek to reduce their anxieties, frustrations, and guilt by putting all of the blame on an identifiable perpetrator. At the end of the day, says Professor Maruna, we have always known this from Aeschylus: "Unanimous hatred is the greatest medicine for a human community." There is a degree of psychopathy in all of us that we need to project into the Other, condemn and possibly persecute, or even execute it (Carveth, 2010, pp. 106–130). This is because if "evil" persons are not the source of evil, then "the more disturbing possibility must be entertained that evil might be a relatively diffuse and commonplace phenomenon that normal people get caught up in" (Ellard, Miller, Baumle, & Olson, 2002, p. 353).

Just as the typical mechanism at work in spectators facing a cinema screen is projective identification, the temptation of placing evil where it can be located extends to bystanders in all environments where harassment is commonly practised and enablers go easily undetected. In family or work environments alike, enablers witness violence being perpetrated by someone else, with the double advantage of vicarious gratification and the certainty to avoid any censure for themselves.

The relationship between abusers and enablers

The study of what makes an individual a psychopath or someone with an otherwise antisocial tendency is coupled with research on what provides such individuals with the mass of enablers they need to be who they are.

The Frankfurt School had already explored the authoritarian personality in an attempt to address the latent tendency to accept a fascist regime

(Innamorati, 2010), with an empirical investigation on a large scale based on the design of psychological scales to identify personality traits peculiar to individuals who tend to become smoothly integrated in an authoritarian society (Adorno, Frenkel-Brunswik, Levinson, & Sanford, 1950).

Adorno and colleagues argued that deep-seated personality traits predisposed some individuals to be highly sensitive to totalitarian and anti-democratic ideas and therefore were prone to be highly prejudicial. Clinical interviews revealed situational aspects of their childhood, such as the fact that they had been brought up by very strict parents or guardians, characteristic of participants who scored highly on the F-scale (F for fascism). These aspects were seldom found in the backgrounds of low scorers. Therefore, the study indicated that individuals with a very strict upbringing by critical and harsh parents were most likely to develop an authoritarian personality. Adorno believed that this was because the individual in question was not able to express hostility towards their parents (for being strict and critical). Consequently, the person would then displace this aggression/hostility onto safer targets, namely those who are weaker, such as ethnic minorities.

Adorno and colleagues felt that authoritarian traits, as identified by the F-scale, predispose some individuals towards "fascistic" characteristics. In other words, according to Adorno and colleagues, the Eichmanns of this world are there because they have authoritarian personalities and therefore are predisposed to indulge in cruelty, and this is as a result of their upbringing.

Erich Fromm sought to refine Marxist theory by using psychoanalysis as a tool for the analysis of contemporary society, thereby founding Freudo-Marxism. His starting point was a notorious flaw in Marxist theory. Marx expected that sooner or later the exploited masses would rebel and overthrow the whole sociopolitical order, yet the poorest Germans and Americans didn't display the slightest urge for political change.

The new element that Erich Fromm introduced into the discourse was the concept of the family as a psychological agency of society. As a matter of fact, the individual only makes his first direct contact with the actual societal world fairly late in his life. Fromm argued that the family constitutes the true foundation of political authority, since the relationship established by children with their father will later be the prototype of their attitude towards any authority. The prevailing social model in its turn determines the family structure, namely the type of relationships that are to be established between parents and children (Horkheimer, Fromm & Marcuse, 1936).

Indeed the dynamics occurring in a particular family also affect the relationship with the children, and it is well known that the mother acts as a transmission belt between the father and children, whether for the good or for the bad. Henry Dicks' work (1967) on couples revealed that the unconscious choices of partners, unconscious exchanges between spouses (powerful dynamics based on projection, splitting, and identification), as well as the relevance of conflicts within the couple, clearly affect their relationship with their children (Lancini, 2007). In fact systems theory as applied to family therapy works precisely on this principle.

Another useful approach is Adlerian family therapy. Based on the original ideas of Edith Dewey, a classification of family atmospheres was developed by Hugh Misseldine in his book *Your Inner Child of the Past* (1963), along the lines of Alfred Adler's concepts as they were elaborated by Adlerian psychoanalyst Henry T. Stein, director and senior training analyst at the Alfred Adler Institute of Northwestern Washington.

There are fifteen different family atmospheres in which children can grow up (democratic, authoritarian, high standards, competitive, suppressive, materialistic, overprotective, overindulgent, inconsistent, inharmonious, disparaging, rejective, martyrising, pitying, and hopeless) of which only the democratic atmosphere prepares a child for cooperation, whereas the others may provoke a lack of trust, drain his courage, and emphasise the false value of superiority over others. Some atmospheres may also breed self-centredness and emotional distance and inhibit the development of empathy for others (Stein, 2018a).

This classification of atmospheres overlaps with another classification by the same author, that of parental styles (democratic and encouraging, overindulgent, over-submissive, over-coercive, perfectionist, excessively responsible, neglecting, rejecting, punitive, hypochondriac, and sexually stimulating). As a response to the punitive parental style, children will long for retaliation, feel guilt, and think of themselves as bad, hate their parents, lie to avoid punishment, and fear their own impulses for revenge. Another parental style is even more relevant to our discourse. Children who have grown up in a family with an over-coercive parental style divide life into the "top dog" and "underdog" and their attitude towards others may be one of imitation, compliance, internalisation, rebellion, and resistance (Stein, 2018b).

Responses similar to these have been observed in children of parents with narcissistic disturbances. For Irwin Gootnick, there are three common types of responses by children to the interpersonal problems presented to them by such parents: *identification*, *rebellion*, and *compliance* (Gootnick, 1997).

Identification is a response to the parent seeing the child as a representative of him- or herself, and is the price of connectedness with the parent. It results in the child becoming a narcissist.

In regard to narcissistic parents, the child must exhibit the same qualities, values, feelings, and behaviour which the parent employs to defend his or her self-esteem.

Rebellion refers to the state of fighting to not accept the dictates of the parent by behaving in opposition to them. The child therefore acts in a self-defeating manner in order to try to maintain a sense of independence.

Compliance refers to the co-narcissistic adaptation described earlier, wherein the child becomes the approving audience sought by the parent. The child is complying with the parent's needs by being the counterpart the parent seeks.

All three forms of adaptation (identification, rebellion, and compliance) can be seen as compliance in a larger sense, since, in every case, the child complies in some way with the needs of the parent, and is defined by the parent. What defines compliance in this sense is that the child becomes the counterpart the parent needs from moment to moment to help the parent manage threats to his or her self-esteem.

Both narcissism and co-narcissism are adaptations that children have made to cope with narcissistic parenting figures (Gootnick, 1997). Miller reports that most of her patients' parents were likely to have narcissistic disturbances, they were extremely insecure and often suffered from depression.

> The child, an only one or often the first-born, was the narcissistically cathected object. What these mothers had once failed to find in their own mothers they were able to find in their children: someone at their disposal who can be used as an echo, who can be controlled, is completely centred on them, will never desert them, and offers full attention and admiration. (Miller, 1979, p. 35)

More recently Rappoport (2005) brings this concept even further and reports that every narcissistic and co-narcissistic client that he has encountered has had narcissistic parents:

> A high proportion of people in psychotherapy have adapted to life with narcissistic people and, as a result, have not been able to develop healthy means of self-expression and self-directedness. ... Commonly, one parent was primarily narcissistic and the other parent primarily co-narcissistic, and so both orientations have been modelled for the child. ... Those who are primarily co-narcissistic may behave narcissistically when their self-esteem is threatened, or when their partners take the co-narcissistic role; people who primarily behave narcissistically may act co-narcissistically when they fear being held responsible and punished for another's experience. (pp. 1–2)

This last observation is one more reason to consider narcissistic disturbances (with other psychopathic manifestations) as a cross-phenomenon, non-individual in nature.

The good, the beautiful, the true ... and the powerful

Much has been written about companies, leadership, human resources, governance, and management, but the conceptual insights thus gained have not made it to the family as organisation: whoever researches "power games within the family" will have a hard time finding anything at all. To date, no one has questioned the nuclear family model in relation to mental illness, all the more so because the birth of psychoanalysis coincides with the beginning of industrialisation and of the migration from country villages to urban metropolis.

Truth and power are two incompatible psychological principles, whose interplay shapes the personality when facing abuse and mistreatment in the family. Some individuals devote their lives to power at the expense of their own inner truth. Those who venture into the realm of truth have to face the invalidating gaze of others and are constantly challenged in their adult lives at the expense of their status: those who embark along this road face an increasing isolation.

The presence (or lack) of a helping witness can make a world of difference in the life of a child, particularly for a child who might not have been lucky enough to be raised by a mother available to be cathected narcissistically, to be a function of the child's narcissistic development.

> A healthy development is still possible, if she only refrains from preventing the child from acquiring what the mother lacks from other people. Various investigations have shown the incredible ability that a healthy child displays in making use of the smallest affective "nourishment" (stimulation) to be found in his surroundings. (Miller, 1979, p. 32).

How on earth is any nuclear family supposed to provide this? And when did nuclear families become the norm? Recent studies indicate that the nuclear conception of the family is inadequate, misleading, and extremely pernicious when relied on for an understanding of the dynamics of family functioning or as a guide for therapeutic intervention. The nuclear family has systematic issues in the areas of intimate partner conflict, problematic behaviours or concerns in one partner, emotional distance, and impaired functionality in children (Bowen, 1978). Anxiety may lead to fights, arguments, criticism, under- or over-performance of responsibilities, and/or distancing behaviour. Besides, it is common for children to become triangulated within their parents' relationship (Wang & Crane, 2001). Yet clinical practitioners and psychological theorists play a notable role in fostering the nuclear myth by assuming that there is no viable model other than that (Uzoka, 1979).

A small family of two, three, or four people offers little in terms of human resources to a child. It is easy to become singled out, harassed, alienated, or otherwise neglected. Psychosis kicks in much more easily in an environment where a single individual finds himself isolated, with no ally, no witness, none to turn to when everybody else teams up. In poor environments, a nuclear family is even more at risk, because the lack of variety within cannot be easily compensated by external system figures, not without costs. Even sexual drives get thwarted and may find it difficult to be directed outward in particular circumstances. The well-known dynamics occurring between parents and children in puberty can be explained in these terms.

Wilhelm Reich observed that the Oedipus complex itself is only conceivable in a society based on the nuclear model of a family and marriage, implying the ownership of women, whereas societies that have neither our sexual repression nor adultery are not compatible with the Oedipus complex. This is why the Oedipus complex is so inadequate: it is culture-specific.

The gap between the biological and the psychosocial maturation of the human offspring, as well as his or her long-lasting cultural dependency (in "developed" civilisations), are key factors to guarantee the maximum evolutionary development, but they also provide the context in which adults can impose their dominion, often insensitive to children's needs. This amounts to perverting their child-rearing functions to their own advantage, something which then gets reinforced by bending family history with biased and self-serving narratives, and by controlling relationships, institutions, and political choices.

The unnamed enemy

The birth of a child can be unsettling and threatening for a parent, because it upsets a pre-established order on all levels: familial, institutional, and cultural. This leads to a defensive attitude, generated by the fear that the emerging generation will make claims and undermine the power, identity, and social control already acquired by the members of the adult generation. This fear is as intense as the adults' projections onto the members of the new generations of their fantasies and drives: competition, hatred, and desire of sexual appropriation. Such fantasies are often bound to become reality: the truth of myth and fairy tales, seen from the angle of Freudian interpretations, is there to confirm this. It is Laius who first wants to get rid of Oedipus, because he fears he could be ousted by him; it is the stepmother who wants to get rid of Snow White, as she is envious of her beauty and her ever-growing competence and charm (Ghiano, 1996).

Sándor Ferenczi was one of the few who clearly highlighted the catastrophic effects of adults lacking identification with childhood in their educational and relational interventions. In his lectures on educational aims, Ferenczi recalls that in 1908 Professor Czerny, a paediatrician, complained to parents about their inadequacy in the upbringing of their children, and identified the cause in their not remembering, or misremembering, their own childhood. Ferenczi goes on to say that humankind is in pain due to exaggerated repression, and that could be done away with by means of a mass clarification: a sort of inner revolution would be needed. In his opinion, that would be the first revolution to really benefit humankind (Ferenczi, 2006).

Ethnocentrism, eurocentrism, anthropocentrism, and so on are all categories of committed cultural militancy, elaborated within diverse discourses, all with a common denominator: a strong critique of forms of totalising domination that impose unfavourable life conditions on the dominated, and manipulate the relevant forms of knowledge and the very representation of reality, by warping and centring them on the dominator's interests. The condition of children as regards the adult world has similar characteristics and the neologism "adultocentrism" has already appeared in political discourse.

Adultocentrism is a way of seeing and operating that expresses a failure in the growth of an adult, in that it reveals some kind of repression and splitting from one's own childhood. It signals the inability to dialogue with one's own past, to acknowledge it, and to integrate it into the present dimension. Adultocentrism is the position of an unfinished adult, which was once an unfinished child, and who later truncated the vital roots of the pleasant and unpleasant experiences of childhood (Associazione Rompere il Silenzio, 2004).

Violence on the child is often accompanied by a heavy use of rationalisations that justify or deny it and by a weak activation of sensitivity. Adultocentrism brings the limits of conceptualisation of subjective experience to the extreme; such limits, which are related to the acquisition of language on one hand, and the biology of the infant on the other, bring the conflict between symbolisation and experience to breaking point (Stern, 1985).

There is a deep link between an adult's domination of children and other forms of political and social domination: they all require a split between rationality on one hand and emotions on the other, that is, the ability to empathise with the Other. According to Eagle (2010) technology has made possible a kind of mass destruction that requires and implies an affectivity, indifference, and a kind of rationality that is completely disconnected from the acknowledgement of other human beings. This has led us to an endless loop and a form of madness.

Adultocentrism worsens the break between adult language and rationality on one side, and sensorial experience and emotions on the other. The former is privileged in order to fulfil the defensive need to control and suppress the affective dimension, in which all sorts of painful experiences have accumulated: suffering, powerlessness, frustration, etc. Consequently, a commitment against adultocentrism on many levels (prevention, training, etc.) can only be aimed at reinstating interest in affect and emotions, as opposed to adultocentric contempt and suppression towards a balance between adult competencies and children's needs (Foti & Foti, 1995).

References

Adorno, T. W., Frenkel-Brunswik, E., Levinson, D. J., & Sanford, R. N. (1950). *The Authoritarian Personality*. New York: Harper & Brothers.

Associazione Rompere il Silenzio (2004). *Adultocentrismo: Il Mondo Dominato dagli Adulti*, Sie Editore (Italy).

Bowen, M. (1978). *Family Therapy in Clinical Practice*. New York: Jason Aronson, 1994.

Carveth, D. L. (2010). Superego, conscience, and the nature and types of guilt. *Modern Psychoanalysis, 35*(1): 106.

D'Silva, K., Duggan, C., & McCarthy, L. (2004). Does treatment really make psychopaths worse? A review of the evidence. *Journal of Personality Disorders, 18*(2): 163–177.

Dicks, H. V. (1967). *Marital Tensions*. New York: Basic Books.

Drexler, K. (2013). Transgenerational weitergegebene Traumata der Bearbeitung zugänglich machen. *Zeitschrift für Psychotraumatologie, Psychotherapiewissenschaft, Psychologische Medizin, 11*(1): 65–74.

Eagle, M. (2010). *From Classical to Contemporary Psychoanalysis: A Critique and Integration*. New York: Routledge, 2011.

Ellard, J. H., Miller, C. D., Baumle, T.-L., & Olson, J. M. (2002). Just world processes in demonizing. In: M. Ross & D. T. Miller (Eds.), *The Justice Motive in Everyday Life* (pp. 350–364). Cambridge: Cambridge University Press.

Ferenczi, S. (2006). *L'enfant dans l'adulte*. Paris: Pétite Bibliothèque Payot.

Foti, C., & Foti, C. (1995). *Giocare per Mettersi in Gioco*. Turin, Italy: Centro Studi Hansel e Gretel.

Fromm, E. (1941). *Escape from Freedom*. London: Macmillan, 1994.

Fromm, E. (1973). *The Anatomy of Human Destructiveness*. New York: Henry Holt.

Garland, D. (2001). *The Culture of Control: Crime and Social Order in Contemporary Society*. Chicago, IL: University of Chicago Press, 2012.

Ghiano, D. (1996). Il complesso edipico, dal modello pulsionale al modello relazionale. In: *Educare alla sessualità e all'affettività*. Turin, Italy: Centro Studi Hansel e Gretel.

Gootnick, I. (1997). *Why You Behave in Ways You Hate: And What You Can Do About It*. Granite Bay, CA: Penmarin.

Hemphill, J. F., & Hart, S. D. (2002). Motivating the unmotivated: psychopathy, treatment, and change. In: M. McMurran (Ed.), *Motivating Offenders to Change: A Guide to Enhancing Engagement in Therapy* (pp. 193–219). Chichester, UK: John Wiley.

Hesse, M. (2009). Portrayal of psychopathy in the movies. *International Review of Psychiatry*, *21*(3): 207–212.

Horkheimer, M., Fromm, E., & Marcuse, H. (1936). *Studien über Autorität und Familie* [Studies on Authority and Family]. *Schriften des Instituts für Sozialforschung*. Paris: Félix Alcan.

Innamorati, M. (2010). La prospettiva culturalista di Erich Fromm e Karen Horney: guarire la nevrosi della società. In: A. De Coro & F. Ortu (Eds.), *Psicologia Dinamica: I Modelli Teorici a Confronto*. Rome: Editori Laterza.

Lancini, M. (Ed.) (2007). *Genitori e Psicologo: Madri e Padri di Adolescenti in Consultazione*. Milan, Italy: Franco Angeli.

Miller, A. (1979). *Das Drama des begabten Kindes*. Frankfurt am Main, Germany: Suhrkamp. Trans. *Prisoners of Childhood: The Drama of the Gifted Child and the Search for the True Self*. New York: Basic Books, 1981.

Miller, A. (1980). *Am Anfang war Erziehung*. Frankfurt am Main, Germany: Suhrkamp. Trans. (H. Hannum & H. Hannum). *For Your Own Good: Hidden Cruelty in Child-Rearing and the Roots of Violence*. New York: Farrar, Straus & Giroux, 1983.

Miller, A. (1984). *Thou Shalt Not Be Aware: Society's Betrayal of the Child*. New York : Farrar. Straus & Giroux [reprinted London: Pluto, 1998].

Miller, A. (1988). *Der gemiedene Schlüssel*. Trans. *The Untouched Key: Tracing Childhood Trauma in Creativity and Destructiveness*. New York: Anchor, 1991.

Miller, A. (1990). *Abbruch der Schweigemauer: die Wahrheit der Fakten*, Hamburg, Germany: Hoffmann und Campe. Trans. *Breaking Down the*

Wall of Silence: The Liberating Experience of Facing Painful Truth. New York: Dutton/Penguin, 1991.

Miller, A. (1998). The political consequences of child abuse. *Journal of Psychohistory*, *26*(2): 573. (Retrieved June 1, 2020, from https://psychohistory.com/articles/the-political-consequences-of-child-abuse/.)

Miller, A. (2004). Saddam Hussein and the cardinals. Article published on the website www.alice-miller.com, January 1.

Miller, A. (2007). *Dein gerettetes Leben: Wege zur Befreiung*, Frankfurt am Main, Germany: Suhrkamp. Trans. *Free from Lies: Discovering Your True Needs.* New York: W. W. Norton, 2009.

Missildine, W. H. (1963). *Your Inner Child of the Past.* New York: Simon & Schuster.

Oliner, S. P., & Oliner, P. M. (1988). *The Altruistic Personality: Rescuers of Jews in Nazi Europe.* New York: Free Press.

Perry, B. D. (1994). Neurobiological sequelae of childhood trauma: post-traumatic stress disorders in children. In: M. Murburg (Ed.), *Catecholamine Function in Post Traumatic Stress Disorder: Emerging Concepts* (pp. 253–276). Washington, DC: American Psychiatric Press.

Rappoport, A. (2005). Co-narcissism: how we accommodate to narcissistic parents. *The Therapist*, *1*: 1–8.

Ronningstam, E. (2005). *Identifying and Understanding the Narcissistic Personality.* New York: Oxford University Press.

Sapolsky, R. M. (1994). *Why Zebras Don't Get Ulcers: An Updated Guide To Stress, Stress-Related Diseases, and Coping.* New York: W. H. Freeman.

Schatzman, M. (1973). *Soul Murder: Persecution in the Family.* London: Allen Lane.

Sibaldi, I. (2012). *Agenda degli Angeli.* Milan, Italy: Sperling & Kupfer.

Stein, H. T. (2018a). The Impact of Family Atmospheres on Children. Retrieved January 31, 2020, from www.adlerian.us.

Stein, H. T. (2018b). Adult Consequences of Childhood Parenting Styles. Retrieved January 31, 2020, from www.adlerian.us.

Stern, D. N. (1985). *Die Lebenserfahrung des Säuglings*, Stuttgart: Klett-Cota. Trans. *The Interpersonal World of the Infant: A View from Psychoanalysis and Developmental Psychology.* New York: Routledge, 2018.

Symington, N. (1996). *The Making of a Psychotherapist.* Madison, CT: International Universities Press [reprinted London: Routledge, 2006].

Uzoka, A. F. (1979). The myth of the nuclear family: historical background and clinical implications. *American Psychologist*, *34*(11): 1095.

Vaknin, S. (1999). *Malignant Self-love: Narcissism Revisited (10th Revised Impression)*. Rhinebeck, NY: Narcissus, 2007.

Wang, L., & Crane, D. R. (2001). The relationship between marital satisfaction, marital stability, nuclear family triangulation, and childhood depression. *American Journal of Family Therapy*, *29*(4): 337–347.

Winnicott, D. W. (1986). *Babies and Their Mothers*. Reading, MA: Addison-Wesley Reading, 1992.

CHAPTER EIGHT

Diversity: notes from the inside and from the outside

Tomasz Fortuna

> I think there's something wrong with my liver. But I understand damn all about my illness and I can't say for certain which part of me is affected. I'm not receiving treatment for it and never have, although I do respect medicine and doctors. What's more, I'm still extremely superstitious—well, sufficiently to respect medicine. (I'm educated enough not to be superstitious, but I am superstitious.) Oh no, I'm refusing treatment out of spite. That's something you probably can't bring yourselves to understand. (Dostoyevsky, 1864, p. 3)

This extraordinary short novel, Fyodor Dostoyevsky's *Notes from Underground*, was written before Sigmund Freud published *The Interpretation of Dreams* or even his papers on hysteria. The underground seems to stand here for isolation from and opposition to the outside world—the outside group—as well as for the unconscious mind and the related sense of alienation. The main character, referring to his "liver problems", clearly *feels his bile rise* when giving us his account of the outside world through his lens, the particular vertex—a hostile treatment of himself (his *superego*). What is *external* and what is *internal* becomes simultaneously less clear.

Liver and bile, being crucial to the processes of digestion and detoxification, become here a symbol of the capacity to relate to the experience of diversity, to tolerate difference and to embrace those experiences. The underground man knows and he does not know at the same time, he is full of emotion and he misses the point when facing a suffering person.

In this text I am concerned with the internal experience of difference and its external manifestations in behaviour and language, trying to link these two territories together. Psychoanalysis offers a complex multifaceted understanding of the mind as well as intra- and inter-group relationships.

There is a danger that the word *diversity* may become a hollow term conforming to the current social and political climate losing thus its edge—turning into a kind of Orwellian *newspeak*, in that it could become stripped of its momentum and true meaning. Diversity constitutes nowadays parts of policies; people know its definition by heart when attending job interviews—becoming this way as if a smokescreen for the surrounding reality. From time to time something erupts in organisations, psychoanalytic societies, in politics or the world of arts, and perhaps these are the moments when we suddenly are in touch with the real experience of difference, with superstition, bias, and prejudice, which supposedly had been managed by our culture and education. These are the moments when we realise we are facing wars and international conflicts, migration, and discrimination.

Then, of course, there is the other side of the story, of the experience of difference—the enriching and liberating qualities of diversity in both the external and internal sense.

The premise of emotional freedom

The opening quote sets two vantage points here, that is, the discovery of contradictory ambivalent feelings, and the unconscious mind. Important here is one's mind's attitude towards the recognition and assimilation of psychic and external truth. Or as Wilfred Bion (1962) described it, the capacity to *get to know* and *learn from experience* (K), an emotional capacity to metabolise and dream one's emotional experiences—as opposed to denial and omnipotent *possession of knowledge* (-K), which can dominate experience and psychic functioning. The third element here is the global sociopolitical context with unexpected events and shifts or disasters in the making, such as those which may result from the attitudes and management of climate change. The interrelation of those elements seems crucial.

Referring to the linguistic research by Giles (1973), Pieter Seuren gives this straightforward but evocative example of the relationship with difference, expressed in the use of speech and behaviour. He writes,

> In simple terms, speakers from different social classes who have positive feelings with regard to each other tend to move their settings [accent, vocabulary, grammar] closer to each other, whereas speakers who have negative feelings with regard to each other start accentuating the differences between them, the differences becoming greater as the feelings are stronger. (Seuren, 2015, pp. 189–190)

He adds that this also happens in groups and between groups of speakers.

Psychoanalysis threw a particular light on the nature and complexity of this kind of behavioural adjustments, demonstrating that this dynamic change in attitude and speech has to do with the internal world of objects and phantasies, as well as the actual interaction between persons or groups. It is a sign of the momentary shifts in the internal reality or rather the activation, as well as containment, of particular kinds of anxieties resulting in the dominance of the particular defensive strategies. These phenomena are dynamic in nature.

The constellations of anxieties, defences, and associated unconscious phantasies, described by Melanie Klein (1940, 1946) as positions, depressive with a concern for the object, and paranoid–schizoid with an underlying sense of threat, are descriptions of states of mind, which tend to determine the way we deal with perceptions of external and internal realities. Although the capacity to tolerate depressive anxieties (such as a sense of separateness, guilt, loss of object love, etc.) is considered an achievement of a fairly mature personality, it is important to note the equation developed by Bion demonstrating an ongoing dynamic interplay between the two positions, Ps<—>D. Thomas Ogden (1989) added the autistic-contiguous mode of generating experience—dominated by the sense of boundedness and the experience of autistic shapes and objects—as a primitive version of object relations. Those shifts between such states of mind may be flexible or rigid, adaptive or maladaptive.

Ron Britton (2001) introduced yet another important aspect of those shifts and changes. In a mind that can register experience and learn from it, there never is a return to exactly the same state of mind, that is, exactly the same paranoid–schizoid or depressive position. There can however be a movement towards the pathological versions of those mental positions, corresponding to the notion of *psychic retreat*, representing complex systems of defences of the personality (as described by O'Shaughnessy, 1981; Rosenfeld, 1964; and Steiner, 1987) that protect from the experience of anxieties relevant to each of those modes of generating experience.

The presence of the dynamic movement described reflects the capacity of the mind to learn from experience and retain memory and the capacity to form creative links. It results in the experience of complexity and richness of relationships and is crucial to preserve a sense of freedom and curiosity, as opposed to feelings of entrapment in a particular emotional experience—for example, as described by "container".

Another way of describing those processes is as the shifts between Ptolemaic and Copernican perspectives, as developed by Jean Laplanche. In his theory of the origins of the unconscious mind, Laplanche (1999) touches upon two important facets of our experience, that is, the shifting of Copernican and Ptolemaic points of view and the experience of otherness. In an earlier essay I wrote,

> By its very nature, our mind is egocentric but at the same time decentred through experience of the unconscious, in terms of an internal otherness of the unconscious mind as well as the otherness and strangeness of another person. According to Laplanche, there not only takes place a phantasy about the existence of another person contrasted with the objective presence of another, but also a communication coming from this other person that provides one with a sense of being different as well as with the sense that there does exist someone or something outside oneself. (Fortuna, 2014, p. 27)

The *otherness* in us, on the one hand, demands understanding and trans-
lation bringing about curiosity and apprehension, and on the other, it
colours our experience of the actual difference in others.

In other words, this is an experience of something from the outside,
residing on the inside.

Groups and difference

One can see Freud's (1930a) notion of the *narcissism of minor differences*
in similar terms, namely as a reaction to the challenge of the continuous process of negotiating difference in order to preserve separateness
and at the same time to secure a sense of cohesion. Acuteness of the
reactions to difference is due to the wish to preserve the integrity and
stability of the psychic apparatus, reflected in the cohesion of the group.
The difficulty, however, lies in the fact that there always is a difference
and a conflict present in the group itself (as well as in one's mind) and
this leads to a constant search for the enemy—the outside group (e.g. as
depicted in Orwell's *Nineteen Eighty-Four*). In both cases, anxieties are
being mastered but the emotional growth is stifled.

Hanna Segal reminds us, "Freud contended that we form groups for
constructive libidinal reasons, to bind ourselves to one another and to
address ourselves to reality (forces of nature) [which seems to correspond
to Bion's *work group*], but also to solve our psychological problems—like
merging our superego into a group superego which leaves us capable
of committing any crimes provided they are sanctioned by the group"
(2006, p. 116).

The psychotic anxieties (unbearable on an individual level) are
located—projected—in the group, which can become a container when
the *work group* predominates, or the process can lead to enactment,
when the *basic assumption functioning* takes over (Bion, 1961). In this
instance, there always seems to be a phantasy of the outside threat—the
world appears to be polarised and hostile. There is an enhanced sense of
difference, as we have seen in the case of the use of speech.

Two unconscious phantasies of triumph and threat clash in those situations resulting in the narcissism and the sense of omnipotence being
punctured or even shattered. The response is often fuelled by another
omnipotent phantasy and the sense of righteousness. As, for example,

described in Sophocles' *Oedipus at Colonus* (406 BC; Steiner, 1990), where Oedipus turns away from the true understanding.

The polarised perception of external and internal realities can be stabilised by rigid systems of defences functioning as an internal mafia-gang (Rosenfeld, 1971). This way splitting and projection as defences against feelings such as rejection, abandonment, separation, or fear of annihilation are maintained. The familiar mafia-like structure supports a belief that as long as one (or a part of the self) submits and cooperates with the omnipotent and superior mafia, one secures its "kindness" and "protection". Aggressive impulses are then employed to preserve the cohesion. When enacted externally these processes shape the structure of gangs and power/dominance relationships.

Although initially described as a tyranny of the psychotic/narcissistic part of the personality over the neurotic one (Bion, 1957), there also is a question of perverse relationships between parts of the personality, that is the non-psychotic parts of the personality, able to register realities, perversely collude (Steiner, 1982) with the omnipotence and omniscience of the psychotic/narcissistic mind—a version of turning a blind eye. This is yet another attack on the link between the outside and the inside.

Diversity on the social level and the intra-psychic experience

Fakhry Davids (2006, 2011), introducing his concept of *internal racism*, a version of a narcissistic defensive organisation of the personality, identified three steps in which the racist response occurs. After the real difference between the subject and object is established (e.g. their accent, skin colour, ethnic or class background, sexuality, etc.), splitting and projection of the split-off undesired aspects of one's self take place. The recipient of the projections is now seen as possessing those qualities and feelings. The further missing piece of the puzzle is an established internal organisation perceiving the object in light of such projections, a template that secures the deal (Davids, 2006). The hierarchy of power, superiority/inferiority relationships, is established and the organisation remains invisible until this balance is upset, for instance by the demand for equality or disagreement. This is supported by social scripts and inequalities existing in the social/collective consciousness. When the balance is disturbed, an acute and often violent response occurs. It seems to play a part when the groups are singled out and violent repercussions take place.

Zadie Smith, writing about the Brexit vote in the UK, addresses the issue of diversity and existing social divisions.

> For many people in London right now the supposedly multi-cultural and cross-class aspects of their lives are actually represented by their staff—nannies, cleaners—by the people who pour their coffees and drive their cabs, or else the handful of ubiquitous Nigerian princes you meet in the private schools. The painful truth is that fences are being raised everywhere in London. Around school districts, around neighbourhoods, around lives. One useful consequence of Brexit is to finally and openly reveal a deep fracture in British society that has been thirty years in the making. The gaps between north and south, between the social classes, between Londoners and everyone else, between rich Londoners and poor Londoners, and between white and brown and black are real and need to be confronted by all of us, not only those who voted Leave. (Smith, 2016, p. 25)

She also tells us about an unspoken tension between her and a young white British mother Smith met at the school her daughter attended. It never seemed possible to arrange anything together due to a sense of "fear and loathing" that Smith felt the other mother had for her. She explains that it was not because she was black but because she was black and middle class at the same time. This perhaps was seen as a transgression of the *agreed* social norms—an element of Davids' configuration of the internal racism. In this process, Smith becomes here an agent of otherness coming from the outside and unsettling the existing order.

Smith's ideas are not far from Bauman's description of "gated communities". He uses the word "community" here with unease. "Inside 'gated communities' the streets are mostly empty. And so if someone who 'does not belong', a stranger, appears on the sidewalk, he or she will be promptly spotted as an out-of-the-ordinary event—before a prank or damage can be done" (Bauman, 2010, p. 159). This expresses no intent to mix, integrate, or get to know each other—there is no community life happening in the usual sense. The real aim is "... to be secure from the daunting, harrowing, incapacitating fear of insecurity. They hope that the walls will protect them from that fear" (p. 160). The concrete spatial division between inside and outside is striking and we are familiar with the real and imagined walls and gates being built to keep the other out.

Ida and *Aftermath*

The films *Ida* (2013) and *Aftermath* (2012) attempt to give an account of the tragic events which took place in occupied Poland during World War II. The conflict between difference and similarity leads here to a wish to protect and preserve as well as to murderousness with intent to wipe the difference out, manage primitive anxieties, and preserve some sense of coherence. Pogroms in some areas of the country at the time took place under the Nazi occupation but were largely committed by inhabitants of Polish villages. The history of pogroms in central and eastern parts of Europe precedes the described events and it raises an urgent question of what had led to such a tragic breakdown in relationships between communities.

Both films look at those painful events retrospectively and deal with the return of the truth and the knowledge about committed crimes. In *Aftermath*, a Polish man, Franciszek Kalina, returns to his home village to find his brother, Jozef, in a conflict with his fellow villagers. The initial impulse to go back was the break-up of his brother's family (his sister-in-law and children left Poland for the US—the first breakdown of a structure) and at this point his lack of understanding of what went on. He realises that the discovery of Jewish gravestones, used during and after the war as a building material in the village, mobilised a violent response. Jozef decides to recover them, removing parts of the road, elements of the church and houses, and place them in his field. He also learns Hebrew to be able to read the inscriptions (Bion's K). Later on, he was perversely accused of a "destruction" of the road after removing the gravestones (a sense of the second breakdown of a kind of structure). His deeply human attitude meets here with a hateful response. Franciszek, trying to support his brother, uncovers further truth, namely that Polish neighbours took over Jewish land and homes after the killings. Together with the actual murder, the truth and knowledge of what had happened were *murdered* as well. The old parson, who represents here reconciliation, capacity to see, contain, and link thoughts and experiences, is removed from his position and replaced by a younger priest, who supports the polarised view of the villagers and denial of the truth. The field that belongs to Jozef is set alight and Jozef is beaten up.

Despite this, everything now was to be uncovered and exposed. There is a sense of paranoid annihilation anxiety in the film—perhaps corresponding to the breakdown points described above. Return of the unbearable sense of guilt equals, in experience, a fear of merciless retaliation, which strips one of any goodness or dignity. The victims, kept in contempt until now, were to return. Projections seem here to support splitting, resulting in feelings of hatred on both sides. Franciszek tries to protect the sense of equilibrium, holding in mind the reality and the proportions of the uncovering events. What however leads to a dramatic resolution of this stand-off is yet another painful discovery, namely that the brothers' father was one of the direct perpetrators of the killings. This information becomes unbearable for Jozef (the third breakdown), who now wants to reverse everything and bury the truth once again.

Bion (1958) confronts us with the difficulty in tolerating knowledge and insight, describing Oedipus' arrogance, which turns out to be catastrophic, as he pursues uncovering the truth regardless of the costs and consequences. Oedipus pays for his actions with blindness and exile, which symbolise departure from knowledge. The blindness and the exile provide him with a shelter, a peculiar kind of oasis born out of a version of events, which lifted the weight of responsibility, opening the way to a defensive psychic retreat (Steiner, 1990). The falsehood of this version of events is due to the obliteration of the complexity of this situation with its actual implications. The omnipotence relinquished for a moment has to be recovered in whatever available form.

In a similar way, the breakdown in *Aftermath* occurs when Jozef cannot take the full truth in—in his experience, he has to move to the other side and he chooses denial and obliteration of knowledge, which has to be murdered and buried (Bion's -K).

Aftermath portrays a version of psychic retreat on the scale of the whole community, with a combination of denial—no tombs to remind anyone of the crimes, no knowledge, no memories or correct historical accounts—with splitting and disavowal—the knowledge exists in the minds of some people but the whole community *turns a blind eye*. People felt protected from the punishing superego but only through those mechanisms. On the personal level, the more or less fragile psychic structure had to be protected because the emergence from such a psychic asylum threatens a sense of confusion and persecution, accompanied by guilt, shame, and humiliation (Steiner, 2011).

Ida is a story of a novice in a female convent. The events are being uncovered through the eyes of their victims. One of the senior nuns feels that it is important for Ida to understand her roots before taking vows. For the first time, Ida is going to meet her maternal aunt, a prosecuting lawyer, who turns out to be the Red Wanda (or Bloody Wanda), infamous for her part in cruel political trials that led to many executions. They are the only remaining members of the Jewish family. The others lost their lives in one of the pogroms.

Ida survived only because she did not seem different—she was little, not circumcised (as the boys were), and had ginger hair. Symbolically (and literally) she, and the knowledge of these tragic events, were removed behind the *walls* of the convent. The reality of her origins was split off and partly denied.

There is an unexpected twist in this story—we find out that it is the son who is the perpetrator, and not the initially suspected father who tried to protect the Jewish family. The father represents here concern and human values but he becomes impotent and perhaps reluctant to defend his stance when confronted with his son's murderousness. Here again, an illusion of safety is present when the difference is eliminated in response to primitive psychotic annihilation anxieties.

Both films describe a period in history when there was an actual brutal attack on human values and the value of human life. As works of art, they convey a particular symbolic depiction of the events and the complexity of psychic experience. In both films, there is a point when the acknowledgement of human suffering and values, as well as a more realistic perception of the events, takes place—for example when Jozef decides to recover the gravestones as well as the memory of Jewish neighbours and their tragic deaths. In *Ida*, it is the rediscovery of her roots together with the painful truth; it also is the meeting with her aunt and Ida's curiosity what life is about. Interestingly, in an early scene, she noticed the rigidity of the structure provided by the convent, when she laughs during a very orderly meal drill. In the end, she, however, retreats back to the convent to take her vows after her aunt, Wanda, acknowledging her loss and the destructive way she managed it in her life (cruelty and promiscuity), commits suicide. Ida as if repeats Wanda's life and a version of her suicide in one day only to retreat back to the convent.

Recently, both films and the knowledge they carry have become unwelcome in some spheres of Polish society and they are considered anti-Polish by the right-wing nationalist politicians. This has led to severe restrictions in screenings of both films in cinemas and on the national television (Kublik, 2016), revealing strikingly similar political and societal reactions to the issues they tried to portray.

Artistic creativity and the experience of difference

Artistic creativity and symbolic representation can at least partly help to process, to work through, such difficult collective experiences. The spectator is affected by the experience and connects with the internal world of the artist (Segal, 1952). Real art brings the aesthetic experience and at the same time disturbs and unsettles the spectator.

In one of the health centres in a diverse and economically deprived part of London, posters for the 2012 Olympic Games were put up on the walls. One of them was *For the Unknown Runner* (2011) by Chris Ofili, depicting a simple drawing of a running man with a Greek vase in the background. In the course of redecoration works, in order to choose the appropriate pictures, patients and staff were asked to leave their comments on each of them. The described poster was labelled "disturbing". This meant that the *Unknown Runner* was to be removed. A person who had funded those posters asked then why did the image seem disturbing: "Was it because the runner was unknown, black, and naked?" I think the image represents movement, corporeality, rawness, diversity, but at the same time loss of employment, funding cuts, and restrictions to care provided to people who often come from ethnic minority backgrounds. For many members of staff it also meant abandonment and loss, sense of resentment and guilt. The attempt to remove this image, even if in good faith, showed the unconscious need to deny painful reality and feelings which had been evoked. The emotional links and connections were unconsciously attacked and the meaning disguised. For real art has to emotionally unsettle, upset the balance, shake the sense of comfort, to subsequently bring awe about.

These processes of negotiating various conflicting thoughts and phantasies and associated emotions never settle and therefore the need to find effective psychic defences to alleviate such experience is no surprise. The ability, however, to manage this confusion and uncertainty is perhaps the only way to engage with what is different and unsettling because of its unfamiliarity. It offers a chance for a European clinician and an African patient to intimately connect intuiting a sense of migration and displacement. The experience of a foreign funeral and mourning traditions may seem strikingly alien and yet may bring about the same experience of loss.

The real difficulty is not only the acceptance of difference but the management of the conflict between the wish to deny it, on the one hand, and to emphasise and embrace its otherness on the other.

Sociopolitical changes closer to home

The UK's vote to leave the European Union and the election of Donald Trump as president of the USA could be seen as symptoms, compromise formations, which avoid the direct unrest but also paradoxically disguise the real cause of this dismay. The urge to build the wall that is supposed to shield the US from Mexicans, another one closer to home in Calais for similar reasons, seems to have the same kind of wishful paranoid thinking and longing for idealised comfort and security. *Gated nations/ countries*, the US and perhaps the post-Brexit United Kingdom, seem to be dreams (or perhaps nightmares) come true. The outside group has been identified and the task is simple—to keep them away. Apparently, in the digital age, the control over borders and security will be assured by the concrete land borders, instead of trust and close international cooperation.

The divisions and projections sanctioned this way work the other way round too, so it is not only the threat that is projected into refugees and immigrants but also the prejudice and racism that is located in the political class. We come here across the question of what the phantasies are and what the reality—how much one demonises Donald Trump and how much he acts on those projections located in him. Someone like

Trump becomes here a convenient receptacle of those qualities, instead of the more objective assessment whether or not he is up to the job and what might the actual dangers be.

The reluctance to see reality is nothing new of course, as we know from Freud's paper "Formulations on Two Principles of Mental Functioning" (1911b) and the further elaborations by Bion and others, but there is something to say about the scale of this phenomenon in the light of current advances in communication technologies and the role of the media. Earlier in this chapter, I referred to Orwell's *newspeak* as it appears in his *Nineteen Eighty-Four* novel (1949), and you will not be surprised that this association is not an original one—comparisons to this classic work have been proliferating in the press (e.g. Seaton, Crook, & Taylor, 2017). We hear about the "alternative facts" and "fake news" and witness a systematic dismantling of the truth.

In one of his earlier essays, not without humour, Orwell gives us a sample of the new qualities of the English language he witnessed in the 1940s, making a case for the relationship between sociopolitical shifts and changes in the use of language,

> As I have tried to show, modern writing at its worst does not consist in picking out words for the sake of their meaning and inventing images in order to make the meaning clearer. It consists in gumming together long strips of words which have already been set in order by someone else, and making the results presentable by sheer humbug. The attraction of this way of writing is that it is easy. It is easier—even quicker, once you have the habit—to say in my opinion it is not an unjustifiable assumption that than to say I think. (Orwell, 1946)

The process of stripping the language of meaning, either by radical replacement (e.g. Orwell's ministries of love, truth, peace, and plenty) or nearly invisible loss of clarity and the real meaning, is striking.

Another example of this is a description of the beginnings of the Americas as we know it:

> There's no doubt that there was a meeting of two worlds. But the phrase "discovery of America" is obviously inaccurate. What

> they discovered was an America that had been discovered thou-
> sands of years before by its inhabitants. Thus, what took place
> was the invasion of America—an invasion by a very alien culture.
> (Chomsky & Dieterich, 1999b, p. 10)

The language used in the recent political debates is also striking. The European Union was labelled a *bloc* and the appalling maltreatment of Greece by the EU, when Greece was on the brink of financial collapse, as well as some of the EUs inflexible structures, did not help. Instead of engaging with a *good enough* European Union this polarisation has been maintained. The word *bloc* is a reminder of the Soviet bloc with all relevant associations. *Brexiteers*, like musketeers, are portrayed as the progressive force, while *Remainers* as the inhibiting obstacle. The rhetoric is not dissimilar from the other side of the channel, for example, *Little Britain* and the comparisons between British and Continental cuisine—a mixture of denigration and contempt for the other side combined with grandiosity and omniscience. This applies to some of the exchanges between the supporters of the union with Europe and the supporters of Brexit.

Leaving the EU is a choice with its chances and consequences, yet on an emotional level it taps into the deepest fears, easily provoking the excitement so present in political discourse. The ongoing bidding: who is going to have it better after Brexit—Commonwealth citizens? Welsh steel workers?—seems to be missing the point, turning a blind eye to the prevailing agenda promoting hostile response towards any kind of vulnerability—be this refugees, economic immigrants, the NHS, a need for adequate police resource, or social housing. David Bell (1996) earlier wrote about some aspects of these processes—the processes that strip the organisations which are designed to care and support human values and a sense of solidarity of those very values. What is forgotten here is the sense of alliance and cooperation, unity, friendly relations, openness, freedoms, mutuality, the Human Rights Act, or the European Court of Justice and the possibility to appeal against unfair in-house rulings. European working directives, protection of the rights of workers, and safety of patients were once criticised as reasons behind the crisis in the NHS.

If you remember the earlier quote by Chomsky, it looks like the US nowadays has to protect itself from immigrants and refugees, as it had to protect itself from native civilisations ever since the arrival of Christopher Columbus.

The effect of this upside-down rhetoric, supported by the previously described processes, is that the real diagnosis is missed and the solutions do not seem to address the problems: the negative consequences of globalisation, and the omnipresence of neoliberal market-driven philosophy entering those aspects of our lives it should not. For example, the use of market incentives to solve a range of social problems (such as a charity paying women dependent on illicit substances to undergo sterilisation), paid access to politicians and medical treatments, even upgrades of living conditions in prisons (Sandel, 2013, 2015). Other crucial factors here are climate change and military conflicts, which are closely linked to the former two.

In effect, there does not appear to be much thinking about how to improve the living conditions of citizens and immigrants, and how to accommodate the global process of migration, which is accelerated by the above factors. Instead, there is a dangerous but psychologically understandable denial and illusion that global migration could be reversed or at least stopped *at the gates*.

Conclusions

In order to manage our perceptions of internal and external realities and their effect on us—the anxieties they evoke—a degree of emotional freedom, expressed as the interplay of different states of mind, different modes of generating experience, is crucial.

We are familiar with the repertoire of defence mechanisms, which play a significant role in keeping the balance right, but at the same time when applied in excess they obliterate awareness and real knowledge. Projective processes were described as a means of keeping split-off parts of the self and internal objects in particular configurations to protect from awareness of vulnerability, sense of dependence, rejection and humiliation, and the associated anxieties, linked in phantasy to the threat of annihilation. This constellation of defences becomes secured by the unconscious allocation of "roles and places" associated with the perception of difference, which often corresponds to social scripts (Davids, 2006, 2011). This kind of outlook can prevail when the needs and rights of the refugees or European workers are considered. These are the scripts allocating a place *inside or outside the wall*.

The loss of the third position (Britton 1989, 2004) leads to concrete solutions before the underlying concerns are even addressed. Triangular psychic space creates the outside/inside divide—when observing the relationship between parents we are outside the parental couple. If this triangularity is experienced as too dangerous to psychic equilibrium, there is a temptation to create exclusive couplings, regressing this way to dyadic relationships with a clear opposing third party located outside. In her elaboration of Freud's concept of the *murdered father*, Rosine Perelberg (2009) shows how the triangular space and the oedipal law get further dismantled, in all their complexity, when the notion of the father is actively wiped out. I tried to illustrate these processes in my analysis of two recent Polish films, *Ida* and *Aftermath*.

The phantasies in the societal sphere refer not only to citizens versus foreigners but also to images of various organisations seen as hostile *blocs* or *negative oppressive containers*, which denude our experience of meaning and emotional freedom. Bion (1967) described a *"crushing, depleting morality, a container that crushes life and liveliness"* (Symington & Symington, 1996, p. 148). This was the way the European Union had been portrayed by the Leave campaign and I think this has been one of the major underlying phantasies present in the social sphere. However, the sense of unquestionable morality seems to be identified with on both sides—Leave and Remain.

Manifestations of these kinds of complex defensive systems against psychotic and depressive anxieties on the organisational level have previously been described by Elliott Jaques (1955) and Isabel Menzies Lyth (1970). The Organisation for Promoting Understanding of Society (Khaleelee & Miller, 1985) took it further and demonstrated a possibility to extrapolate group dynamics onto the societal level and the study of social change. Society as a large and complex group, however, could be thought of as an interacting agglomeration of smaller and more homogenous groups behaving according to Bion's description of basic assumptions functioning. Identity politics, otherwise an inevitable and important aspect of societal dynamics, led however to the experience of parts of society finding themselves in the role of minority (outside) groups (Rustin, 2017). This unavoidably results in a sense of existential threat.

Although one can find enclaves of relative freedom in different kinds of democratic systems, the neoliberal ideology seems to promote pseudo-autonomy, as it is a double whammy—a promise of autonomy if one only strives to profit, leading to consumer dependency both ways in the end. Prosperity, *being better off*, is a promise in return for submission and "trust". Greedy "siblings" from the EU (and previously the Commonwealth) threaten in phantasy to take everything away—jobs, schools, health care, and prosperity. In some parts of Polish society, a phantasy about a "resurrected" twin and his "messianic" mission to revive the "real" Poland and fight its enemies is strongly established. Or in a similar way there are the unspoken sentiments and dreams of recreating entities such as the British Empire or the Soviet Union—rooted in a peculiar misguided form of *nostalgia*. Those phantasies seem to be closely linked with the described annihilation anxieties.

Such a state of affairs seems to lead to the long-term collusions, disavowal and denial, resembling the model of chronic and acute enactments (Cassorla, 2001, 2005), where prolonged collusions can lead to dramatic decisions and actions, if not sufficiently understood. The problem is that the sign is recognised, diagnosis is wrong, and prescribed treatment seems to be further collusion and enactment. One could say that unhappiness about austerity and neoliberal market values seems to be receiving treatment with a higher dose of austerity in the same market milieu with a pinch of isolationism and boast.

Not everything seems to be lost, however, and we are familiar with the cyclical turns and shifts in sociopolitical relationships and in our minds. Reversing a quote from Tennyson, Segal says, "But we have minds of our own. We could say: 'Ours is to reason why, ours is to live and strive.' I still think that silence is the real crime" (Segal, 2006, p. 120).

Thinking therefore about recent political events, there is a sense of unrest, uprising-like spirit in the way the votes were cast, or for example in the formation of the Occupy movement, with its mutual wisdom—people intuitively know what is missing and what is essential. Those rebel aspects are being continuously hijacked by different kinds of politicians but there is at the same time a healthy assertiveness at its heart.

I think that the growing interest in psychoanalysis and psychoanalytic trainings is a recognition of the pitfalls of modern reality, where there is rarely the time and space to feel human and to approach others in a deeply human way with its most intimate subjectivity.

I have been reminded of the more hopeful attitude to diversity and difference, relationships between communities and individuals, and the human and cultural wealth diversity brings to London.

(I should have started this way but instead) I will conclude my chapter with this quote:

> If you assume that there is no hope, you guarantee that there will be no hope. If you assume that there is an instinct for freedom, that there are opportunities to change things, then there is a possibility that you can contribute to making a better world. That's your choice. (Chomsky & Dieterich, 1999a, p. 6)

References

Bauman, Z. (2010). Strangers are dangers … Are they, indeed? In: *44 Letters from the Liquid Modern World* (pp. 157–162). Cambridge: Polity.

Bell, D. (1996). Primitive mind of state. *Psychoanalytic Psychotherapy*, *10*: 45–57.

Bion, W. R. (1957). Differentiation of the psychotic from the non-psychotic personalities. *The International Journal of Psychoanalysis*, *38*: 266–275.

Bion, W. R. (1958). On arrogance. *The International Journal of Psychoanalysis*, *39*: 144–146.

Bion, W. R. (1961). *Experiences in Groups and Other Papers*. London: Tavistock.

Bion, W. R. (1962). *Learning from Experience*. London: Tavistock.

Bion, W. R. (1967). *Second Thoughts: Selected Papers on Psycho-Analysis*. London: Heinemann Medical.

Britton, R. (1989). The missing link: Parental sexuality in the Oedipus complex. In: R. Britton, E. O'Shaughnessy, M. Feldman, & J. Steiner (Eds.), *The Oedipus Complex Today: Clinical Implications* (pp. 83–101). London: Karnac.

Britton, R. (1993). The missing link: parental sexuality in the Oedipus complex. In: Birksted-Breen, D. (Ed.), *The Gender Conundrum: Contemporary Psychoanalytic Perspectives on Femininity and Masculinity* (pp. 83–101). London: Routledge.

Britton, R. (2001). Beyond the depressive position: Ps (n+1). In: C. Bronstein (Ed.), *Kleinian Theory: A Contemporary Perspective* (pp. 63–76). London: Whurr.

Britton, R. (2004). Subjectivity, objectivity, and triangular space. *The Psychoanalytic Quarterly, 73*: 47–61.

Britton, R., O'Shaughnessy, E., Feldman, M., & Steiner, J. (1989). *The Oedipus Complex Today: Clinical Implications.* London: Karnac.

Cassorla, R. M. (2001). Acute enactment as a "resource" in disclosing a collusion between the analytical dyad. *The International Journal of Psychoanalysis, 82*: 1155–1170.

Cassorla, R. M. (2005). From bastion to enactment: The "non-dream" in the theatre of analysis. *The International Journal of Psychoanalysis, 86*: 699–719.

Chomsky, N., & Dieterich, H. (1999a). Introduction. In: *Latin America: From Colonization to Globalization* (pp. 6–8). Melbourne, Australia: Ocean.

Chomsky, N., & Dieterich, H. (1999b). The first invasion of globalization. In: *Latin America: From Colonization to Globalization* (pp. 9–16). Melbourne, Australia: Ocean.

Davids, M. F. (2006). Internal racism, anxiety and the world outside: Islamophobia post-9/11. *Organisational & Social Dynamics, 6*: 63–85.

Davids, M. F. (2011). *Internal Racism: A Psychoanalytic Approach to Race and Difference.* London: Palgrave.

Dostoyevsky, F. (1864). *Notes from Underground.* R. Wilks (Trans.). London: Penguin, 2009.

Fortuna, T. (2014). Tension at the border, emotional freedom and creative process. In: *Art and Freedom: Psychoanalytical Reflection on the Meaning of Creativity* (pp. 24–31). Krakow, Poland: MOCAK.

Freud, S. (1911b). Formulations on the two principles of mental functioning. *S. E., 12.* London: Hogarth.

Freud, S. (1930a). *Civilization and Its Discontents. S. E., 21.* London: Hogarth.

Giles, H. (1973). Accent mobility: a model and some data. *Anthropological Linguistics, 15*(2): 87–105.

Jaques, E. (1955). Social systems as a defence against persecutory and depressive anxiety. In: M. Klein, P. Heimann, & R. Money-Kyrle (Eds.), *New Directions in Psycho-Analysis: The Significance of Infant Conflict in the Pattern of Adult Behaviour.* London: Tavistock.

Khaleelee, O., & Miller, E. (1985). Beyond the small group: society as an intelligible field of study. In: *Bion and Group Psychotherapy* (pp. 354–385). London: Routledge & Kegan Paul.

Klein, M. (1940). Mourning and its relation to manic-depressive states. *The International Journal of Psychoanalysis, 21*: 125–153.

Klein, M. (1946). Notes on some schizoid mechanisms. *The International Journal of Psychoanalysis, 27*: 99–110.

Kublik, A. (2016). Półkowniki Jacka Kurskiego. Niektóre filmy Stuhra, Szumowskiej, Pasikowskiego i Pawlikowskiego zakazane, Gazeta Wyborcza. http://wyborcza.pl/7,75398,20996698,polkownicy-jacka-kurskiego-lista-nazwisk-zakazanych-w-tvp.html (accessed November 18, 2016).

Laplanche, J. (1999). The unfinished Copernican revolution. In: *Essays on Otherness* (pp. 52–83). J. Fletcher (Trans.). London: Routledge.

Menzies Lyth, I. (1960). A case study in the functioning of social systems as a defence against anxiety: a report on a study of the nursing service of a general hospital. *Human Relations, 13*: 95.

Ogden, T. H. (1989). On the concept of an autistic-contiguous position. *The International Journal of Psychoanalysis, 70*: 127–140.

Orwell, G. (1946). *Politics and the English Language*. London: Horizon.

Orwell, G. (1949). *Nineteen Eighty-Four*. London: Secker & Warburg.

O'Shaughnessy, E. (1981). A clinical study of a defensive organization. *The International Journal of Psychoanalysis, 62*: 359–369.

Perelberg, R. J. (2009). Murdered father; dead father: revisiting the Oedipus complex. *The International Journal of Psychoanalysis, 90*: 713–732.

Rosenfeld, H. (1964). On the psychopathology of narcissism: a clinical approach. *The International Journal of Psychoanalysis, 45*: 332–337.

Rosenfeld, H. (1971). A clinical approach to the psychoanalytic theory of the life and death instincts: an investigation into the aggressive aspects of narcissism. *The International Journal of Psychoanalysis, 52*: 169–178.

Rustin, M. (2017). Questions of identity and the British psychoanalytic tradition. *Bulletin of the British Psychoanalytical Society, 53*(3): 10–16.

Sandel, M. (2013). *What Money Can't Buy: The Moral Limits of Markets*. London: Penguin.

Sandel, M. (2015). Are There Things Money Shouldn't Be Able to Buy? Oxford Union lecture, https://youtube.com/watch?v=zMg9Gjz8PKs (accessed November 18, 2016).

Seaton, J., Crook, T., & Taylor, D. J. (2017). Welcome to dystopia—George Orwell experts on Donald Trump. *Guardian*, January 25.

Segal, H. (1952). A psycho-analytical approach to aesthetics. *The International Journal of Psychoanalysis, 33*: 196–207.

Segal, H. (2006). September 11. *Psychoanalytic Psychotherapy*, *20*(2): 115–121.

Seuren, P. A. M. (2015). Unconscious elements in linguistic communication: language and social reality. *Empedocles: European Journal for the Philosophy of Communication*, *6*(2): 185–194.

Smith, Z. (2016). Fences: a Brexit diary. *New York Review of Books*, August 18.

Sophocles (406BC) Oedipus at Colonus. In: *The Three Theban Plays: "Antigone", "Oedipus the King", "Oedipus at Colonus"* (pp. 279–388). R. Fagles (Trans.). London: Penguin, 1982.

Steiner, J. (1982). Perverse relationships between parts of the self: a clinical illustration. *The International Journal of Psychoanalysis*, *63*: 241–251.

Steiner, J. (1987). The interplay between pathological organizations and the paranoid–schizoid and depressive positions. *The International Journal of Psychoanalysis*, *68*(1): 69–80.

Steiner, J. (1990). The retreat from truth to omnipotence in Sophocles' Oedipus at Colonus. *International Review of Psycho-Analysis*, *17*: 227–237.

Steiner, J. (2011). *Seeing and Being Seen: Emerging from a Psychic Retreat* (The New Library of Psychoanalysis), London: Routledge.

Symington, J., & Symington, N. (1996). The phenomenology of psychosis. In: *The Clinical Thinking of Wilfred Bion* (pp. 143–165). London: Brunner-Routledge.

Films

Aftermath (2012). dir. Władysław Pasikowski, Apple Film Productions.
Ida (2013). dir. Paweł Pawlikowski, Opus Film.

CHAPTER NINE

George Orwell: politics and the avoidance of reality

Roger Hartley

Befpre considering Orwell, I want to establish a preliminary critical context by describing some psychoanalytic concepts that are concerned with thinking (and avoiding thinking) about reality. The framework is loosely that of the Kleinian account, where we have two mental or psychological "positions", positions which reflect the significant relations between the ego and its objects. In the paranoid schizoid position (which is taken to be genetically prior) the ego implements defensive measures in order to protect itself against a range of anxieties and conflicts, some of which arise from internal sources, some from external or environmental circumstances. These defensive measures, like splitting the ego and projective identification, provide a solution of sorts, but only at the expense of the integration of the ego. A degree of ego integration is taken to be necessary to recognise reality in the sense of it being something separate from the self.

While the psychology of the paranoid schizoid position is descriptively complex, one of the effects of the defensive measures is to create, in terms of the relation between the ego and its objects, a sense of simplification, a solution, as it were, to the anxieties faced by the ego. The sense of simplification arises because the various elements of the ego's object relations are kept apart from each other (splitting), and appreciated each in turn, as it were, rather than as the various features of the same complex object. Similarly, different values are kept apart from each other, or located in different places of the self, or other people (projective identification). As a result values do not appear to conflict with each other. It follows that this mode of thinking implies a process of disintegration, to the point where the qualities and features of the object, either internal or external, have disappeared.

In the Kleinian account the paranoid–schizoid position is contrasted with the depressive position. In this position the ego establishes more secure and integrated relations with internal and external objects, and as a result external reality is perceived and understood as something separate from the ego and the self. What this means in general terms is that the complexity of the object is recognised, as well as the fact that it has properties which are separate and distinct. We can characterise this mode of thinking as the recognition of complexity, bringing with it a state of mind, beliefs, and thinking which can be described as complex thinking. There is also a recognition of the strains and difficulties involved here, bringing with them a constant temptation to resort defensively to a simplified thinking instead. Most people working in this tradition today would recognise a constant fluctuation in the mind between these positions, rather than some permanent overcoming of the paranoid–schizoid position.

From the point of view of the culture of a group or larger collective, one can see a relation between cultural beliefs and unconscious beliefs/myths, particularly so in the Kleinian system, where the concept of unconscious phantasy can be reconfigured as the psychoanalysis of unconscious beliefs, or a kind of personal mythology. An object relation, even if coloured by unconscious phantasy, carries with it, or produces, or implies, a belief or a disposition. It is possible to think of something dispositional which goes from a primitive "I don't like that, I will spit it out" and "I like that, I will take it in" to "That is bad" and "That is good". So we can get from a primitive experience to a wider cultural value, even if the pathway isn't straightforward. The investment here is not just the particular disposition but also the way in which the beliefs are held, either in simplified, literal, fundamentalist ways, or with a complex recognition.

What would a collective entity or a group operating on these levels look like? What would be its main dispositions? One feature of such a group or larger society at the paranoid–schizoid level would be the awareness of the danger of disintegration, as it is for the individual. Such a group would have to invest the larger part of its energies and resources in maintaining the system of irrational collective beliefs and simplifications which support the paranoid/schizoid unconscious positions. This would mean that other social and economic functions and activities which require rational organisation and beliefs would be neglected, resulting in threats to basic standards of living, the environment, and to the material fabric of society. There would be a conflict between the irrational beliefs and those beliefs, more contextually rational, necessary in order for basic social and economic functions to take place. This difficulty can be observed most typically in authoritarian regimes, especially when internal contradictions become pronounced, so that the justification for blatant inequalities and failures to meet basic material needs become increasing irrational. Propaganda then becomes a central activity sustaining the regime.

It doesn't follow that the type of thinking associated with the depressive position, complex thinking about reality, is characteristic of liberal social democracies, because such societies also require irrational beliefs and simplified thinking to support the dominant social and economic functions, even if there are other mechanisms for the redistribution of wealth, material goods, and social capital which soften the impact of material and social inequalities, and which provide support for a belief in the rational or fair basis of the wider society. Would it be going too far to say that it is difficult to imagine a society without a preponderantly paranoid/schizoid basis? Similarly, if it were the case that key political functions and beliefs—the nature and the exercise of a legitimate sovereign authority for instance—were largely conducted psychologically at the paranoid–schizoid level (because of the particular psychological resonance of authority conflicts), then the difference between political positions to do with sovereign authority or the legitimate monopoly of violence claimed by the state that on the face of it are different would be diminished, as would the rational choice between them. It is a question of the sort of beliefs that support the claims any regime will make about the legitimacy of the social and political order, the relationship between rational beliefs and unconscious states of mind.

By the time in the 1940s when Orwell wrote *Animal Farm* (1945) and *Nineteen Eighty-Four* (1949), some of these political issues were of a central concern to him, but it is by no means obvious how his thinking had developed. Orwell's political development in the 1930s was idiosyncratic. By comparison with other intellectuals on the left he took longer to identify a political position for himself, and when he did so it wasn't in response to quite the same events and circumstances. For many intellectuals the key events of the period were the great crash of 1928 and the subsequent economic depression in the early 1930s. The collapse of capitalism created the focus on radical alternatives of the left and right, and on political events in Germany and the Soviet Union. Yet while this history came to be an essential framework for Orwell's thinking about politics, it happened much later than was typical for the European intelligentsia, so that it was only by 1937/8 that Orwell became fully engaged with the European political perspective, and even then from a rather personal and marginal point of view.

One way of understanding this difference is to look at Orwell's background in the 1920s and 1930s. Orwell spent the period after leaving Eton in 1921 as a member of the Imperial Indian Police in Burma, and this experience was highly unusual, at least in relation to his contemporaries. It was international but not European, and produced a peculiar version and experience of being English, domestic, and foreign at the same time. We have the fictional account in his novel *Burmese Days* (1934), and an autobiographical account in the second part of *The Road to Wigan Pier* (1937). The critique that Orwell made of imperialism and colonialism is the same in both cases. The colonial regime was seen as a mixture of commercial exploitation and the civilising mission. In fact the history of the British relationship with Burma since the nineteenth century had always been more obviously commercial than was the case in most other British possessions, and the civilising mission in Burma, which only appeared as a part of the imperial programme at the end of the nineteenth century, was always superficial. In this colonial situation it was a matter of understanding what was going on on the surface, and not perceiving or coming to understand a "deep" or "complex" political reality. The politics of the colonial surface, the dubious and contested

legality of the colonial presence, was the overt truth of the colonial situation, and the colonial situation was a simplified form of rule. This I think
is the source of one's sense that Orwell came eventually to hold left-wing
views, without the same political formation as other people who held
similar views.

The question of the surface was important for Orwell, because it raised
the difficulty of how he was to place himself in relation to contemporary
reality if he was to get beyond the surface to an alternative, if indeed that
were possible. How he placed or situated himself and what it led to could
then become the basis of what he wrote about subsequently. The version of
Orwell as a journalist—a writer merely in search of copy—is misleading.
In fact the question of action was unusually important for Orwell's project
as a writer. In his 1940 essay *Inside the Whale*, Orwell described the state
of the ordinary person in relation to contemporary events as essentially
passive. Action though was a way of resisting those events, acting on the
world rather than being acted upon, and any assessment of Orwell has to
take his actions into account, as a form of acting on the world, especially
when considering what is sometimes described as his undue pessimism.

However, we can see a connection between the passive person and
the psychology of the paranoid–schizoid position, a connection between
passivity, organised behaviour of a compliant kind, and simplification.

In the second part of *Wigan Pier*, Orwell relates the process by which
he left the Burmese police force in 1927 and went down and out. He
describes this as a moral matter, but in a very stark, binary way. He says
that he had to get out and away from the world of the oppressors, and
this led him towards the social worlds he describes in *Down and Out in
Paris and London* (1933). But you could ask why there wasn't a different
analysis and a different positioning, and why everywhere between top
and bottom was excluded. One explanation of this is to think of Orwell
as operating primarily from within a paranoid–schizoid view of reality,
a stark and simplified version of the world, but searching for a more
comprehensive alternative nevertheless. For Orwell, as for the French
philosopher and theologian Simone Weil, with whom he has much in
common, the purpose of action was to demonstrate and experience a
solidarity with the oppressed and the exploited of the world, an authen-
ticating self exposure which, by virtue of a free and significant act, indicated a point outside the world of oppression.

Orwell's moment of political clarification came in 1937 during the Spanish Civil War. As Bernard Crick (1980) has described, Orwell went to Spain to fight Fascism even if he had journalistic and literary objectives as well. He was accredited by the Independent Labour Party, Marxist in orientation, and joined the POUM, also an independent Marxist party, though described by the communists as Trotskyite. What he encountered in Spain was the egalitarian culture of the POUM militia, especially on the Aragon front, which had a great effect on him, and led him to say in a letter to Cyril Connolly that he finally believed in socialism. But there was also the persecution of the POUM (and himself) by the government in Barcelona, under communist sponsorship, an entirely different kind of politics which involved the suppression of political freedoms, the misrepresentation of events that amounted to invention, and a resort to violence and illegality with the aim of destroying the supposedly Trotskyite POUM. It was a stark binary politics, to meet the requirements of the internal politics of the soviet regime and its associated foreign policy, a world away from the constitutional legality of politics in Britain in the 1930s, especially in the period of the Conservative dominated national government.

The simplified binary politics which Orwell described and exposed in *Animal Farm* and *Nineteen Eighty-Four* has its origins here, a political method developed by a new political or managerial elite (described by James Burnham in *The Managerial Revolution* 1941), a new class, interested in power and in the domination or the destruction of civil society. What this required for the general politics, as displayed in the Soviet Union, was a narrow view of political reality, maintained by the threat to the supposed common interest from heretical or traitorous leaders and their followers. Snowball in *Animal Farm* and Goldstein in *Nineteen Eighty-Four* are the type of the heretical opposition leader, whose names are routinely invoked by the regime to create an atmosphere of fear and a climate of crisis, and to suppress legitimate doubts and discontents about the regime.

This conception of politics is crucial if we are to see how the rational pursuit of binary politics by a political elite has a calculated effect on the mentality of the political public, and their capacity to think about political realities. The regime produces a view or version of political reality which must be mindlessly accepted rather than thought about. The result is a total absence of thought, but supported by a highly charged emotional and psychological content manipulated by the regime according to current political requirements. This is the world of the Outer Party in *Nineteen Eighty-Four*, the functionaries of the regime, who share an emotional world which corresponds to a paranoid–schizoid schema to a remarkable degree, not just in its emotionality, but in the extent to which it allows group manipulation because of the dispersed ego structure. Freud said something similar in *Group Psychology and the Analysis of the Ego* (1921c), a psychology which he thought was based on social or political identifications which diminished the independence of a coherent integrated ego.

In *Nineteen Eighty-Four* the novel culminates in Room 101, the place where O'Brien, the Inner Party member, will torture and re-educate Winston Smith, a member of the Outer Party. O'Brien has beguiled and misled Winston into the belief that he (O'Brien) is secretly a follower of the heretic Goldstein, and has access to Goldstein's theories. But this is merely the prelude to Winston's arrest by the Thought Police, when he is taken to Room 101 in the Ministry of Love. There O'Brien begins the assault on Winston's rationality and emotional attachments. The Party determines that $2+2 = 5$ if the Party says it does—referring to both Stalin and Swift. O'Brien destroys Winston's moral integrity and capacity to resist by exposing his fear of physical torture, and his capacity for betrayal. Winston is psychologically broken by O'Brien—weeping tears of gratitude, he has won the victory over himself, and loves Big Brother. Slogans have replaced thought. Orwell shows how the binary politics of *Nineteen Eighty-Four* involves a simplification and narrowing of thought, as does the regime's language, Newspeak. Equally essential to the manipulative purposes of the Inner Party is the labile emotional and psychological environment, the fear-ridden mental world of the Outer Party, whose political mobilisation depends upon a lack of integration at a personal level.

This leaves a central question. If *Animal Farm* and *Nineteen Eighty-Four* are Orwell's satires of a binary politics, what kind of politics lay outside a binary politics, on which a progressive politics, a politics of hope could be based? In an important sense, Orwell never produced a satisfactory answer to this question.

His experiences in the Spanish Civil war in the POUM militia provided a transformative experience of equality and solidarity, the background of his later socialist commitments. In *The Lion and the Unicorn*

(1941), he outlined the possibility of an imminent revolution to be carried out by the English people, whose consciousness of the need for radical change had been raised by the conduct of the war. His vision was of an English society as a historically based social organism. It was, he said, a family with the wrong members in control. If the controlling members were removed there was the basis for a new type of socialist society, as long as the binary manipulative politics of a newly emergent political elite could be avoided. It was binary Leninist politics that was the danger, with its emphasis on the destruction of civil society, the most significant obstacle to implementing the rule of the new elite. It was this civil society he described in *The Lion and the Unicorn*, and later *The English People* (1947), and perhaps we can think of the recognition of civil society as forming the basis of a politics which requires complex thinking, susceptible to the values of the depressive position.

The difficulty in assessing Orwell's thinking on a hopeful politics is that his later and most famous work suggests a darkening of his mood and a growing pessimism, and this cannot be discounted. To say that *Nineteen Eighty-Four* and Big Brother present a paranoid–schizoid world is an uncontentious claim, but it also appears that Orwell is unbalanced about it, that there is no perspective in the novel on other possibilities, that it is too simplified—in other words, the novel has too much in common with what it depicts. The satirical reduction doesn't always succeed. *Animal Farm* by contrast, although it is simple, is not simplified, the satire is handled adequately, and as a result the fable is more balanced and hopeful, though hardly optimistic.

In this context we must consider how Orwell thought about the relationship between politics, language, and literary style. He developed a simple style, non-literary, as he suggested prose like a window pane, the antithesis of the florid manipulations of literary language. The political writer had an important role to play in polemic, but this raised the question of style and the mode of writing. The literary uses of language could drift away from the political subject and from a political point of view. Of course, the alternative, the simple direct style, could look simplistic, or thoughtless, or even like propaganda, unless it was invested with a sense of the moral authority of the author. Orwell acquired that authority from how he lived and where he went, vital non-literary supports to his writing.

There was the question, perhaps the question of Orwell's time, as to whether politics was so central to contemporary reality that the avoidance of politics represented an intellectual and moral abdication. The difficulty was that a liberal mode of literature, only occasionally political, could be construed as such an abdication of responsibility. However, a committed literature appeared to have abandoned the freedoms, the critical distance, and the complexity associated with a liberal literature, or perhaps abandoned literature altogether. Orwell's writing of the 1930s reflects and explores this problem of a marginal literature with a blend of journalism, documentary, and satirical naturalism in his fiction.

Orwell wanted to achieve a way of writing about politics in a polemical way, and so with a direct reference to reality, but which was also literary, an art as he put it, with the examples of Swift and Dickens as his models. It was a tension, perhaps between immediacy and distance, that he never wholly succeeded in reconciling or overcoming, apart from in the fable of *Animal Farm*.

I want to conclude by returning to some of the psychoanalytic assumptions I started off with, and the possibility, to put it generally, of a politics which doesn't depend on simplified thinking—in Kleinian terms, the possibility of a politics of the depressive position, in which psychological reality as such is recognised. Most importantly, complexity will involve a recognition of the imperfections of actual reality, a capacity to learn, and a tolerant attitude when political ideals aren't realised. These requirements are more of an attitude than a political programme, but are at least viable within a liberal social democracy, even if such a polity can also display the characteristics of *Nineteen Eighty-Four* and authoritarian regimes. What is noticeable about the politics of *Nineteen Eighty-Four* is the constant idealisation of the regime, a continuing description of reality completely at odds with the facts, and the unavoidable controlling supervision of the regime. Thought, reflection, and the recognition of psychological reality are replaced by slogans and mindless propaganda.

So from within a Kleinian account it is possible to distinguish two different kinds of politics, which can be identified by their observable features and characteristics, to do either with the recognition of the constraints of reality, the facts, or with a politics of manipulation with the objective of dissolving the constraints of reality. At best there will be an uneasy coexistence, at worst something like the wholly paranoid–schizoid world of Big Brother. Thus a psychoanalytically informed understanding of politics along these lines can be made which addresses the problem of describing the unconscious factors that can subvert any political programmes that set out to conserve, reform, or radically change the given social and political circumstances.

References

Burnham, J. (1941). *The Managerial Revolution: What is Happening in the World*. New York: John Day.

Crick, B. (1980). *George Orwell: A Life*. London: Secker & Warburg [reprinted Toronto: Sutherland House, 2019].

Freud, S. (1921c). *Group Psychology and the Analysis of the Ego. S.E., 18*: 65–144. London: Hogarth.

Orwell, G. (1933). *Down and Out in Paris and London*. London: Gollancz.

Orwell, G. (1934). *Burmese Days*. London: Gollancz, 1935.

Orwell, G. (1937). *The Road to Wigan Pier*. London: Gollancz.

Orwell, G. (1938). *Homage to Catalonia*. London: Secker & Warburg.

Orwell, G. (1940). *Inside the Whale*. London: Gollancz.

Orwell, G. (1941). *The Lion and the Unicorn*. London: Secker & Warburg.

Orwell, G. (1945). *Animal Farm*. London: Secker & Warburg.

Orwell, G. (1947). *The English People*. London: Collins.

Orwell, G. (1949). *Nineteen Eighty-Four*. London: Secker & Warburg.

Orwell, G. (2002). *Essays*. J. Carey (Ed.). London: Everyman.

CHAPTER TEN

In the union: the psychodynamics of solidarity

Elizabeth Cotton

> *... Let me re-state the key issue again. Work-related stress is a hazard created by employers ... [this union] does not support the idea that individual members of staff can or should be given the "resilience" to deal with poor working conditions created by the employer.*
> —*Correspondence between senior members of a UK Health & Safety trade union network, 2014*

Despite the global trend of trade union decline, trade unions have shown remarkable durability in a context of neoliberal economic policies and economic crises. Many trade unions, particularly in developing countries, have shown immense resourcefulness in organising and mobilising workers (Cotton, 2013), including the growing number of precarious workers (Standing, 2011) who have historically been under-represented by organised labour.

The traditional "counter-power" argument for trade union organisation is that it provides an organised challenge to the internationalisation of capital. As early as the 1920s, Edo Fimmen, in his seminal book *Labour's Alternative*, argued that both national and international trade union structures are a necessary response by labour to the internationalisation of capital and growth of European companies and monopolies. Fimmen predicted the development of "concerns" and "combines"—cartels that consolidate capital in order to reduce risk and eliminate competition, and the "mingling" of interests between entrepreneurs from different countries bringing with it a potential for a "world-wide monopoly" (Fimmen, 1924, p. 58). This political analysis of the growth of MNCs, concentration of capital, increased insecurity of investment, and decline in state regulation, predicted themes now mainstream within popular globalisation (Stiglitz, 2012) and inequalities literature (Wilkinson & Pickett, 2011) with a growing body of research linking social and health inequalities (Marmot, 2020).

For several decades, there has been a general decline in traditionally strong trade union memberships across Europe, with the number of UK shop stewards falling by two thirds between 1984 and 2004 (Charlwood & Forth, 2009) and with a "de facto enterprise unionism" prevailing in the private sector (Gumbrell-McCormick & Hyman, 2013).

Since 2008 we have seen a decline in national level collective bargaining, particularly in Western Europe and a return to "concession bargaining" and bipartite agreements as a way of maintaining job security (ibid.). Additionally there have been large-scale cuts in public sector jobs, and renewed privatisation, and a dramatic growth in unemployment and temporary contracts in Europe and North America. This has contributed to a decline in public sector union membership, the stronghold of trade unionism globally, and has put a downward pressure on union power in relation to wages and job security (ibid.).

Since the 1990s, liberal and coordinated market economies have experienced large-scale reorientation towards global markets and flexible work structures (Dicken, 2016). This has led to a deregulation of workplace protections, downsizing, and outsourcing—often involving the relocation of jobs to low wage and "non-union regions" (Peters, 2011, p. 88). In developing countries working conditions are heavily influenced by the growth of multinational corporations and their extensive use of global supply chains (Dicken, 2016; Doogan, 2009).

The emergence of the gig economy as a framework to understand the tide of precarity driven internationally through financialisation and technology is now commonplace in our everyday discussions about work; as are online platforms facilitating both virtual exchange of assets popularised through platforms such as Airbnb, and the use of virtual employment—such as Deliveroo and Uber. One of the characteristics of online platforms is that corporations attempt to evade employers' costs and duties by relying on insecure contracts such as zero hours contracts, and virtual management through technologies to establish the fiction of self-employment and the independent worker. This "Uberisation" (Cotton, 2019b) exists across all sectors, even in the mental health and therapy sector (Cotton, 2019a), accelerated during the 2020 coronavirus crisis.

The rise of these virtual employers is not a new story of technological innovation, it is an older one about the spread of precarious work. It is the ideological mantra of neoliberalism to reduce restrictions on trade with the promotion of flexible labour and loss of labour protections a key part of this. The global increase in contract and agency labour—with the thousands of different contracts of employment used globally—has created both an acceptance of precarious work, often facilitated through online technologies and platforms, and an organised corporate resistance to improving working conditions.

What is new is that the battle line for precarious work has shifted to the use and abuse of self-employment where this category of workers earns on average half the wage of directly employed staff, allowing certain evasions such as minimum wage legislation, sick pay, and pensions. A large percentage of these precarious workers work for private employment agencies—a 224bn euro industry dominated by ten multinational companies. Despite campaigns against the abuse of "disguised employment" seen globally, the use of externalised labour continues to expand into new sectors—education and health top of the list—and into geographical regions such as Eastern Europe (Cotton, 2015).

One of the consequences of this precarity is that levels of discrimination creep back into the workplace. Bluntly, most precarious workers are young, black, migrants, old, or women. In the UK, the Equalities and Human Rights Commission published a shameful report in 2016 on discrimination at work. It included the data that BAME workers are twice as likely to be precarious as white workers. Part of the reason for this might be that a higher percentage of BAME workers are underemployed—either involuntarily working part-time or just not able to make up the hours. Many are highly skilled—in fact precarious groups like women or BAME workers have a long history of being overqualified for downgraded jobs because of the belief that they have to work ten times as hard as their white male counterparts in order to survive. The UK has gone backwards in terms of social mobility, and social class matters more now than it did thirty years ago (H M Government, State of the Nation Report, 2014). If you are born into a rich family with a father in a senior position you are twenty times more likely to have a senior job.

Precarious work has up until this point made people compliant for fear of losing work. It is this insecurity that silences the millions of people working under these conditions and one explanation why the public debates about the future of work (RSA, Good Work, 2017) are often at best ill-informed and at worst a fiction. But it is possible that we are nearing a tipping point, where such large numbers of people are living under precarious conditions from which they see no way out other than to self-organise. Whatever the fictions about the sharing and gig economies, you cannot actually spin yourself out of in-work poverty. So that leaves us with a genuine problem, how will our society respond to the inevitable social consequences of inequality and the downgrading of working life?

With this externalisation of work comes an externalisation of the employment relationship (Theron, 2005) away from a binary employer/ employee relationship to include third parties, notably contractors, suppliers, and private employment agencies. With this shift in the nature of the employment relationship come other externalisations: projections of risk and duties away from the principal employer and a decline in state regulation including the right to join a union and engage in collective bargaining (Croucher & Cotton, 2011).

Over the last twenty years the majority of large companies have made extensive use of outside finance—debt and equity—for funding, which has led to short-term investment strategies and management practices designed to deliver faster and higher returns on investment. The 2008 economic crisis, which was felt acutely by alternative investment funds (AIFs) leading to sharp losses, raised concerns about the risk of bankruptcy in a wider range of non-financial companies in the future and subsequent job losses (Applebaum, Batt, & Lee, 2014).

These changes in the nature of the employment relationship have led to the introduction of management techniques aimed to introduce flexible working and lean production methods (Peters, 2011). Often these techniques are linked to work intensification and production processes which increase managerial control. Research on the service sector and health care, for example, reveals widespread use of "command and control" systems of management, linked to work intensification, funding cuts, and the use of targets (Carter et al., 2013; Cotton, Kline, & Morton, 2013).

This precarity is not just about the way work is organised but impacts our experience of work and our states of mind. In the context of a global recession and the growth of insecure work, there is an evidenced increase in mental health problems associated with work. The emerging crisis in mental health relates also to austerity policies and the winding down of welfare provision. Even in the traditionally advanced welfare capitalist countries of continental Europe welfare provisions are being dismantled. Funding for public health systems are in decline with mental health services disproportionately affected.

The quote above comes from correspondence between senior trade union HSE officials in the UK, in relation to the growing body of mental health work that has emerged over the last decade in response to the distress experienced by working people. Trade union attitudes towards mental health are diverse and expose a tension within trade unions, both ideological and practical. On an ideological level there has been a widespread rejection of resilience and positive psychology models of well-being at work viewed as an attempt to ignore employers' responsibilities to provide decent conditions of work (Cotton, 2017). On a practical level, trade unions with increasingly limited resources are often constrained in the support they offer memberships whose needs are increasingly outside the bread and butter functions of collective bargaining and policing employment rights.

One question that preoccupies unions is how to maintain sufficiently strong levels of solidaristic ties between increasingly diverse and insecure groups of workers. That is not to say that all precarious workers do not organise—many do, and all over the world, sometimes organised through established trade unions, other times despite them. From the Colombian contract miners (Cotton & Royle, 2014) to the Deliveroo workers organised through the International General Workers Union—push people far enough and they will organise as the motivation to join a union that provides genuine protection is getting stronger.

In addition to changes in employment relations, the question of solidarity in action relates also to societal changes—the decline in cohesive working-class groups and shrinking social-democratic political power (Kjellberg, 2011). Solidarity understood as an identification between homogenous groups of working people is increasingly not responsive to the diversity of working people's lives and political positions (Cotton, 2017). The issue that unions are constantly needing to address is how to build relationships between increasingly insecure and precarious working people sufficient to mobilise collective action.

This chapter explores the psychodynamics of creating and maintaining solidaristic ties between groups of workers in a context of economic crisis and proposes a move away from an ideological model towards a relational model of solidarity. It proposes a re-emphasis on social justice to underpin collective action and the emancipatory practices of trade union education as an important resource for putting solidarity into action.

Solidarity in practice

Solidarity is a central organising principle for trade union activity, referring both to the principle of common action with others and to the identification of one's own interests with theirs (Hyman, 1997). Although some conceptions of solidarity presuppose a shared collective identity— such as class—increasingly the diversity of workforces and trends in labour migration cannot assume a homogeneity of identity.

Although the working class has grown on a world scale (Martinez Lucio, 2010), trade unions have always had to aggregate and prioritise a huge diversity of interests that exist within their memberships. Trade union legitimacy, usefully framed by Hyman (1997), rests on their ability to represent and defend four categories of interests; the "bread and butter" issues of wages and conditions; workplace rights/security/career opportunities; issues of political economy such as welfare and social wages; and finally community and environmental issues looking more broadly at society and social justice.

Solidarity can be conceived in three senses: first, as a normative or moral principle that creates an obligation to support other workers and groups; second, as enlightened self-interest motivated by the belief that an injury to one is an injury to all representing only a weak moral imperative. This has been described as "solidarity as a mobilising myth" (Gumbrell-McCormick & Hyman, 2015)—a classic rationale for motivating collective action often in highly complex and international industrial settings.

At national and international levels trade unions often move between these two different modalities although there is an increased emphasis on mutual and concrete benefits from solidarity within this period of economic globalisation and political conflict (Stirling, 2007).

A third idea of solidarity, taken from the work of Richard Hyman, is a model of "mutuality despite difference" (Gumbrell-McCormick & Hyman, 2015, p. 2). This formulation emphasises the fundamental need for solidarity in practice precisely because of the lack of cohesion between working people. It is a model that accepts as fundamental the difference and conflict between individuals and groups and an acknowledgement of the tendency for groups to exclude and retreat into black and white thinking and action.

It is important not to underestimate that what are often presented as general interests of working people have traditionally been shaped by the particular interests of "relatively advantaged sections" (Hyman, 1997, p. 517) of trade union membership. This is particularly the case with the industrial sector memberships as compared with precarious members who tend to be more attuned to broader social justice and political economy issues such as welfare reform and living wages.

The notion of solidarity appealed to by unions is influenced by their institutional setting and organisational cultures—from the highly politicised trade unions of Latin America to the functionalist models of the former Soviet Union. As a result, national and international levels of trade unions often move between ideological and more pragmatic and concrete formulations of why solidarity matters in order to mobilise members.

A solidaristic model of cooperation has historically been underpinned by class identification and a focus on collective interests. For members of trade unions, this involves the commitment to support other members in response to conflicts with employers, a concrete task as well as a political one, but as the economic and political crisis deepens there is often a pressure to deliver concrete outputs. From climate change to the living wage, we want to see solidarity in action.

Solidarity

Hyman (1997) usefully divides classes of workers into four main groups; elite, core, periphery, and excluded. These groups are constructed differently in different national contexts but trade union membership patterns can be understood using these four categories, where elite and core workers tend to dominate and there is still a relatively low level of activity relating to periphery workers. Periphery workers include relatively visible categories such as temporary agency workers and self-employed workers. Excluded workers include the large majority of informal workers in developing countries who remain outside labour and trade union protections.

There is an inherent tension between the two faces (Gumbrell-McCormick & Hyman, 2013) of trade unionism, the "sword of justice" where unions defend the oppressed and underprivileged and a model of vested interests where the focus is on defending particular interests of a smaller group of predominantly elite workers.

This tension may explain the relative lack of attention paid by trade unions to precarious work until the early 2000s (Standing, 2011). Trade unions have had to place a growing strategic importance on developing field-enlarging strategies (Cotton & Royle, 2015) for organising precarious or atypical workers, often through education programmes looking at organising strategies and broad social justice campaigning, exemplified by the USA Justice for Janitors and the UK's Organising Academy (Simms, Holgate, & Heery, 2013). This organising work often focuses on the "zone of higher unionisation" (Hyman, 1997) where workers are between the core and the periphery, such as temporary agency workers (Cotton, 2015), who are relatively easy to organise in comparison to more precarious workers such as homeworkers or self-employed workers.

Furthermore, as social movements and activist networks expand in response to the economic and social crises in many countries, solidarity action requires working with an expanded range of social actors. Social movements and spontaneous worker organisations are increasingly important vehicles for social change. This engagement with social justice and civic movements is crucial to build a sufficient base for unions to mobilise around immediate political issues.

The fundamental questions for trade unions rest on how they can mobilise workers in defence of collective interests and values. Kelly (1998) categorises the necessary elements of mobilisation into: a conception of common interest; some form of collective organisation; and a perception of opportunities for successful outcomes. The biggest challenge to trade unions is to build engagement with members and more broadly across social movements to create a sufficiently powerful conception of common interest to motivate collective action.

Trade union organisations

Although the dominant narrative about trade unions within liberal and coordinated market economies is that they are outdated and defunct organisations, the current economic conditions have increased rather than decreased a demand for the work of trade unions (Gumbrell-McCormick & Hyman, 2015) both at the level of providing individual support to workers and coordinating international negotiations and actions against international capital (Croucher & Cotton, 2011). It is also worth noting that aside from religious groups, trade unions continue to be the largest membership organisations across the world.

Solidarity is often understood within unions as solidarity against a political or economic actor. For unions in hostile environments a common defensive position is to locate and project all problems in external actors, as a way of creating a cohesive group identification. Although this is, at times, an important driver of solidarity action such cultures can have the consequence of arresting the development of social and political capital at membership level. Censorship of dialogue and denial of the diversity of opinions and conflict inherent within large groups (Main, 1975) is a "strategy of survival rather than development" (Armstrong, 2005, p. 89) leaving members without the authentic relationships and political framework that they need.

The psychology of activists and people working in unions also shapes union organisational cultures. In most parts of the world trade union activists are unpaid and voluntary—many risking their jobs and sanctions because of their union activity. The motivations for political activity are varied—sometimes ideological or ethical, and always deeply personal. Many are motivated by a profound sense of fairness and a need to find an alternative social and political space. Others are more motivated by a vocational commitment to supporting others—and experience the dilemmas and pressures of responding to an increasingly unmanageable tide of individual cases and conflict at work. Activists are vulnerable to overwork and burnout—often deflated by their limited capacity to respond to the workplace issues their membership are facing. The limitations of what can be done to help members comes into direct conflict with the internal pressures activists are prone to put themselves under to make super-heroic efforts to address systemic workplace problems (Money-Kyrle, 1951).

Acts of solidarity carried out against an employer, for example, can powerfully build what Turquet (1975) calls "oneness", observable in groups of workers engaged in workplace organising. This can be understood as something like the Greek idea of *storge*. In this sense activism is prone to paranoia, where "fear simplifies the emotional situation" (Winnicott, 1950) creating the potential for a gang-like state (Canham, 2002) positioned against the capitalist class.

For trade unions there is a strong potential for becoming ideologically defended, a defence of "being in the union" that denies difference and relies on a group mentality that maintains a sense of belonging despite the fragmentation of working groups. Taking this broad political perspective presents trade unions with the problem of how to reconnect members to a sense of belonging (Gallin, 2014) to an internationalist and solidaristic perspective.

This defence, combined with the demands activists make on themselves and each other, exposes trade unions to the risk of fundamentalism (Britton, 2015). This can be experienced as a traumatic splitting into rights and wrongs, them and us. In the words of Ron Britton "It's not what we believe but how we believe that determines whether destructiveness is the outcome." That is, when beliefs become facts we lose our necessary position of "moderate scepticism", which allows us to function on the basis of probability rather than falling into absolute certainty or absolute doubt.

In large-group settings such as union congresses, there are risks of reinforcing basic assumption experiences (Bion, 1961), such as "oneness" (Turquet, 1975) or pairing in the attempt to create cohesion. Projective processes where aspects of the union are split off and projected into external actors (Main, 1975) and a "generalised" black and white think-ing dominate union activities. This way of functioning tends to highlight intra-group conflict (Money-Kyrle, 1951) while underplaying inter-group conflict.

Although less likely, small groups as well as large groups can be vul-nerable to strong identification with the union, which can lead to gang states of mind (Canham, 2002) where the diversity of memberships and individual difference are denied (Hoggett, 1992; Winnicott, 1950). This "oneness" can even be reinforced by organisers where the tendency for "like" to attract "like" (Clawson, 2005, p. 40) can dominate and replicate patterns of exclusion.

In a situation of organisational overwhelm (Perini, 2010) there is often a reluctance to engage realistically with the problems that unions face or to address the individual psychological development of mem-bers, in an attempt to avoid catastrophic change (Sedgwick, 1982) and reflecting the immense challenges that unions and activists face on a daily basis. This intolerance of ambiguity and difference is reflected in the widespread undervaluing of the daily work of organising and educa-tion within trade unions.

Trade union organising

A key function of trade unions in most parts of the world is to support members to build their individual and collective capacities in the face of employers, particularly in response to sectoral, technological, or political changes such as introducing collective bargaining into the newly inde-pendent trade unions of the former Soviet Union (Khaliy, 2005; Sogge, 2004). One of the principal ways that they do this is through educational programmes using active learning methodologies, well established in most parts of the world.

There are two main roots to the methods used in trade union educa-tion programmes. The first is trade union education in Western Europe developed out of the Swedish Working Men's Institutes of the 1880s and the German workers education system (Eiger, 1994). The principal aim of both traditions was to build workers' participation and build their confidence to deal with workplace issues. The Swedish model of study circles is less formalised than the German system and more grassroots focused with a limited role for tutors and a focus on small-group work and participant selection of areas of study.

The second root of trade union education comes from the Brazilian pedagogue, Paulo Freire who developed his methods throughout the 1970s and until his death in 1997, and his model of emancipatory education (Freire, 1970), sometimes called active learning methods (ALMs) or participatory education. Emancipatory education builds solidaristic relationships and collectivisation by using dialogic methods, consciousness raising, and collective problem-solving activities. It is a dialogic model of education, emphasising small-group dynamics and collective tasks (Klandermans, 1986). It is underpinned by a number of principles, including confidentiality and solidarity, and activities aim to provide a safe and containing (Bion, 1952) space for expressing and processing experience and a vital source of support in the workplace.

Additionally, education programmes provide important opportunities to widen the pool of collective experience and to learn from diverse strategies and union responses to globalisation. This is a key resource for trade unions in developing strategies for renewal on the basis of gains made by other unions. These methods are highly effective at building social capital, understood as the resources built up through relationships to provide mutual aid and development.

Over the last five decades these methods have been adopted by unions in most parts of the world, principally through the work of international trade union structures such as the Global Union Federations and the International Labour Organization (ILO) (Croucher & Cotton, 2011; Croucher, 2004). Millions of euros are raised and spent annually to disseminate these education methods to national and local trade union structures in developing and transition economies in a conscious attempt to build trade union capacity and international solidaristic networks. These methods require only limited resources and can have high returns for unions with only small financial resources in capacity building of local organisations.

Trade union education is work that creates spaces or "cognitive frames" (Culpepper, 2002, p. 778) where new ideas, politics, and action can be determined by activists and trade unionists within a protective framework. The psychosocial (Sedgwick, 1982) basis of Freire's model regards union building as essentially a project of emancipation.

Emancipation is understood as a dual task of addressing the external reality of oppression, as well as internal psychic oppression, where individual psychological empowerment, or building ego strength, is central to the political project of organising.

This is not a process of building "organic solidarity" (Hyman, 1997, p. 529), rather it is precisely this educational model's capacity to contain differences and conflict that gives it relevance to the task of building collective organisation in the current political and social climate. Emancipatory education requires working with groups and individuals, managing the politics of difference while maintaining the cross-sectional demands (Sedgwick, 1982) of diverse memberships and organisations.

Relational models of solidarity

Although unions rely on organising to survive, education work is consistently undervalued by union leaderships and decision-making structures, reflected in the lack of funding and decision-making power that trade union education structures have (Croucher & Cotton, 2011).

One of the reasons for this relates to the inherent difficulties in carrying out educational work. Trade union education is not a straightforward process because it involves managing the diversity of individual, organisational, and political perspectives that exist within the workplace (Hoggett, 1992) while being critical of them. Adult education by its nature can raise difficult emotions for participants in the process of identifying problems, looking realistically and critically at our working lives, and engaging in collective action. The process inevitably involves acknowledging our dependency on others and being able to challenge often strongly held ideological views and positions about society and our place in it. As a result, the tens of thousands of experienced educators who carry out trade union education programmes are often regarded as ancillary to their organisations, a status reflected in their temporary contracts and lack of power within union decision-making structures (Croucher & Cotton, 2011).

This is despite the important contribution that an emancipatory model of education makes to building solidaristic relationships. This model allows a deeper and broader exchange between trade union organisations and individual activists and can be understood as a "relational process" (Roseneil & Ketokivi, 2016): one which allows us to build relationships with others in a way that acknowledges our separateness and differences while at the same time accepting our ultimate dependency on each other.

Relationality, from a psychoanalytic perspective, is premised on our developmental reliance on our relationships for survival and the shaping of our identities. Within a psychoanalytic model our subjectivity is fundamentally shaped by others throughout our lives. Within the British Kleinian tradition, infant development hinges on processes of introjection and identification with the people around us (Klein, 1948; Winnicott, 1958). It is through this exchange that our identities are formed and our capacities to form relationships fundamentally shaped (Bowlby, 1969).

This process of relationality, and the difficulties involved in accepting our dependency on our inherently insecure relationships (Morgan & Ruszczynski, 2007), is accepted within psychoanalysis as a difficult and fundamental fact of life (Money-Kyrle, 1951). It is this important human experience of the dynamic nature of relationships and groups (Long, 2002) that emancipatory education is, in part, designed to address.

Emancipatory education is a powerful tool in "political subject-making" (Lazar, 2013, p. 114) where our political identifications are formed through a process of identification and taking in of the experiences and views of the people around us. Working in small groups both exposes differences and lack of "oneness" in groups while at the same time makes it possible to build strong emotional ties sufficient to build a sense of altruism (Freud, 1930a) and reinforce an understanding of the importance of collectivism. The advantage of working in small groups using educational activities is that the setting offers a containing (Douglas, 2007) space which is helpful in building ties where solidarity is un-self-conscious (Olmsted, 1959). This developmental process uses identification as the "glue" holding groups together (Long, 2002)—emphasising relational rather than ideological connectedness.

Trade union education's attention to developing realistic plans in the final stage of activity is helpful in overcoming fragmentation and an absence in group working. It places the responsibility for future action firmly in the hands of the participants and in so doing reinforces their sense of agency (Pogue White, 2006) and builds confidence in the direct benefits of collective action (Flavin, Pacek, & Radcliff, 2009). This can be understood psychoanalytically as a process where members develop an identification with the task, however it is defined (Long, 2002).

This is in part because small groups provide an important holding environment (Praglin, 2006) where people can potentially feel secure enough to speak honestly and with authenticity allowing meaningful relationships to be formed. As a result, being in small groups allows a sense of identification and belonging (Bion, 1961; Turquet, 1975) where people can generalise about their connectedness, but at the same time offer individuals a specific and unique role in the group. This sense of belonging could be understood as a workplace equivalent of secure attachment, a necessary basis for solidarity.

For the leadership of some trade unions this relational model of solidarity is not believed to be the legitimate work of trade unions. One of the consequences of trade unions denying emancipatory education's dynamic model of development is that education becomes marginalised, understood as a support service rather than the principal tool for building structures that can deliver solidarity in practice.

Future solidarities

This relational model of unionism emphasises the capacity for mobilisation, defined as a way of turning association (numbers of people forming a collectivity) into organisation (capacity for collective action in opposition to capital and the state) (Sullivan, 2010).

It is a relational model of organising in which trade unions create spaces where working people can understand societal and industrial changes taking place, and build dialogue and strong solidaristic relationships in situations of industrial conflict that can mobilise members. This is consistent with union traditions that emphasise "social-capital formation and mutual-aid functions" (Jarley, 2005, p. 1) in order to build union organisation.

This is a much broader understanding of unionism than the Webbs' idea of unions improving employment conditions for wage earners (Webb & Webb, 1913). This orientation regards unions' organisational legitimacy as based on their capacity to serve human welfare rather than narrow interests such as wage claims or collective bargaining. This is important not just in developing social capital in changing societal and workplace settings, it also provides unions, which are often working in isolation, with field enlarging strategies (Cotton & Royle, 2014).

Increasingly, labour movements are integrated into broader social movements and work with a wide range of civic and single-issue groups. The majority of these in developing countries operate informally, with trade unions considered exceptional in their levels of organisation and financing as well as their capacity to disrupt economic and political activity. For many unions, their solidaristic networks are dense and their leaderships are capable of adopting the role of visionaries (Sullivan, 2010) within often unfocused collective organisations that come out of specific protests and disputes, including the yet to be determined fallout of the coronavirus crisis.

These societal changes mean widening the organising model from a simple one of recruiting union members as the sole basis for union revitalisation (Sullivan, 2010) towards an expanded model of building relationships with existing and often spontaneous groups of working people.

In order for this model to work it has to transform "individual dissatisfaction into collective grievance" (Gumbrell-McCormick & Hyman, 2013, p. 177): unions have to create a collective sense of injustice, including a sense of who is responsible for it and sufficient organisation to shape collective demands and action.

In defence of international solidarity, Fimmen steadily reminds us that the work of trade unions involves two objectives which, at times, are in tension: to operate within the existing economic system in order to negotiate the best conditions for working people but at the same time to develop alternatives to it. In a context of declining leverage and therefore affiliation fee income, the argument of this chapter is that trade union activity will need to be re-calibrated towards a wider political project of social justice in a context of aggressive neoliberal economic policies and the rise of nationalism and religious fundamentalism. In this context, the political work of trade unions has to be built—not as an ideological project but rather as a developmental one. The central argument is that the primary value of trade unions is that they are able to create spaces for dialogue between diverse interests and provide a safe environment out of which new political ideas can grow.

References

Applebaum, E., Batt, R., & Lee, J. E. (2014). Financial intermediaries in the United States: development and impact on firms and employment relations. In: H. Gospel, A. Pendleton, & S. Vitols (Eds.), *Financialization, New Investment Funds, and Labour: An International Comparison* (pp. 53–85). Oxford: Oxford University Press.

Armstrong, D. (2005). *Organization in the Mind: Psychoanalysis, Group Relations, and Organisational Consultancy*. London: Karnac.

Bion, W. R. (1952). Group dynamics: a review. *The International Journal of Psychoanalysis, 33*(2): 235–247.

Bion, W. R. (1961). *Experiences in Groups and Other Papers*. London: Routledge.

Bowlby, J. (1969). *Attachment and Loss. Volume 1: Attachment*. London: Basic Books.

Britton, R. (2015). *Between Mind and Brain: Models of the Mind and Models in the Mind*. London: Karnac.

Canham, H. (2002). Group and gang states of mind. *Journal of Child Psychotherapy, 28*(20): 113–127.

Carter, B., Danford, A., Howcroft, D., Richardson, H., Smith, A., & Taylor, P. (2013). "Stressed out of my box": employee experience of lean working and occupational ill-health in clerical work in the UK public sector. *Work, Employment & Society, 27*(5): 747–767.

Charlwood, A., & Forth, J. (2009). Employee representation. In: W. Brown, A. Bryson, J. Forth, & K. Whitfield (Eds.), *The Evolution of the Modern Workplace* (pp. 74–96). Cambridge: Cambridge University Press.

Clawson, D. (2005). Response: organising, movements and social capital. *Labor Studies Journal, 29*(4): 37–44.

Cotton, E. (2013). Regulating precarious work: the hidden role of the Global Union Federations. In: M. Sergeant & M. Ori (Eds.), *Vulnerable Workers and Precarious Working* (pp. 71–91). Cambridge: Cambridge Scholars.

Cotton, E. (2015). Transnational regulation of temporary agency work: compromised partnership between private employment agencies and global union federations. *Work, Employment and Society, 29*(1): 137–153.

Cotton, E. (2017). Constructing solidarities at work: relationality and the methods of emancipatory education. *Capital & Class*, *42*(2): 315–331.

Cotton, E. (2019a). The industrial relations of mental health. In: C. Jackson & R. Risq (Eds.), *The Industrialisation of Care: Counselling, Psychotherapy and the Impact of IAPT*. Monmouth, UK: PCCS.

Cotton, E. (2019b). *UberTherapy: Working in the Therapy Factory*. London: Surviving Work. ISBN 978-1-9998637-9-1.

Cotton, E., Kline, R., & Morton, C. (2013). Following Francis: reversing performance in the NHS from targets to teams. *People & Strategy*, *36*(1): 63–65.

Cotton, E., & Royle, T. (2014). Transnational organising: a case study of contract workers in the Colombian mining industry. *British Journal of Industrial Relations*, *52*(4): 705–724.

Croucher, R. (2004). The impact of trade union education: a study in three countries in Eastern Europe. *European Journal of Industrial Relations*, *10*(1): 90–109.

Croucher, R., & Cotton, E. (2011). *Global Unions, Global Business: Global Union Federations and International Business. Second Edition*. London: Libri.

Culpepper, P. D. (2002). Powering, puzzling, and "pacting": the informational logic of negotiated reforms. *Journal of European Public Policy*, *9*(5): 774–790.

Dicken, P. (2016). *Global Shift: Mapping the Changing Contours of the World Economy. Seventh Edition*. London: Guilford.

Doogan, K. (2009). *New Capitalism? The Transformation of Work*. Cambridge: Polity.

Douglas, H. (2007). *Containment and Reciprocity: Integrating Psychoanalytic Theory and Child Development Research for Work with Children*. London: Routledge.

Eiger, N. (1994). A comparison of trade union education in the Federal Republic of Germany and Sweden. *Labour Studies Journal*, Spring: 31–55.

Fimmen, E. (1924). *Labour's Alternative: The United States of Europe or Europe Limited*. London: Labour Publishing Company.

Flavin, P., Pacek, A. C., & Radcliff, B. (2009). Labor unions and life satisfaction: evidence from new data. *Social Indicators Research*, *98*: 435–449.

Freire, P. (1970). *Pedagogy of the Oppressed*. New York: Continuum.

Freud, S. (1930a). *Civilization and Its Discontents*. S. E., *21*: 59–148. London: Hogarth.

Gallin, D. (2014). *Solidarity: Selected Essays by Dan Gallin*. London: LabourStart.

Gumbrell-McCormick, R., & Hyman, R. (2013). *Trade Unions in Western Europe: Hard Times, Hard Choices.* Oxford: Oxford University Press.

Gumbrell-McCormick, R., & Hyman, R. (2015). *International Trade Union Solidarity and the Impact of the Crisis.* Stockholm: Swedish Institute for European Policy Studies.

H M Government (2014). *State of the Nation 2014 Report.* London: Social Mobility & Child Poverty Commission.

Hoggett, P. (1992). *Partisans in an Uncertain World: The Psychoanalysis of Engagement.* London: Free Association.

Hyman, R. (1997). Trade unions and interest representation in the context of globalisation. *Transfer: European Review of Labour and Research, 3*: 515–535.

Jarley, P. (2005). Unions as social capital: renewal through the return to the logic of mutual aid? *Labor Studies Journal, 29*(4): 1–26.

Kelly, J. (1998). *Rethinking Industrial Relations: Mobilization, Collectivism and Long Waves.* London: Routledge.

Khaliy, I. (2005). *The Effects of Foreign-funded Trade Union Education in Russia.* Moscow: Academy of Sciences.

Kjellberg, A. (2011). The decline in Swedish union density since 2007. *Nordic Journal of Working Life Studies, 1*(1): 67–93.

Klandermans, B. (1986). Psychology and trade union participation: joining, acting, quitting. *Journal of Occupational Psychology, 59*: 189–204.

Klein, M. (1948). *Contributions to Psycho-Analysis.* London: Hogarth.

Lazar, S. (2013). Citizenship, political agency and technologies of the self in Argentinean trade unions. *Critique of Anthropology, 33*(1): 110–128.

Long, S. (2002). The internal team: a discussion of the socio-emotional dynamics of team (work). In: R. Weisner & B. Millett (Eds.), *Human Resource Management: Challenges and Future Directions.* Milton, QLD, Australia: John Wiley.

Main, T. (1975). Some psychodynamics of large groups. In: L. Kreeger (Ed.), *The Large Group: Dynamics and Therapy* (pp. 57–86). London: Karnac.

Marmot, M. (2020). *Health Equality in England: The Marmot Review 10 years on.* The Institute of Health Inequality. Available at: https://health.org.uk/sites/default/files/upload/publications/2020/Health%20Equity%20in%20England_The%20Marmot%20Review%2010%20Years%20On_full%20report.pdf (last accessed April 6, 2020).

Martinez Lucio, M. (2010). Labour process and Marxist perspectives on employee participation. In: A. Wilkinson, P. J. Gollan, M. Marchington, &

D. Lewin (Eds.), *The Oxford Handbook of Participation in Organizations* (pp. 105–130). Oxford: Oxford University Press.

Money-Kyrle, R. E. (1951). *Perversion and Delinquency*. London: Duckworth.

Morgan, D., & Ruszczynski, S. (2007). *Lectures on Violence, Perversion and Delinquency*. London: Karnac.

Olmsted, M. S. (1959). *The Small Group*. New York: Random House.

Perini, M. (2010). "Si vis pacem para bellum". Psychoanalysis, peace, education and conflict literacy. In: H. Brunning & M. Perini (Eds.), *Psychoanalytic Perspectives on a Turbulent World* (pp. 17–40). London: Karnac.

Peters, J. (2011). The rise of finance and the decline of organised labour in the advanced capitalist countries. *New Political Economy, 16*(1): 73–99.

Pogue White, K. (2006). Applying learning from experience: the intersection of psychoanalysis and organisational role consultation. In: L. J. Gould, L. F. Stapley, & M. Stein (Eds.), *The Systems PPsychodynamics of Organizations: Integrating the Group Relations Approach, Psychoanalytic, and Open Systems Perspectives* (pp. 17–45). London: Karnac.

Praglin, L. J. (2006). The nature of the "in-between" in D. W. Winnicott's concept of transitional space and Martin Buber's "das Zwischenmenschliche". *Universitas, 2*(2). Retrieved from http://uni.edu/universitas/currentissue/art_praglin.pdf.

Roseneil, S., & Ketokivi, K. (2016). Relational persons and relational processes: developing the notion of relationality for the sociology of personal life. *Sociology, 50*(1): 143–159.

RSA (2017). *Good Work: The Taylor Review of Modern Working Practices*. Independent Report.

Sedgwick, P. (1982). *Psycho Politics*. London: Pluto.

Simms, M., Holgate, J., & Heery, E. (2013). *Union Voices: Tactics and Tensions in UK Organizing*. Ithaca, NY: Cornell University Press.

Sogge, D. (2004). Turning the problem around: FNV Mondiaal in Eastern Europe and the Soviet Union. Amsterdam, The Netherlands: Report for the Netherlands Ministry for Foreign Affairs and FNV Mondiaal.

Standing, G. (2011). *The Precariat: The New Dangerous Class*. London: Bloomsbury.

Stiglitz, J. E. (2012). *The Price of Inequality: How Today's Inequality Endangers Our Future*. New York: W. W. Norton.

Stirling, J. (2007). Globalisation and trade union education. In: S. Shelley & M. Calveley (Eds.), *Learning with Trade Unions: A Contemporary Agenda* in *Employment Relations* (pp. 207–224). Aldershot, UK: Ashgate Publishing Limited.

Sullivan, R. (2010). Organizing workers in the space between unions: union-centric labor revitalization and the role of community-based organizations. *Critical Sociology*, *36*: 793–819.

Theron, J. (2005). Employment is not what it used to be: the nature and impact of work re-structuring in South Africa. In: E. Webster & K. von Holdt (Eds.), *Beyond the Apartheid Workplace: Studies in Transition* (pp. 293–294). Pietermaritzburg, South Africa: University of KwaZulu-Natal Press.

Turquet, P. (1975). Threats to identity in the large group: a study in the phenomenology of the individual's experiences of changing membership status in a large group. In: L. Kreeger (Ed.), *The Large Group: Dynamics and Therapy* (pp. 57–86). London: Maresfield Library.

Webb, S., & Webb, B. (1913). *Industrial Democracy*. London: Workers' Educational Association.

Wilkinson, R., & Pickett, K. (2011). *The Spirit Level: Why Greater Equality Makes Societies Stronger*. New York: Bloombsbury.

Winnicott, D. W. (1950). Thoughts on the meaning of the word democracy. *Human Relations*, *4*: 171–185.

Winnicott, D. W. (1958). *Through Paediatrics to Psychoanalysis: Collected Papers*. London: Tavistock.

CHAPTER ELEVEN

On the psychology of religious fundamentalism

Lord John Alderdice

Introduction

It is understandable that many current writers begin their published reflections on the phenomenon of religious fundamentalism by acknowledging the significance of September 11, 2001 and the suicide attacks on the United States of America, in particular on symbols of its economic, military, and political power. However, there are certain problems with this starting point. First, there is an implied conflation of religious fundamentalism with the use of terrorism and politically motivated violence, a connection that merits further exploration, and second, it disconnects, by setting to the other side of that watershed, the importance of the Protestant fundamentalism which was substantially mobilised in the US presidential election campaign of George W. Bush the previous year. In addition to Islamic and other religious fundamentalist movements, Protestant fundamentalism had been on the rise in various parts of the world for some time. BBC News reported on July 13, 1999, "Heresy trials are to be brought back by the Church of England. After a gap of 150 years tribunals are to be reintroduced for clergy accused of not believing in God." Since then the matter has continued to rumble slowly through the governing structures of the Church of England at the same time that the worldwide Anglican Communion is near to schism over the question of the Church's attitude to homosexuality. This demonstrates a profound divergence and antagonism between those who may be described as liberals or modernists and those taking action against them who we might describe as fundamentalists. That the latter group are not merely conservatives is shown by their intolerance of the position of the liberal modernists. The Anglican Communion has always prided itself on being a "broad church" of liberals, conservatives, and others, and the views being expressed by the modernist tendency are by no means new, so the threats of schism and formal discussions within the courts of the Church about the reappearance of heresy trials seem to represent something significant about the growth and development of fundamentalism.

The heresy trial of J. Ernest Davey

The last really significant heresy trial in a major British religious denomination took place in the Irish Presbyterian Church in 1927 when Professor J. Ernest Davey was cleared of the charge after an extensive trial during February and March of that year. This was followed by an appeal by his accusers that was then rejected by the General Assembly in June 1927. The action was taken against the young professor by fundamentalists within the Presbyterian Church in Ireland and despite the fact that the trial took place more than eighty years ago it is important in our wider consideration of the psychology of religious fundamentalism for a number of reasons.

Professor Davey was one of the brightest theologians of his day. Born in 1890, a son of the Irish Presbyterian manse, he was showered with prizes from his school days on. He entered King's College, Cambridge in 1909, taking a series of prizes, and first-class honours, and was awarded a fellowship in theology in 1916, the first such fellowship to have been awarded in twenty-six years. He proceeded to the University of Edinburgh with more "firsts" and the professor of Hebrew and Semitic studies at Edinburgh described the quality of his papers as "rarely seen in my thirty years' experience". He returned to Belfast in 1917 and was elected to the chair of Church history in the Presbyterian College aged twenty-seven. In 1923 he published *The Changing Vesture of the Faith* based on a series of lectures he had delivered to members of the public in Northern Ireland, and this book, along with *Our Faith in God* which had come out the previous year, were substantial contributors to his being arraigned on charges of heresy. In *The Changing Vesture of the Faith* he espouses a psychological approach to understanding the changes and developments of Christian beliefs, institutions, and observances over the centuries and he writes in very approving terms of the recent develop-ments of psychoanalysis and how they shed light on these subjects. The Rev. James Edgar in his later published challenge to Professor Davey's position (1928) singles out his espousal of this psychological approach and his acceptance of evolution as some of the most toxic aspects of his "modernism", calling for "a little more repression and a little less expression". While this challenge, written in the aftermath of the trial, claims a self-sacrificial engagement in the struggle and denies any wish to criticise Davey as a person, it is couched in strident and angry terms and is dismissive and disrespectful of Davey's intellectual work, espe-cially where it involves higher criticism, liberal social ideas, evolutionary principles, and psychology. Even more interestingly he betrays a clear political position by appealing to the Sons of Ulster (a commonly used term in Northern Ireland, meaning Protestant Unionists) and making regular references in deprecating terms to Germany, recently defeated in the First World War.

As Dr Austin Fulton (also a later Moderator of the Presbyterian Church in Ireland) pointed out in his biography of Davey (1970) there were a number of elements of the context in which the heresy trial arose that may well have contributed to the fundamentalist/modernist dispute reaching such a pass. World War I had a profound impact on the political framework of Europe, bringing some empires to an end, and beginning the "unstitching" of those that remained, including the British Empire itself, where that unstitching had already begun with the partition of Ireland in 1921. While there had been no conscription in Ireland during the war, young men had answered the call to arms by the tens of thousands, going to their deaths in unimaginable numbers at the Battle of the Somme and all along the front line. This legacy of sacrifice still has an effect reflected in the special meeting of Belfast City Council held every July 1 for the sole purpose of remembering those who fought at the Somme, though the last survivor died years ago.

Protestants and partition politics in Ireland

The Great War, as it is still known, was followed by the War of Independence in Ireland in which the Irish Republican Army (IRA) rebels took on the victorious forces of the British Empire and drove them out of most of the island. Only the six Northern counties remained within the United Kingdom after the partition of 1921, while the twenty-six southern counties went on to form their own independent and almost totally Catholic nationalist state. Northern Protestants in the early 1920s were therefore terrified that either they would be abandoned by Britain and taken over by the South, or that their province would be destabilised by internal elements of the IRA supported by the Roman Catholic Church and people.

Into this frightened Protestant population arrived a fiery fundamentalist preacher called Rev. W. P. Nicholson. A native of the North he had trained with the Presbyterian Church in the USA. He returned with the militant certitude and fundamentalist evangelistic techniques being deployed in the fight against modernism in the United States, as exemplified in the 1925 trial of biology teacher John Scopes, accused of breaking the law by teaching evolution to students in Dayton, Tennessee. It is said that after W. P. Nicholson arrived home he was warned by a representative of the new Government of Northern Ireland not to use his gifts to stir up trouble with the Catholics because of the potential political risks, and he is reported to have reassured his interlocutor that he would "lay off the Papishes" and concentrate his fire on those of whom he disapproved in the Protestant community—in particular the Plymouth Brethren (a small isolated Protestant sect) and "liberals, modernists, higher critics and Unitarians". Fulton expresses the view that without this charismatic focus of discontent the plaintiffs in the heresy case might not have been able to get their case off the ground, and while they lost in an overwhelming vote—707 supporting Davey and only 82 against—their impact was to be long-lasting.

Davey went on to become principal of the Presbyterian Theological College in Belfast and moderator of the Presbyterian Church in Ireland, but he wrote relatively little after the trial, other than his life's work on the Gospel of St John published more than thirty years later in 1958. By that time a new W. P. Nicholson had arisen in the form of the young

Ian Paisley. Northern Ireland seemed more stable, and his fundamentalism was not taken so seriously for a while, but as he gradually became more of a threat, it was noticeable how reticent the mainstream Presbyterian Church was to rebut his stance. It was as though no leading figure wanted to risk becoming the sacrificial lamb in a new heresy trial. The Free Presbyterian Church that Ian Paisley established grew in size and influence and his sermons and writings viciously attacked both modernists and "Romanists" who he put in the same camp. He participated in anti-civil rights demonstrations and actively contributed to the breakdown into street violence with the resultant burning of Catholic houses, and the reappearance of the IRA and their Protestant alter egos—the Ulster Volunteer Force (UVF), named after those who had fought in World War I, and the vigilantes of the Ulster Defence Association (UDA). Northern Ireland slid rapidly into what became a thirty-year nightmare of terrorism and violence, with more than 3,000 people killed and tens of thousands injured out of a population of only one and a half million people. In the resultant chronic political uncertainty over the constitutional future of Northern Ireland Ian Paisley's political party slowly emerged as a significant political force, and eventually after the prolonged Irish Peace Process of the 1990s (which Paisley opposed and tried to undermine) had resulted in the Good Friday Agreement (a name he abhorred because of its clear religious connotations), his party became the largest political party in Northern Ireland, and he finished his career in 2008 leading the new power-sharing government as the first minister of Northern Ireland. Interestingly, because of the compromise represented by his going into government with Sinn Fein, the political wing of the IRA, he was forced to relinquish the moderatorship of the fundamentalist Free Presbyterian Church which he had founded and led for fifty years.

Fundamentalist certainty and political uncertainty

It is difficult to avoid the conclusion that in the history of Northern Ireland, there is an intimate connection between the strength and aggressiveness of fundamentalist religious views, and the instability and uncertainty about the political and constitutional future of the province. Despite the insistence of fundamentalists that faith is an individual matter and that each person must make a personal commitment based only on their convictions and relationship with God, there is much evidence that this is more generally a group phenomenon related to political anxiety and fear. Indeed, many authors have attributed the rise of fundamentalism among Protestants in the United States of America and among Muslims from Indonesia to Morocco to various aspects of social, economic, and political instability and change in the world as they experience it, and I have been struck in my own conversations with religious Islamists how they are keen to emphasise the importance of the political problems rather than religious differences with the West.

It is worth exploring Davey's writings in some more detail because he was one of the first eminent theologians to apply the emergent ideas of psychoanalysis to religion, and one could reasonably assume from the extent of their profound reaction against this modest and shy academic, that what he wrote and said must have struck a particularly notable if dissonant chord with his fundamentalist accusers.

Psychoanalysis, faith, and religion

Davey starts from the observation that at what he calls "the higher end of the scale", Judaism, Christianity, and Islam are remarkably alike in the lines and forms of their development, and proposes that this is due to the similarity of human nature the world over. His first thesis is that life, which is invisible, can only be observed as it is expressed in visible forms. While diversities come from the creativity of individuals, they are then adopted by groups and communities, and the resultant forms give to life what he describes as habit, consistency, and coherence, but also limit spontaneity. The treatment of religion then, from the individual and social psychological viewpoint is, he believes, the truest way of understanding what religion means since individual and social psychology is the study of human nature. An important function of religious forms including those of his own Christian faith is the reassurance they give in the presence of fear of death, danger, and discomfort. When sincerely engaged upon such studies, he maintains, the serious thinker must reach the conclusion that there can be no complete certainty in life. Those who seek such a thing must depend on short-cuts to reassurance which, in intellectual terms, will often require the vehement defence of every link in their chain of argument for fear the whole edifice collapses. He contends that in religious faith it is the authenticity of experience and the reality of one's nature that are the truly important matters rather than the details of belief and doctrinal systems, but it is the latter that are misleadingly depended upon for reassurance rather than faith.

For the average man then, religion is less a matter of faith than an ethical system with authoritative sanctions, and as such it is an essential of a social being. The institutions of the Church are the answers to man's craving for ethical and spiritual guidance. These change—"the changing vesture of the faith"—and at any time in history they represent to a great degree the culture and temperament of the people concerned. He observes that northern Europeans lean towards Protestantism with its Calvinistic or Augustinian points of view, while the Catholics of the South lean towards semi-Pelagian or Scotist tendencies. Ironically the more there has been a concentration on the writing of creeds and confessions of faith, the more the central and indeed common themes of faith, love, and the value of the human soul have been ignored, even in the wording of the creeds. The common things of faith and human existence are passed by and the creeds and confessions focus instead on the areas of contention and often contemporary error. This masks what is for him the key to faith, that the search for ideals, for self-completion, is the search for God, a hunger that is part of the human condition and which can only be satisfied in the experience of personality. The expression of such experience is the key to the forms of religion, at least at their best and most authentic, and this is not a matter of logic so much as one of proportion, fitness, and balance, "keep(ing) abstract reason in its place of servant to life".

This leads him to conclude that the forms of the Church in any age (by which he refers to beliefs, institutions, and observances) tend to reflect the political forms and interests of the social organism as it exists in that age. He then moves to consider the tendency to regard matter as evil and so to build an edifice of self-denial and self-mortification, but he points out that actually it is usually the desire which is associated with the body, rather than the matter itself which is the problem, and that "instinct for sacrifice" should represent something temporary for the sake of gain, rather than something in itself. This takes him to the universal presence in societies everywhere of taboos and sacrifices in various forms, and proposes that the special contribution of Christianity in its higher forms is to emphasise consecration rather than renunciation as redemptive.

In the early 1920s when Davey's lectures were given to a mixed lay and clerical audience there was a good deal of discussion about the application of psychoanalysis to society. *Social Aspects of Psychoanalysis*, for example, was published by Ernest Jones in 1923, containing a series of lectures given by senior psychoanalytic figures to the Sociological Society in London. It is not difficult to see how Davey's observations as a very intelligent and scholarly young man, soaking up the new findings of psychoanalysis and evolutionary biology before, during, and after the First World War, when there was the most profound turmoil of thought, society, and world order, should lead to such insights into the normal form and function of religion. As psychiatrists, we know that in the study of disturbances of personality and mental life in the psychiatric patient, where the phenomena are easily seen because they are exaggerated and inappropriate, we learn not only about mental pathology, but also about normal mental evolution and function. So it is that in the extremes of social upheaval we may hope to appreciate more of the how and why of large group life. At such a time of frightening uncertainty, however, it is also easy to see why his message was not a reassuring one and was responded to with attacks and denigration. While his intention was to adumbrate the best of the higher forms of faith, he inevitably, if gently, pointed up the rigidities and pathology of what he referred to as "the lower end" of religion, and in doing so from within the theological faculty of the Church rather than from a more remote academic perch, he opened himself up for vitriolic abuse from those who by this time were part of a fairly coherent network of religious fundamentalism.

Fundamentalism and Holy Scripture

The term "fundamentalism" is generally regarded as having come from a series of twelve essays by two American brothers, Lyman and Milton Stewart entitled *The Fundamentals: A Testimony to the Truth*, published between 1910 and 1915 and promoted by conservative elements in the United States. These views made their way to Britain through various evangelists including those involved in the Keswick movement. Not all those who held to such views wished to be identified as fundamentalists, but they did all share a commitment to defend a supernatural as distinct from a scientific approach to faith. In their very useful survey of *The Psychology of Religious Fundamentalism*, Hood, Hill, and Williamson recognise the work of Carpenter, Marsden, and others in the more recent Fundamentalism Project, which identifies militant opposition to modernity as the key to understanding Protestant fundamentalism, and also see this as applicable more generically to describe the religious and cultural phenomena of religious fundamentalism worldwide including within Judaism, Islam, Hinduism, and other religions. While applauding much of its work, Hood and colleagues are concerned that the approach of the Fundamentalism Project may be too broad and "obscures more than it illuminates", and they have developed a model which they believe accommodates both an appreciation of the commonality of fundamentalisms as well as a respect for the specifics of each fundamentalist faith.

They rightly point out that all attempts to identify a particular personality type as identifying fundamentalist believers has proved nugatory, and maintain that the historical and sociocultural context is vital in appreciating it as a meaning system. They focus on the importance of a sacred text within fundamentalism as providing the centrepiece for understanding it and propose a cognitive model of what they call "intra-textuality". This principle focuses on the absolute prerequisite of reading a sacred text as the text itself prescribes, accepting as absolute the "truths" which the text itself prescribes as such. The Divine has spoken and the recorded text is treated as being the only legitimate version of absolute truth, not to be measured by any external measures, but providing meaning to the believer and guidance for life and for the interpretation of all other knowledge. It is not necessarily the case that all elements of the sacred text be considered to have the same level of significance, but the issue can only be resolved "intra-textually", that is to say, under the instruction of the text itself. The value of this model, as the authors point out, is that it not only allows for the differences between fundamentalists who adhere to different sacred texts, but also, because interpretation of the intra-textual meaning will itself vary from individual to individual and from group to group, it allows for the considerable variations between different fundamentalist groupings who hold to the same sacred text, for example within Protestantism.

It is certainly the case that they demonstrate the way in which an intra-textual reading provides a coherent, meaningful, unifying philosophy of life, and they identify five key features among Protestant fundamentalists—belief in the inerrancy of scripture, a literalist interpretation of the text, the importance of evangelism, separatist behaviour, and commonly (but not essentially) the doctrine of pre-millennialism. They are also right to urge caution in assuming too close a connection between fundamentalism and violence. The overwhelming majority of people who hold to fundamentalist views do not support overt violence in the form of terrorism; however, that is not to say that there is not a degree of militancy in their attitude. There is a different emotional tone in fundamentalism than in conservatism. Fundamentalists press their case in a more vigorous and less tolerant manner. One is unsurprised when fundamentalists grasp the opportunity of a heresy trial, for example. While conservative minded people and so-called evangelicals within Protestantism hold to many of the same doctrinal positions as fundamentalists, they tend to be more prepared to accept that other people have a different perspective, of which they may at times despair, but which they generally accept as part of society and even of Church society. I am not entirely convinced by the inclusion of the Amish as fundamentalists by Hood and colleagues. It seems to me that they are instead a rather particular, small conservative group. The intra-textual model also tells us very little about why fundamentalism appears at particular points in history. The intra-textual approach appears meticulously respectful to fundamentalists by dealing with doctrine entirely within the encapsulated bubble of the interpretation of the sacred text, however as far as the fundamentalist is concerned this isolates his convictions from the wider world from which he wishes to separate himself, but with which he is also inevitably, though conflictually engaged. Protestant fundamentalists may relate their strivings to changes that have taken place in the intellectual and religious order of things, and are then reflected in political and other unwelcome changes that have taken place. The question for observers is whether the "truth" is the reverse—that is, that the intellectual and political changes have created an unwelcome uncertainty and instability to which their religious fundamentalism is a response of some kind. The approach of Hood and colleagues is certainly more thoughtful and respectful than the simple contention that fundamentalists are misled by wrong teaching, or worse, however to separate it off and deal with it as a phenomenon of intra-textuality to avoid disputes about causes and motivations, also strips it of the key to understanding it, both from within and without the religious perspective.

Fundamentalism and group psychology

Vamık Volkan tries a different route of exploration. The FBI were confronted in the USA by a number of crises with fundamentalist groups, notably in 1993 when the FBI attacked and burned the Waco cult compound in Texas. Volkan was invited to chair an advisory committee to the agency's Critical Incident Response Group and he became interested in what he has described as "encapsulated" fundamentalist organisations, not only David Koresh's Davidians in Waco, but Jim Jones in Jonestown, Shoko Sahara's Japanese Aum Shinrikyo, Joseph's DiMambro's Order of the Solar Temple, and others. These are movements that remain isolated within the larger society and tend to induce negative feelings, including fear, in those outside the encapsulated group. From these groups Volkan identified ten common characteristics—a divine text; an absolute leader who is the interpreter of the divine text; a demand for total loyalty to the group and the yielding up of all aspects of life and choice to the group and its leader; tangible benefits for members; feelings of being both omnipotent and yet victimised; extreme sadistic and/or masochistic acts; alteration of the shared "morality"; creation of borders (psychological and sometimes physical) between the group and the rest of society; changing of family, gender, and sexual norms within the borders; and negative feelings and fear amongst outsiders. These ten observations from so-called "encapsulated" fundamentalists are clearly not entirely separable items. The setting down of a border for the group and the creation of different ways of thinking and behaving based on the divine text as (idiosyncratically) interpreted by the single inspired leader will not surprisingly contribute to the sense of omnipotence, the negative attitudes of outsiders, and the resultant and ambivalently unwelcome sense of victimisation.

Volkan further postulates that when for some reason a significant number of outsiders begin to become sympathetic rather than have negative feelings about the group, perhaps because the wider society has

undergone a massive trauma that has resulted in feelings of humiliation and helplessness, the idea of a "saviour" becomes attractive. He
refers to the remarkable growth and power of the Taliban in post-Soviet
Afghanistan and describes as especially powerful the symbolic link
established with Mohammed through the leader, Mulla Omer, publicly
putting his arms into the sleeves of a cloak believed to have belonged
originally to the prophet Mohammed—this symbolic link collapsing
the passage of time and the separateness of the two individuals concerned. While Professor Khurshid Ahmad has disputed the authenticity
of reports of this particular event, Volkan has demonstrated a similar
mechanism in a number of other case studies in the Balkans, Baltic states,
Cyprus, and elsewhere. Volkan, who was senior Erik Erikson scholar at
Austen Riggs Hospital, sees the phenomenon of fundamentalism as representing a regression in the functioning of a group in the face of a threat
or threats to the identity of the large group, an idea that he has developed out of a revision of Erik Erikson's description of individual identity
(2009). Large-group identity—whether it refers to religion, nationality,
ethnicity, or shared ideology—he defines as the subjective experience
of thousands or millions of people who are linked by a persistent sense
of sameness while also sharing some characteristics with "others" who
belong to foreign groups. He describes this identity as being part of the
psychic development of the large group which emerges out of its, often
mythologised, history, and describes how, in a fashion analogous to that
of the individual under threat, it is possible for the large group to regress
to points in its earlier development where chosen glories and traumas
(analogous to fixation points) become infused with emotion and significance and lead to a series of defences. An example would be the appearance in a people of "entitlement ideologies" such as irredentism where
the nation's difficulty in mourning the loss of people, land, or prestige,
in, for example, the loss of empire, leads to attempts to deny the losses
and seek to recover them either in fact or in symbolic form, sometimes
at great cost, and with a continuing significance that is not much diluted
by time, and can be reignited after years or even centuries. Another
example are the "purification" practices where words are purged from a
language, symbols removed from view, or worst of all, ethnic cleansing
is embarked upon, to repair the damaged sense of identity, in a defence
analogous to externalisation/projection in the individual.

The idea that identity might form a useful bridge between the psychology of the individual and the group has been around for some time. The social anthropologist, John Blacking, for example, explored it in South Africa in the 1970s using musical culture because it showed the link between individual and group feelings and action and the power of something which has affective significance, even if transitory in its performance and experience. He also showed (1983) how identity has continuity even when its external cultural expressions adapt to take account of changes in the political context and climate, especially where there is stress or conflict—a musical/cultural version of Davey's "changing vesture" thesis in the religious aspect of large-group identity.

One of the important things about Volkan's work is that he not only applies the concept of identity to the large group but he also sites it within an evolutionary or developmental process, which can be put into reverse in the context of trauma. This evolution/dissolution model is familiar to psychoanalysts but as was demonstrated in a lifetime of work by Henri Ey, the French psychiatrist, it comes from the pre-psychoanalytic work of Hughlings Jackson in neurology and psychiatry. Ey (1962) developed a neo-Jacksonian approach which he called organo-dynamic because it paid due attention to both biological and psychological aspects of psychiatry, and was based on a model that was congruent with both.

Regression and the loss of temporo-spatial functions

The key features of this model are his explication of mental life as being our construction of "reality" and his application of the development/ regression model to that experience of reality. Mental illness in his description is not only a shrinking of human existence and a pathology of freedom, but also a disturbance of our capacity for experiencing reality. We have to understand, he says, the limits set to the sick man's comprehension of the mental disturbance that makes him sick with a "disease of reality". The reality of the disease consists precisely of the unreality, or the "imaginary structure" of the basic experiences, what Ey calls "pathologies of the field of consciousness and personality", though he uses these terms in a particular way. In the regression or dissolution of the experience of reality, whatever the cause, there are negative features coming from the loss of higher functions, as well as positive symptoms coming from the release of the remaining mental functions, but there is also reconstructive or reparative work which follows, given time. The negative effect of the illness involves the loss of temporo-spatial functions—the temporal function being the capacity to distinguish in the experiencing of time between what is past, present, and future, and the spatial function being the experience of what is inside me and what is part of someone else. Such regressions may be sudden, temporary mental crises, or may become chronic in which case there are adaptations or reconstructions of the personality from the remaining and regressed capacities.

In applying such a phenomenological model to large-group identity we can note, as Volkan has pointed out, the temporal regression or "collapsing of time" such that events from the distant past may evoke powerful images and emotions, as though they happened only yesterday. The loss of spatial function in the individual is experienced in primary process thinking, both in the normal and regular dream life from which we can voluntarily wake up, and also in the more terrifying loss of ego boundaries, characteristically with the release phenomena of transitivism and appersonation and the appearance of hallucinations, where the patient's thoughts or memories are felt to be outside themselves and directed at them, rather than internal and proceeding from them. Sometimes the dissolution of the self is actually experienced directly in psychosis or in the pre-psychotic period. Various attempts are made by the remaining mental function to make sense of the experience, or repair the "reality", for example through delusion formation.

If one applies this to the large group, whatever the cause or trauma, regression would involve a loss of the higher functions which enable history to be experienced as past (temporal function), and for differentiation between individuals within the group as well as between the group and other groups (spatial function). The loss of these functions leads to the collapse of time so that the past invades the present, and the loss of differentiation between individual people and between the large group and other large groups leads to what Girard calls a "mimetic crisis" with the attendant danger of violence.

Violence and the Sacred

The importance of the differentiation between individuals and groups in controlling violence is identified in great detail by the French-American,

René Girard in a series of books, but for the purpose of this chapter *Violence and the Sacred* (1972) is probably the most relevant. In human beings, he says, there are not only the instinctual appetites for food or water and so on, which we share with the animal kingdom, but also imitative desire—"I want that because I observe that you have it." This fundamental mechanism of mimesis or non-conscious imitation of desires inevitably leads to rivalry and in Girard's view the social constructions of law, culture, and religion were essentially mechanisms that set down boundaries for rivalry, which, if uncontrolled, would lead by rapid mimesis to a violent rivalrous crisis. The particular device at the centre of this boundary setting is the scapegoat mechanism, by which, instead of everyone being set against everyone in violence, all turn against one individual who is demonised, victimised, sacrificed, and then, since his sacrifice brings peace, is ultimately divinised. Girard identifies this mechanism as key to understanding the foundational myths of what he calls archaic religions. In every repetition of the phenomenon the lynch mob feels itself justified in their violence against this individual who is regarded as the embodiment of some sort of evil. The difference between such myths and Judaeo-Christian religion in particular (as exemplified in the crucifixion of Christ and its ritualisation in the Eucharist), he says, is the recognition that the identified victim is actually innocent and that he is being sacrificed, not because of his wickedness, but to rid the community of its evil/violence. The problem is that once the myth of the wickedness of the victim is exposed as a lie the power of the mechanism is destroyed for no one can feel so justified in scapegoating. In a post-9/11 expression of his thinking Girard (2005) says that while the realisation of the hypocrisy or "lie" behind the scapegoat mechanism has ensured that we have in many ways become less violent through our insistence on the rights of women, racial and religious minorities, the disabled, and other victims or potential victims, this demythologising has also contributed to more violence through the release of the old mimetic violence which the sacrificial violence was instigated to control.

Regression and reconstruction of large-group identity

As I have outlined elsewhere (2003), if one puts these observations together, the rise of religious fundamentalism may be seen as resulting from a societal regression brought about by the fear of the loss, or in some cases the trauma of actual damage or loss, of large-group identity resulting from a combination of rapid sociopolitical changes in the past century. These might be summarised as follows—the advances in evolutionary science which remove the boundaries between humanity and the rest of the animal kingdom and introduce complexities of thinking which a majority of the population may find difficult to construe; the collapse of traditional authoritarian forms of government (monarchies, empires, and tribal chieftains) with the advance of participatory democracy; the developments in information and communication technologies, greater speed and ease of travel, and the borderless capacity for destruction in the nuclear age, all of which both excite interest and threaten large-group identity; the end of the Cold War, the collapse of communism, and the widespread espousal of free market economics; in short the forces which we describe as rapid globalisation represent the loss of boundaries and our experience of time and space is shaken.

Interestingly however, fundamentalists do not generally see their movements as merely going back to the past. They certainly feel that they are identifying key strands from the roots of their faith and tradition, which they feel to have been overlooked, lost, or denied, however they describe their activities as "revival", and many readily espouse new technology in their own lives. Professor Ahmad starts his paper on Jama'at-e-Islami (2006) in precisely this way, and in conversation I found him very clear that the Islamist approach was about addressing the modern world, not trying to recreate the past. Hamas and Hizballah also say they are not trying to recreate an old way of living, and there is nothing Amish-like in their style of life. They are instead developing new ways of constructing social and economic models for their communities. From a Jacksonian point of view fundamentalism is not merely a form of regression but also includes the release of functions from an earlier time or lower level of structure and complexity, and most importantly also incorporates an attempt at reconstruction from a position of dissolution. Given what Girard describes as the fundamental mechanism of mimesis (or non-conscious imitation), large-group identity regression may result in a reparative attempt to re-erect the boundaries that could obviate mimetic rivalry, but have been removed by the traumatic loss of or damage to large-group identity. It is as though the unspoken message from the frightened community is, "We do exist; we are different and we may be acting in an aggressive (scapegoat) way, but it is in order to prevent worse (mimetic) violence." This is of enormous importance because it makes clear that it is possible to identify within fundamentalism an innate reparative or reconstructive component, something that is often missed or dismissed by observers. It may not be impossible to relate to this component if it is recognised.

Fundamentalism, radicalisation, and violence

Finally, I return to two of the problems identified at the start of the chapter, the relationship between different fundamentalisms, and the relationship between fundamentalism and violence. Girard's emphasis on mimetic behaviour and the infective nature of violence should alert us that different fundamentalisms will imitate each other and create a cycle of regressive thinking and action. Hence the growth of Protestant fundamentalism within the USA is not hermetically sealed from the growth of fundamentalism elsewhere, and not only Protestant fundamentalism, but other religious fundamentalisms too. As the boundaries are dissolved, so the possibility of mimesis of thinking increases.

Further, as Volkan points out, and Girard helps to further explain why it is, there is an inherent violence, sadistic and/or masochistic, in the scapegoat mechanism, and therefore insofar as fundamentalists are attempting to reinstitute it, with old and new boundaries there will be an aggressive tone to their approach. It may be militant in its evangelism, aggressive in its language and attitude especially to lukewarm co-religionists who are more of a threat than those who are clearly different, and in its treatment of women in particular, and minorities in general, there will often be abuse and sometimes overt violence. The overwhelming majority of fundamentalists, however, do not become involved in, or supportive of terrorism, and indeed many will abhor it. Those who do become genuinely supportive of, or involved in, terrorism seem to have undergone a kind of radicalisation which they may share with others who are not religious fundamentalists at all. Many of the young people who get involved in suicide attacks and other terrorist activities are radicalised, but not especially religious, though if they survive they may become religious afterwards while in prison or under the influence of radical clerics or other prisoners. This differentiation between fundamentalist religious convictions and radicalised activists is of great importance in managing the deterioration in global security, and we do not yet understand it fully, save to say that one does not necessarily progress to the other, or require the presence of the other, though they can be present and facilitate each other.

A further key question is how far the scapegoat mechanism can really be revived. Perhaps it can no longer work for so long because the "cat is out of the bag" that the mechanism is based on a lie, though I am not yet sure of this because as human beings our capacity for denial is significant. There are in any case possible alternatives. The development of the European Union and some of the other peace processes which have been modelled on it show that in certain contexts a process can be created through which it is possible not only to contain the violence but to work through and transform it by the development of relationships in which differences can be sustained and mimesis limited or directed in positive competition rather than dangerous rivalry. On this, however, I must sound a note of warning because these alternative processes are new and as we can see in Europe, are still susceptible to deteriorate into mimesis and rivalry. While the post-war generations in Europe remembered that the purpose of the "European Project" was to prevent a return to the rivalries of nation states which had resulted in catastrophic wars, all was well. But now that a new generation of leaders is more concerned with economic success and using the EU as a platform for power to rival the USA, Russia, and China, so the dangers re-emerge both within the EU, with the appearance of racism and xenophobia, and also in collusion with a new line of international division with scapegoating of the Islamic world in general, and Iran in particular.

In summary, religious fundamentalism can perhaps best be understood as a phenomenon of large-group psychology which occurs not merely as a direct result of regression in the face of threat or trauma, but showing three related elements—the loss of some more developed social functions, the return to or release of more elementary social characteristics, and the reconstruction of the large-group identity from the remaining functions and faculties of the group. Fundamentalism is characterised by the diminution of individual freedom, a concretising of thinking, and restrictions of behaviour, but its "purpose" is to repair or reconstruct the group identity and as well as to prevent further breakdown and/or violence and this positive component should not be disregarded.

References

Ahmad, K. (2006). Great movements of the 20th century No 2, Jama'at-e-Islami. In: *The Message* (pp. 1–8). New York: Islamic Circle of North America.

Alderdice, J. (2003). Liberalism and fundamentalism. *Liberal Aerogramme, 46*: 13–17.

Blacking, J. (1983). The concept of identity and folk concepts of self: a Venda case study. In: A. Jacobson-Widding (Ed.), *Identity: Personal and Socio-cultural*. Atlantic Highlands, NJ: Humanities Press.

Davey, J. E. (1923). *The Changing Vesture of the Faith: Studies in the Origins and Development of Christian Forms of Belief, Institution and Observance*. London: James Clarke & Co.

Edgar, J. (1928). *Presbyterianism on Its Trial*. Belfast, UK: Privately published.

Ey, H. (1962). Hughlings Jackson's principles and the organo-dynamic concept of psychiatry. *American Journal of Psychiatry, 118*: 673–682.

Fulton, A. (1970). *J. Ernest Davey*. Belfast, UK: The Presbyterian Church in Ireland.

Girard, R. (1972). *Violence and the Sacred*. Baltimore, MD: Johns Hopkins University Press.

Girard, R. (2005). Violence and religion. In: P. Walter (Ed.), *Das Gewaltpotential des Monotheismus und der Dreieine Gott* (pp. 180–190). Freiburg, Germany: Verlag Herder.

Hood, R. W., Hill, P. C., & Williamson, W. P. (2005). *The Psychology of Religious Fundamentalism*. New York: Guilford.

Jones, E. (1924). *Social Aspects of Psychoanalysis*. London: Williams & Norgate.

Volkan, V. (2008). Large Group Identity, International Relations and Psycho-analysis. Presentation at "Psychoanalysis and International Relationships", Gasteig Cultural Center, Munich, Germany.

Volkan, V. (2009). *On Freud's "The Future of an Illusion"*. M. K. O'Neil & S. Akhtar (Eds.) London: Karnac.

CHAPTER TWELVE

The politics of NHS psychiatry

Kate Pugh

Mental health services are currently underfunded and failing young people at risk. The government has announced an increase to NHS England's main budget of just over £20bn by 2023/24; an increase of 3.4% a year on average, and the analysis from *Securing the Future* (NHS Confederation, 2018) suggests that if this is maintained over the next fifteen years, it should be enough to maintain current standards of care, assuming the rest of the Department of Health and Social Care's budget grows at the same rate. However, this is not enough of an increase to allow modest improvements by upgrading areas like mental health provision, public health spending, waiting times, spending on buildings, equipment, and pay. This would require around 4% a year over the fifteen years, which would likely need to be front-loaded as 5% over the first five years.

Research by The Health Foundation also points out that the inadequate support generally available now puts the health of young people at risk in the future. Young people in the UK are not getting the support they need to make a smooth transition into adulthood, putting them at greater risk of experiencing poor health in later life. The findings are the first to emerge from The Health Foundation's Young People's Future

Health Inquiry (2018), which is exploring the support twelve to twenty-four year olds need to enter adulthood with the core building blocks for a healthy future, namely: a place to call home, potential for secure and rewarding work, and supportive relationships with their friends, family, and community. Extensive engagement with young people around the UK identified four assets (described below) that help them secure the building blocks for a healthy future. An accompanying poll asked 2,000 young people aged twenty-two to twenty-six to what extent they had these assets when growing up. Fewer than one in five (16%) young people felt they had access to all assets growing up, despite more than two thirds (68%) recognising they were all important.

Emotional support: 90% of people in this age group said that having emotional support is important, but just 49% felt they fully had this growing up.

Appropriate skills and qualifications: 92% of people in the same age group said that having the opportunity to achieve the right skills and qualifications for their chosen career is important, but just 47% (fewer than half) felt they fully had the opportunity to achieve these.

Personal connections: 89% of the age group said that having the right relationships and networking opportunities to help enter into and progress in the working environment is important, but just 31% felt they fully had these growing up.

Financial and practical support: 77% of the same sample said that having financial and practical support from family is important, but just 46% felt they fully had this growing up.

Jo Bibby, director of health at The Health Foundation, commented:

> Young people today are facing pressures that are very different to those of previous generations. This new research demonstrates that many young people in the UK are not getting the support they need to make a smooth transition into adult life. This support is vital to securing the building blocks they need for a healthy future. Without it we are putting their future health at risk. We hope that the work of the inquiry over the coming months will help us understand the reasons for this and identify the changes needed to address this worrying trend.

Julia Unwin CBE, strategic advisor to the inquiry and former chief executive of the Joseph Rowntree Foundation, commented:

> The future health of our young people is our most valuable asset. The importance of the early years (0–5s) is widely understood, but the 12 to 24 year period offers a similarly important opportunity to affect and influence our health in later life. If we don't take steps now to address the underlying issues, we could be storing up longer term problems for both individuals and society as a whole.

The report finds that, depending on the mix of assets young people have during the years twelve to twenty-four, four "types" of young people have emerged:

"Starting ahead and staying ahead", who generally have the full range of skills, connections, and support to access what they need for a healthy future.

"It's not what you know, it's who you know", who have the skills but lacked the connections needed to get work in their chosen career.

"Getting better together", who have experienced struggles in the past and were working with support from others to move on from these previous challenges.

"Struggling without a safety net", who lacked any support or access to skills or connections needed to build a healthy future.

I will discuss in some detail one patient who most certainly falls into the last category of "Struggling without a safety net", and I will illustrate some of the splits in the mind and in the organisations that care for these patients.

The most powerful defence in psychosis is the denial of ordinary needs. A stark example of this was demonstrated by a young male patient admitted to the ward who was lying in bed, incontinent and refusing food and water. He was convinced that he had no need to get these basic needs met as he was beyond ordinary bodily realities. He believed himself to be all mind and intellect and that his body was floating and fluid like water. He had the fantasy that, like an emperor on a throne, he would have all excretions and ingestion dealt with without him having to attend to anything himself. This seemed to be a recreation of an infantile state, indeed intrauterine state, idealised as the height of privilege with complete denial of the helpless dependency it involved. To seek help was deeply humiliating for this young man who only slowly came to recognise his vulnerability and dependence on others.

I bring this example to illustrate the responsibility in provision of mental health services to recognise the enormous need and dependency of patients even, and indeed especially, when they most deny it themselves. I am concerned that, at times, organisational structures can mirror the split in the patient's mind rather than mend it; that is, there can be a collusion with the psychotic part of the patient's personality (Bion, 1957) which believes that they are omnipotent and without ordinary needs and can then fail to provide appropriate care.

For example, in the provision of early intervention services for young people having their first psychotic breakdown, this need for dependency is recognised with an active outreach model recommended for these patients and their families. The enormous strains on such services, with a lack of adequate resources for the community services that support vulnerable young people, shows a parallel denial of need for care. There is a lack of provision for mental health of adolescents and young adults which is leading to barriers to accessing care across mental health services.

Freud in his *New Introductory Lectures* (1933a), described psychiatry as akin to anatomy and psychoanalytic understanding as akin to histology; psychoanalysis is the understanding of the underlying structures and forces that form the surface picture described in psychiatry: the splits in self and other and the operation of denial and omnipotent defences to vulnerability.

An analytic understanding of the mind is a way of exploring the obstacles to mental health provision. Freud (1933a) went on to describe psychotic breakdown as being like a crystal shattering:

> If we throw a crystal to the floor it breaks, but not into haphazard pieces; it comes apart along its lines of cleavage into fragments whose boundaries, though they were invisible, were predetermined by the crystal's structure … Mental patients are split and broken structures of this same kind … they have turned away

from external reality, but for this very reason they know more about internal, psychical reality and can reveal a number of things to us that would otherwise be inaccessible to us. (p. 59)

We can see similar splits in the structures which are there to provide care for the mentally ill as the NHS is thrown to the floor by efforts to withhold funding and down-shift services. There is currently a crisis in mental health with a great shortage of psychiatric beds and appropriate alternative safe care in the community. At the same time, there is a change in the language around care. Rather than asylum and long-term care, we talk of "recovery model" and the wish to not "encourage dependency". This premature promotion of independence, and the patient as the master of their own recovery and as peer support for others, can appear attractive as a move away from a paternalistic medical model, but it reflects an underlying denial of severe disturbance and need for real help to develop. It is a manic flight to health that covers despair of receiving any real developmental help.

The case of Jason Mitchell, widely reported in the news and subject to an independent panel of inquiry in 1996, is a stark illustration of this crisis and shows it has been in place for decades.

The case of Jason Mitchell: report of the independent panel of inquiry, 1996

I first met Jason Mitchell, a nineteen-year-old boy, on the locked ward at Epsom hospital where he had been admitted following an assault on the caretaker of a local church. I had been asked to do a report for the courts where he faced a charge of attempted murder. The caretaker had called the police when this young man, who had been hiding in the church, approached him and asked him to lie down while he fetched a piece of wood to hit him on the head and kill him. The man was left in no doubt of his seriousness in this intent as he felt terrified for his life.

Jason was an apparently friendly young man willing to tell me his story and describe his experiences. He told me that for six years he had been having strange experiences. This started with just "feeling different" but went on to him changing from "liking things to disliking things" in an abnormally intense way, for example, a television programme took on an emotional significance the "same way you would feel as if you was in love with somebody". Comedy shows on television were making jokes about him and laughing at him. He began to interpret ordinary events as being persecutory. For example, he believed that there were groups of people who flashed their headlights in his face in a threatening way and that people walking past him in the street were talking about him. For the last five years he had heard voices which sounded like people mimicking his father's voice and talking about his past. He would look for these people and search the house for microphones, videos, and heat sensitive lights which he believed must be hidden there. He came to think that he had been a victim from birth of an experiment which deprived him of all privacy and exposed him to constant nagging criticism, or overhearing critical conversations about him. He believed that these voices could control him.

On the day of his arrest, the voices had told him to get on the train to Epsom and had told him that he must kill the vicar: "This is the time that you should kill that man." He was convinced that it was the vicar who was responsible for all his distress. When the caretaker found him in the church, Jason decided he would have to kill him as well as the vicar and he had asked him to lie down on the ground so that he could knock him out with a lump of wood with the minimum of damage. The caretaker ran away to call the police and Jason waited for them to arrive, thinking the voices had tricked him into this situation.

There was a split in Jason Mitchell between the friendly young man he could sometimes appear and his level of psychosis and dangerousness, which sometimes slipped from view. The inquiry noted that in court the more serious charges of attempted murder and assault occasioning actual bodily harm, to which the plea was not guilty, were not pursued despite clear evidence and admission from the patient that his intention was to kill. Instead it was settled that Jason plead guilty to common assault and possession of offensive weapons. These lesser "index offences" were cited in later records on which management of his case rested. The judge did ascertain that if Jason relapsed in his mental illness he could become very dangerous and his decision was to make a Hospital Order under Section 37 of the Mental Health Act 1983, together with a Restriction Order unlimited in time under Section 41.

The inquiry questioned the decision not to place Jason in a forensic psychiatric setting rather than return him to a general psychiatric ward, as there he could have accessed specialist therapeutic help. He seemed to respond to the routine and structure of the hospital setting, and joined in the therapeutic group work that was available.

I think Bion's concept of the psychotic and the non-psychotic aspects of the personality are very helpful in understanding these splits, both in the patient's mind and reflected in the systems in which he relates to, the court and the hospital. In the "brick mother" of the hospital, he can recover his mind and describe and have curiosity about his disturbance, but it can become split off in the minds of the staff. He is not experienced as dangerous and even the court wants to see him as more benign and less disturbed than is the case.

This split is so evident in the case of Jason that only four years later he was recommended for discharge from his detention in hospital and transferred to a hostel back in his home town. The responsible psychiatrist questioned his diagnosis of schizophrenia and the team "had moved to a working diagnosis of drug induced psychosis" to account for Jason Mitchell's past psychiatric history, leading them to regard his reports of "hearing voices as manipulative behaviour" in a young man with a difficult personality disorder. The decision was taken to stop all anti-psychotic medication and place Jason in a low-level care hostel where he lacked the structure and containment afforded by hospital care. This placement broke down and he was housed in independent accommodation despite the social work recommendation that he be in fully supported care in the community to prevent relapse. The split in the patient's mind between a recognition of real disturbance and need for care, and complete denial of this reality was reflected in the services provided to him.

Within six months Jason Mitchell tragically did commit the murders he had felt so compelled to do, one being the killing of his father, the others strangers, a couple unknown to the patient but representing the source of his distress.

The system failed because there was ultimately a collusion with the denial of disturbance characteristic of psychotic functioning, which went along with a belief that suitable containing care was not needed. The inquiry was particularly struck by one piece of evidence that was largely ignored by the psychiatrists in charge of Jason's care. It was a report by an unqualified member of the occupational health team who had, over time, developed a trusting relationship with Jason and come to a detailed understanding of his inner world. This was prepared during the time of his hospital admission when he was contained and in therapeutic group work as well as on anti-psychotic medication. She reported that he was the youngest of five children and that his mother left his father before Jason was a year old. He was then brought up by his father who was very resentful of the mother and gradually developed alcohol dependency, becoming unreliable and neglectful. The extended family were able to support them in the early years but by the time he was seven years old, both his older brothers were in prison and he and his father were isolated. His mother still lived in the same small town and if he met her, she would pretend not to know him and asked him to not acknowledge her as his mother. He became a lonely, strange boy without friends and unable to learn at school. By the age of twelve he was involved with the police. He left school at fifteen with no qualifications and survived with a life of petty crime, drug abuse, and living rough. He made only one friend in his life which was with an older man who offered a homosexual relationship to him and gave affection and gifts. His parents had offered no attention, support, or care through his late childhood and adolescence.

It was at this desperate time in his life that Jason felt his mental illness began. He viewed it like moving from a chrysalis to a butterfly. He felt invincible, elated, and beyond harm. In this state, he became indebted to a gang of drug dealers who punished him by hurting him and hanging him from a multi-storey car park, threatening to drop him to his death. Working for them led to him spending two years in Feltham Remand Prison where he began to develop his fantasies of revenge on those who had hurt him. He devised elaborate ways of killing his enemies and this masterful fantasy sustained him. His father never visited him in prison and on his release, he did not get the warm return home he longed for.

This report concluded that Jason spent a vital part of his life with his basic needs denied and his immediate social structure lost to him. When his reality became unbearable, he formed his own fantasy world which prevented any normal emotional growth. He appeared strong and self-reliant, while denying that his needs were great.

This description closely fits the observations of psychoanalyst Herbert Rosenfeld in his understanding of destructive aspects of narcissism in psychotic functioning. Rosenfeld in his paper on narcissism (1971) describes a particular pathological organisation in which the patient may idealise destructive aspects of the self which are turned to as a source of strength and superiority. The narcissistic patient withdraws from life to an idealised destructive object which pulls or seduces the good parts of the self towards death and destruction. He saw in trying to treat very disturbed patients that they denied their need and dependency on help and turned instead towards a "gang" structure in their minds which promised protection from the persecution of enemies and from the overwhelming guilt of despair. This was a brutal world in which dependency is disavowed. It is not until ordinary dependency is accepted that the patient can begin to develop emotionally.

In current services it is often thought that dependency on services should not be encouraged and many interventions, even for quite disturbed children and young adults, are only brief. There is an encouragement of self-help and peer group support, all denying the real disturbance and level of need. The lack of psychological and specifically psychotherapeutic understanding of patients with severe mental illness is a particular concern of the report of the inquiry into the case of Jason Mitchell:

> In particular there was an absence of any psychological/psychodynamic approach to understanding his emotional and personality development; and little attention was paid to family dynamics and relationships. There was no monitoring of Jason Mitchell's inner life. Indeed there was a deliberate avoidance of his subjective mental state.

The loss of hospital beds for adolescents and young adults having their first psychotic breakdown is part of a sanctioning of a belief that less is more. Only 11% of the NHS budget is spent on mental health while it represents an estimated 23% of social and health needs.

In November 2016, the Royal College of Psychiatrists published research showing that a large number of clinical commissioning groups were spending £10 or less on each child for mental health. The government pledged to invest in child and adolescent mental health services, with £119m of NHS funding allocated to clinical commissioning groups for 2016, another £140m promised for 2017/18, and an additional £30m for eating disorder services—but it is up to local clinical commissioning groups to ensure that money is passed to the front line, based on their assessment of local need.

The RCPsych figures show that children and adolescents' mental health is still underfunded when it comes to the share of NHS spending in many areas of the country. There are 52 clinical commissioning groups in England that are allocating less than 5% of their total mental health budget to services for children and young people. That is despite the fact that one in every ten children aged five to sixteen years has a diagnosable mental health disorder and children under eighteen make up a fifth of the population (21.3%). The president of the Royal College of Psychiatrists, Professor Sir Simon Wessely said:

> Our analysis shows that in many areas of the country, the proportion of money that NHS clinical commissioning groups are planning to spend on the mental health of our children and young people is negligible. We know that more than half of all adults with mental health problems were diagnosed in childhood and less than half were treated appropriately at the time. It is a national scandal that opportunities to prevent mental illness from occurring in childhood are being missed because of unacceptably low investment.

Access to psychotherapeutic understanding for children is very difficult and vulnerable under-eighteens are suffering the effects of increasing rationing of psychological help in the UK. A report by Pulse (July 2016), a GP group, states that NHS child mental health services are failing the next generation; up to four in five children with mental health problems are being denied access to treatment they urgently need in some parts of England and six in ten children and young people across England do not receive treatment for problems such as anxiety and depression, despite the increased risk to them if their condition worsens. Pulse's figures, obtained under freedom of information legislation from fifteen mental health trusts, showed that 61% of children and young people referred for help from CAMHS in 2015 received no treatment. A third were not even assessed for it.

There seems to be a shared denial of the disturbance and need for psychotherapeutic and psychiatric help which will leave increasing numbers of adolescents at risk of breakdown without a net to catch them. This is a split in which there is an apparent commitment while covering real neglect.

One of the main recommendations of the inquiry into Jason Mitchell was that mental health staff should have an understanding of their patient's histories and internal psychic worlds; that it was not enough to note only absence or presence of gross psychiatric symptoms. An understanding at the level of histology, not merely anatomy, to take Freud's medical analogy, was needed.

It is therefore extremely important that medical education has taken this into account with reflective practice groups (where such understanding is developed) now being mandatory for core trainees in psychiatry and recommended for all doctors from medical students through to higher trainees in psychiatry. This needs to be expanded across all disciplines and reflected in a commitment to understanding patients suffering from mental illness.

"Illness is neither an indulgence for which people should have to pay, nor an offence for which they should be penalised, but a misfortune, the cost of which should be shared by the community"—Aneurin Bevan, "father" of the NHS.

References

Bion, W. R. (1957). Differentiation of the psychotic from the non-psychotic personalities. In: *Second Thoughts: Selected Papers on Psychoanalysis* (pp. 43–64). New York: Jason Aronson.

Blom-Cooper, L., Grounds, A., Guinan, P., Parker, A., & Taylor, M. (1996). *The Case of Jason Mitchell: Report of the Independent Panel of Inquiry*. London: Duckworth.

Freud, S. (1933a). *New Introductory Lectures on Psycho-Analysis. S. E., 22.* London: Hogarth.

NHS Confederation (2018). *Securing the Future: Funding Healthcare and Social Care to the 2030s.* London: Institute for Fiscal Studies and The Health Foundation.

Price, C. (2016). A national disgrace: NHS fails to treat child mental health. *Pulse* (July 4).

Rosenfeld, H. (1971). A clinical approach to the psychoanalytic theory of the life and death instincts: an investigation into the aggressive aspects of narcissism. *The International Journal of Psychoanalysis, 52*: 169–178.

Royal College of Psychiatrists (2016). The scandal of underfunded child and adolescent mental health services laid bare in new research from the Royal College of Psychiatrists. Available at: www.rcpsych.ac.uk2016 (accessed May 2020).

Young People's Future Health Inquiry (2018, June 18). London: The Health Foundation.

CHAPTER THIRTEEN

Psychoanalytic activism: historical perspective and subjective conundrums

Mary-Joan Gerson

Leanh Nguyen's paper (2012) stirs the heart and electrifies the mind. My goal as a discussant is to keep that electrical current active, while I channel some of its energy into questions I find embedded in her text. First, I'd like to locate Nguyen's voice in a long history of psychoanalytic activism, a tradition that is not sufficiently honoured by our profession.

Altman (2010) has provided comprehensive documentation of psychoanalytic activism, beginning with Freud's concern about extending psychoanalytic treatment to poor and underserved individuals, which led to a movement between the two World Wars of establishing free clinics throughout Europe. Beginning in the 1920s, members of the Frankfurt School, including Erich Fromm, Norman Brown, Herbert Marcuse, and others, engaged in a Marxist and dialectic critique of psychoanalysis. They were soon followed by Fromm who viewed character and conflict as shaped by economic forces. In the wake of the Nazi scourge, psychoanalysis was transplanted to the United States and became a treatment for the educated and relatively affluent. There were many reasons for this right turn, including new definitions of analysability under the strong influence of ego psychology as well as the press of a capitalist ethic.

A striking exception to the elitist turn in psychoanalysis was the work of Harry Stack Sullivan who, in the last year of his life, participated in three international meetings, including a UNESCO Tensions Project whose mission was to examine the psychological causes of nationalistic aggression (Perry, 1982).

In the 1960s, the community mental health movement was launched in the United States and it engaged many psychoanalysts. Altman (2010) noted that budgetary concerns ultimately strangled an approach that de-emphasised symptoms, but rather focused on prevention and consultation. I worked at a community mental health centre in the 1970s and remember grieving that the initial cut funding for an incredibly low-budget, well-attended, weekly gathering of patients with long-term psychosis, was followed by a reduction in consultative services, such as the community clergy group I was leading. The irrationality of these administrative decisions was more destabilising than any clinical challenge I faced. I do think that there are inherent constraints to psychoanalytic activism. First, many analysts feel emotionally taxed and even drained by the work, and they are not interested in undertaking commitments that involve exposure to more psychic pain. Second, others feel that all of our work is essentially beneficial and restorative to the social fabric. Third, our mandate is to connect to patients of all political persuasions (even those sometimes infuriating to us) and this effort can lead to a subjective sense of dividing our political and clinical identities. I find it inspiring that, in the face of these and all the other personal constraints, many psychoanalysts are involved in activism projects today and this involvement seems to be growing. Here I mention several as exemplars: Deborah Luepnitz's (2002) work with the homeless in shelters; Nina Thomas' (2011) international efforts in Haiti and Palestine; Jane Darwin and Ken Reich's (2006) creation of the SOFAR project (Sex Offender Families Against Registration); and Altman's (2010) efforts in the inner city. Recently, I and another faculty member at the New York University Postdoctoral Program in Psychotherapy and Psychoanalysis surveyed our community to document pro bono and activism efforts and we were immensely impressed with the number of people involved in social justice projects, such as working with asylum-seekers, terminally ill patients, and underserved children.

My own psychoanalytic-activist work has been as a consultant to the staff of two non-governmental agencies: "Day One", which tracks adolescent partner abuse and "The American Jewish World Service", an organisation with a wide reach in global programming, including, for example, refugee displacement, child sexual and physical abuse prevention programmes, and assistance in acute, often tribal conflict. I will refer to my own experience as I turn to the power of Nguyen's paper.

The central message of Nguyen's paper is her conviction that when our work embraces individuals suffering from extreme trauma, our psychoanalytic ideology and methodology are essentially activist. She says, "We save lives by helping these patients to reclaim their willingness to be human. And we also perform a civic service in showing society what it means to be human" (p. 317). She identifies two implicit activist positions. The first she describes as: "… the implicit pledge of our profession is that each life counts, each story needs to be found and retold, and each telling matters infinitely and effects profound ripples in the world—and in our psychic individual selves" (p. 317). But she also identifies another activist stance: "My covert agenda is to tell people about trauma; to show them the costs of torture; to expose the feats and ruins of 'survivorship' and, subliminally, to mitigate the collective dissociation by rendering the human being underneath the 'torture survivor'" (p. 309).

Let me take up the second of these positions. I think that one of the universally disturbing aspects of contemporary life is the media-based accessibility of what we would, in fact, consensually regard as human and non-human behaviour. Perhaps I believe there is less ambiguity about abuses that signify dehumanisation than Nguyen does. Indeed, I am riveted by the obverse dilemma of how we can incorporate into our notion of the human the intentionality of the perpetrator. A Sullivanian colleague believes that this is an issue of group contagion—any behaviour can be sanctioned in what becomes a "normative context". Others have posited the concept of sub-speciation—that in the moment of attack, the victim is viewed as utterly "other", or have pointed to warfare's chaotic dissolution of cultural norms, which inflames and releases psychopathology in vulnerable individuals. Grand (2000) has hypothesised that "evil is an attempt to answer the riddle of catastrophic loneliness" (p. 5).

I want to raise a question about Nguyen's resistance to a narrative thread focused on resilience. She states:

> The representation of what happens after torture or war mostly follows the plot line of normalcy–traumatic blow–devastation–recovery. It employs the tropes of "hero," "victim" or "survivor," which puts us all comfortingly in the genre of a tragedy or an epic. They gratify the spectator-consumer with the illusion of meaning and absolve her of the responsibility of staying "unsettled." (see LaCapra, 2001, pp. 9, 311)

Several years ago, I went to an agonising photographic show called "Children of Bad Memories" by Jonathan Torgovnik (2009), which featured huge Cibachrome portraits of women raped in Rwanda standing next to the child born of the rape. Each photograph was documented with a testimonial statement (Torgovnik, 2009). One woman openly expressed her dislike of her offspring. However, others expressed their need to triumph over dehumanisation, not to sink into it. I was, as I always am, struck by the difference in these journeys. I do not think this is denial or avoidance, but rather it is an expression of my psychological awe at the choice of triumph, the mysteries of character structure. If we could understand the origin of this difference, it would help us understand even more about the human condition, and is this not what we are after as psychoanalysts?

A small point: I think it is crucial for us to retain a certain humility about our particular theoretical or clinical contribution, however passionate our engagement. Nguyen notes that "The activism is in making judges, witnesses and the authorities recognise the human being and in making it possible for them to not turn their gaze away from the human life that lies in their hands ..." (p. 313). I agree that we psychoanalysts are uniquely trained to articulate the individual psyche. However, I also believe that the lawyers and doctors who work with torture survivors care deeply about human life, and I worry about privileging our own ideology and subjectivity, which ultimately restricts possibilities for collaboration. I would like to highlight some points that Nguyen makes in her paper, which struck me as particularly enriching to the literature on trauma. She says:

> In the deadening space that these patients exist, language and life
> are not allowed to move back and forth between me (the witness,
> the living) and the patient (the haunted, living dead). Mortality—
> which comes to us in the little moments of being penetrated and
> disconnected; in meaning being made, re-made, and un-made; in
> speaking to each another; in the flow of people loving us and leav-
> ing us—is evaded by these patients as they insulate themselves
> from life and keep their experiences un-spoken, un-transmitted.
> And there is no longer living, but merely existing. (p. 313)

She brought to my mind Becker's *The Denial of Death* (1973), in which
he wrote that "The irony of man's condition is that the deepest need is to
be free of the anxiety of death and annihilation; but it is life itself which
awakens it, and so we must shrink from being fully alive" (p. 66). From a
more sanguine perspective, Strenger (2009) has described creative work
in midlife as a unique amalgam of both ensuring and denying mortality.
But what I found most evocative was Nguyen's statement that in the resignation to "I am just existing" her clients have erased mortality, and
with it the creativity or Eriksonian generativity that a sense of mortality renders. I would not have associated the experience of being dehu-
manised with the denial of mortality. I found her discussion of narrative
compelling. What is central to Nguyen's commitment is an exquisitely
patient and attuned attentiveness to the terror of narration. She states:

> The narrative desire is corrupted, as speaking would revive the
> wounding. But without the words, they remain ghosts and aliens;
> without engaging in the narrative act, they remain haunted, pos-
> sessed, away and apart from the living; being silent keeps the
> nightmare muted but without the narrative impulse they remain
> alienated from the community of humans. Such is the vicious
> dilemma these patients are caught in. (p. 313)

I think that we psychoanalysts today are privileging non-verbal communication, registering body states and tonal inflection as alternatively
valid means of representation. She does emphasise that "The activism
lies in the commitment to stay with the unspoken and to metabolise
the unbearable so that I can retell the story of the trauma in a tolerable,

recognisable, and usable form" (p. 14). And, of course, we think of enactment as representing what cannot be said. I wonder how Nguyen uses these other registers in locating and activating the narrative pulse in her torture patients.

Second, Nguyen points out that the fragmentation in narrative must be tolerated by the witness. I know that the young people I worked with at the American Jewish World Service were narratively mute when they returned from their overseas assignments. Actually, they have indicated that my group meetings with them are remarkably helpful because they had considered language inadequate to carry the pain of their empathic and identificatory response, and they had feared that, in attempting to convey it, they too would be erased. However, they also felt silenced by another inhibition that Nguyen does not mention in her paper, and which I post here: these young field workers felt that any narrative rendering of trauma was inherently expropriating and violating of those who had shared their story with them.

Lastly, Nguyen cites the immense responsibility of hearing and absorbing the experience of trauma. The telling of that otherwise unavailable reality—of how the person comes back to the living having been nearly erased—is a deep responsibility for society; because, if you get it wrong, then the sliver of life that still pulses amid the narrative ruins, and the space for connection and faith that hangs between the living dead and the unknowing, are forever lost (p. 310).

I wonder about her limits or those of any psychoanalyst deeply grasping hideous experience. Both Sullivan and Donald Winnicott located a private self; the inaccessibility of certain domains of experience to the most penetrating analytic inquiry. When it comes to torture, I think that unknowability is fundamental, partly because of our own annihilating anxiety in the face of it. I have always been struck by Elie Wiesel's warning:

> A plea for the survivors? I know, it seems insane. It is not …
> Accept the idea that you will never see what they have seen—
> and go on seeing now, that you will never know the faces that
> haunt their nights, that you will never hear the cries that rent
> their sleep … And so I tell you: You who have not experienced

their anguish, you who do not speak their language, you who do not mourn their dead, think before you offend them, before you betray them. Think before you substitute your memory for theirs ... (Wiesel, 1978, p. 247)

It is clear that Nguyen deals with unknowability in her work.

The last section of Nguyen's paper focuses on the personal in the political and it is a delicately rendered testimonial of the personal benefit she has accrued from her work with severely traumatised patients. What I most admired was her comfort with taking from her patients. An adage frequently evoked, certainly within the interpersonal tradition, is that if a treatment has not changed us, it has not really been psychoanalytic treatment. But Nguyen is talking about gratitude. She says, "The work is a coming home that is doubled up within a turning away. But, as I dedicate myself to finding and re-telling their unspeakable and unspoken stories, these patients in turn inevitably bring me to questions that allow me to reach into unvoiced questions about my own life ..." (p. 315).

I have been thinking lately about how much I take from patients; how my current issues about ageing and loss are being abetted in my work, and at times I feel notably off-kilter and guilty about this consumption. I think we have talked a lot about mutuality in psychoanalytic treatment and a great deal about envy and rage, but we have not addressed gratitude, that truly hierarchically reversing exchange.

Many of us today feel that psychoanalytic discourse too often devolves into comfortable rhetorical positions, recycling ideas that we curl up with in comfort. We turn to interdisciplinary lenses to refuel our theory, but I think that if we try to psychoanalytically grapple with the most important crises of our era, bending our theory to this purpose, we not only will make a contribution to the human community, we will also enliven our own scholarly enterprise. And Nguyen's paper is an exemplary springboard to that effort.

References

Altman, N. (2010). *The Analyst in the Inner City* (2nd edn.). New York: Routledge.

Becker, E. (1973). *The Denial of Death*. New York: Simon & Schuster.

Darwin, J., & Reich, K. (2006). Reaching out to the families of those who serve: the SOFAR project. *Professional Psychology: Research and Practice, 37*: 481–484. doi:10.1037/0735-7028.37.5.481

Grand, S. (2000). *The Reproduction of Evil*. Hillsdale, NJ: Analytic Press.

LaCapra, D. (2001). *Writing History, Writing Trauma*. Baltimore, MD: Johns Hopkins University Press.

Luepnitz, D. A. (2002). *Schopenhauer's Porcupines: Intimacy and Its Dilemmas*. New York: Basic Books.

Nguyen, L. (2012). Psychoanalytic activism: finding the human, staying human. *Psychoanalytic Psychology, 29*: 308–317.

Perry, H. S. (1982). *Psychiatrist of America: The Life of Harry Stack Sullivan*. Cambridge, MA: Belknap Press of Harvard University Press.

Strenger, C. (2009). Paring down life to the essentials: an epicurean psychodynamics of midlife change. *Psychoanalytic Psychology, 26*: 246–258. doi:10.1037/a0016447

Thomas, N. K. (2011). Working under occupation: psychoanalytic reflections on psychosocial service in Palestine. *The Psychoanalytic Activist*. Retrieved April 24, 2020 from http://apadivisions.org/division-39/publications/news-letters/activist/2011/10/palestine-psychosocial-service.aspx.

Torgovnik, J. (2009). *Intended Consequences: Rwandan Children Born of Rape*. New York: Aperture.

Wiesel, E. (1978). *A Jew Today*. New York: Random House.

CHAPTER FOURTEEN

The rise of the new right: psychoanalytic perspectives

Elisabeth Skale

I would like to begin with a few preliminary thoughts about the political situation in Austria, when a far-right party has participated in government (2017–19), with the rise of the New Right in general, and with the current global role of social media and its unconscious effects which seem to have influenced voters, especially those of the new far-right parties.

It is well known that after a short period of social democratic government from 1918 to 1930, there was a right-wing conservative and later an Austro-fascist government which finally gave way to Hitler's Nazi regime, welcomed by the majority of Austrians. Since 1945 there has been a constitutional law prohibiting National Socialist activities. The governments after the Nazi period were socialist or conservative one-party governments or coalitions. On one occasion Kreisky's socialist party made a coalition with the far-right Freedom Party of Austria (FPÖ) and from 2000 to 2008 there was a coalition of the conservative People's Party with the far-right Freedom Party under Jörg Haider—so the current situation is not without precursors.

But the election of a far-right party in 2017 in Austria can also be seen as closely connected to the growth of nationalist, xenophobic, populistic parties in France, Netherlands, Italy, Germany, Hungary, and Poland together with "movements" like Donald Trump's and the Vote Leave in the United Kingdom. The far-right parties, Front National—now Rassemblement National—in France and Alternative für Deutschland in Germany do have similar programmes to Austria's Freedom Party, but they were able to be kept at bay by strong opponent parties (led by Macron and Merkel). In Austria the conservative, neoliberal party helped the far-right FPÖ to enter government by building a coalition, with the idea of "taming" the latter in the long run and even of diminishing the number voting for it.

Most alarming in these populist politics, beside the xenophobic and racist content, is their attitude towards democracy. Behind the smoke-screen of strengthening "direct democracy" with their calls for plebi-scites, they propagandise an erosion of representative democracy with its separation of powers. In Hungary this culminated in Orban's dictum of the "illiberal" democracy as his idea of a successful nation.

There are many definitions of the populist style of politics, and here I would like to refer to the Bundeszentrale für politische Bildung, a polit-ical education centre which defines it by four elements:

1. Populists are addressing "people", consisting of "ordinary men".
2. Identity politics is central for the agitation of populists, with the demarcation of the "people" from two distinct groups of "enemies":
   a) Political, economic, or cultural elites who are held in antagonistic or hostile contrast, or
   b) Marginalised social, cultural, religious, or ethnic minorities, mostly migrants, who are made into scapegoats for all sorts of grievances.
3. The third characteristic of populism is its dependency on charismatic leadership figures, which use a fixed canon of attention-grabbing stylistic devices: providing radical solutions to complex prob-lems, deliberately breaking taboos, provocations, personalisation, emotionalisation, and fomenting fear and hatred for those "up there" or "the others", and making contact with their audience as directly as possible.
4. Typically, populism organises itself as a "movement", avoiding the term "party". Instead, it is a covenant, league, list, front, or

even movement seeking deep roots in the "people", and the leader often holds a very heterogeneous group of followers through his charisma. Often there is no formal membership with rights and duties, but a strictly hierarchical decision-making structure that is usually tailored to the central role of the leader (see http://bpb.de/politik/extremismus/rechtspopulismus/192118/was-versteht-man-unter-populismus).

The sociopolitical situation in 2015, the so-called "refugee crisis", promoted right-wing and extreme right-wing populism.

Interestingly enough, right-wing populist "movements" made very early use of the possibilities of social media, its dynamics fostering their political style, and indeed seem to be tailored to them. There are also left populist portals, but they have a relatively short range.

The dynamics of social media

There is currently quite a lot of research into the dynamics of specific manipulations via social media. An Austrian journalist, Ingrid Brodnig, published an informative book, *Lügen im Netz* (2017), collating different aspects of this issue.

During the last few years it has been recognised that eliciting anger in the digital debate leads to large numbers of "clicks"; "angry people click more" characterises the dynamics of social media (Brodnig, 2017, p. 39). In a study about the "virality" of online content, Jonah Berger and Katherine Milkman using a data set of all the *New York Times* articles published over a three month period showed that anger is the strongest engine for sharing and sending. But also other "high-arousal emotions" such as amazement and worry lead to increased activity. In addition, Berger described an "infectiousness of emotions", both offline and online: people do not simply share information—the more emotion a content causes, the more likely it is to be spread. False claims are also shared when they trigger the right emotions. So, for digital electoral campaigns, stirring up anger and dealing with not-quite-right claims can be an impressively successful strategy (Brodnig, 2017).

The software, the algorithm of web portals such as Facebook, makes a significant contribution: articles to be read are not ranked logically but are instead listed in order of relevance according to the individual user's "profile". The criteria that assess the relevance, the "filtering", depends on the "interaction", which means the number of "likes", "comments", and "shares" of a specific article, but also takes into account the profile of the user and his or her preferences. The filtering is mainly controlled by profit, because the longer a user stays on a page, the more advertising can be displayed. In this way the algorithm favours high-excitation emotions as they cause high interaction which shows the system that it should make further distribution to selected users. The effect of the "news feed" is that news items are more prominently displayed the more they cause vortex and this makes the "algorithm into a drama machine" says Brodnig (p. 45).

By this dynamic the system creates a phenomenon called "filter bubble", where messages confirming one's own intuition are considered to be more relevant, and the "confirmation bias", a well-known general inclination, is being exploited by the portal's previous experience, the "click history". The filter bubbles are further influenced by the fact that negative news and scary messages attract special attention. Interestingly enough, there are studies showing that citizens who tend to be conservative or politically right-wing orientated tend to show a "negativity-based credulity", trusting warnings about risks significantly more often than leftists. Thus, the propaganda of right-wing extremist movements, which tend to provoke paranoid fears, meets a willingness to adopt a paranoid world view.

Through this, the great new potential of global communication, with huge possibilities of connecting millions of users from all parts of the world, can be exploited by illegal groups. If extremists notice they are not alone, they are cheering each other on, so that radical people online can further radicalise. In a media landscape that is "fragmented" by social media, these dynamics get an additional spin, when users withdraw into so-called "echo chambers" (Sunstein, 2018). These are digital spaces in which people largely exchange views with like-minded people and obtain more information that fits their interests and their world view. In a deeply personalised, digital environment, people only surround themselves with people and information that suits them; the voice of the sceptic is absent, or, conversely, critical voices, if they enter at all, are criticised, dismissed, threatened, and by this the uniformity of existing opinion is reinforced (Brodnig, 2017).

An "isolation index" has been created by Matthew Gentzkow and Jesse Shapiro to describe and measure the ideological segregation of different media, online and offline. It ranged from 1.8 per cent for radio to 10.4 per cent for national newspapers, but only 7.5 per cent for individual surfing on the net. However, for Twitter during the US election campaign, the isolation index was 40.3 per cent.

Far-right populists use these characteristics of social media to create parallel worlds:

1. By discrediting critical press with the suggestion of a large "conspiracy" within the media landscape to fool the population. For example, Heinz-Christian Strache recommended a foreclosure strategy towards the established media to his electorate. Trump also said: "Forget the press, read the internet. Study other things, do not go to the mainstream media" (Colorado Public Radio).

2. To generate a mood through targeted use of misinformation or "fake news". In particular right-wing populist movements, also the FPÖ in Austria, formed their own websites—presenting "alternative facts" and celebrating themselves as "detectives" against conventional reporting, with the aim of increasing mistrust of the "lying press", a term of National Socialist propaganda.

3. By deliberately spreading distrust of democracy. There are a number of websites and blogs such as Der Wächter ("The Watcher"), Breitbart ["Broad Beard"] News by Steve Bannon, unzensuriert.at ("uncensored") of the FPÖ, in which "electoral fraud" or "voter fraud" in Western democracies, especially in the run-up to important elections, are asserted and "proven". This can fuel mistrust in elections, and probably also increase voter turnout and strengthen the "movement" that "protects" against this "scam".

4. False reports about acts of violence by refugees or marginalised communities: one famous example is the denigration of Sweden. A hoax was even officially distributed by Donald Trump.

The creation of parallel worlds is intended to create a paranoid atmosphere of fear, hate, and persecution, characteristic of right-wing extremism, which is then exploited for its own political purposes and "solutions". The strategy of Steve Bannon,[1] FPÖ, and AfD is to cast doubts on the conventional media and to point potential voters to certain "alternative media", which then report particularly positively on right-wing populist content and movements. It seems threatening that "around the right-wing populist movements a separate 'echo chamber' is growing, in which citizens are permanently supplied with alarm messages and half-truths suitable for the party line" (Brodnig, 2017, p. 75).

Interestingly, the strategy of Facebook was changed after the last US presidential election. Since then a message has to be displayed with the notice "disputed" and linked to the respective fact check, when it has been unmasked by at least two fact checking facilities[2] as a hoax.

Unconscious dynamics

To understand the unconscious dynamics of right-wing extremist populism, I would first like to draw on well-known works on anti-Semitism (Otto Fenichel, 1940, and Ernst Simmel, 1946).[3] Fenichel sums up about anti-Semitism in general:

> The anti-Semite arrives at his hate of the Jews by a process of displacement, stimulated from without. He sees in the Jew everything which brings him misery, and not only his social oppressor but also his own unconscious instincts, which have gained a bloody-dirty-dreadful character from their socially caused repression. He can project them on to the Jew because the actual peculiarities of the Jewish life, the strangeness of their mental culture, the bodily (black) and religious (God of the oppressed peoples) peculiarities and their old customs make them suitable for such a projection. (1940, p. 38)

These statements can also be used to understand current racism and xenophobia vis-à-vis Arab asylum seekers in Europe. The demarcation of strangers from the "people" corresponds to one of the described right-wing populist arguments. The recurring arguments of an "invasion" of Europe by asylum seekers from the Middle East and the imminent Islamisation of Europe seem increasingly to function as a "chosen trauma", which serves to unite the population in the "fight" against invaders and through the common fears to "emotionalise" the issue. Heinz-Christian Strache (FPÖ) repeatedly spoke of a third Turkish siege vaguely connected with a fear of "losing a war". Similarly, Vamık Volkan (1999) describes the dynamics of "chosen trauma" and its importance for large-group identity. It is often deliberately created and used by nationalistic leaders to fuel conflicts: find a trauma, feel like a victim, gain the right to revenge, attack or elucidate an attack to create an additional trauma.

In order to understand more fundamentally these phenomena, but above all the rapid spread of racist and anti-democratic ideas and the unconscious dynamics emanating from the various platforms of "social media", I think it is important to refer to Freud's 1921 essay *Group Psychology and the Analysis of the Ego* where he describes characteristics of the "mass", its formation, and alterations of the ego.

Following William McDougall's *The Group Mind* (1920), Freud describes an unorganised mass as exceedingly excitable, impulsive, passionate, fickle, inconsistent, indecisive, and yet ready to do the utmost in their actions, violent in their judgements, easily led and swayed. Individuals in the mass are without self-confidence, self-esteem, or sense of responsibility, but ready to be carried away by their powerful consciousness to commit all the misdeeds that we can only expect from an absolute and irresponsible power (Freud, 1921c, p. 85).

On the other hand Gustave Le Bon (1895) found that once people are united into groups or masses, they have the need for a head and the crowd becomes a docile flock demanding obedience, guidance, and submission to a "leader". It has such a thirst for obedience that it submits instinctively to anyone who appoints himself its master (Freud, 1921c, p. 80).

It is McDougall who writes that in the group emotions are stirred up to a pitch that they seldom or never attain under other conditions; and it is a pleasurable experience for those who are concerned, to surrender themselves so unreservedly to their passions and thus to become merged in the group and to lose the sense of the limits of their individuality. The manner in which individuals are thus carried away by a common impulse is explained by McDougall by means of what he calls the "principle of direct induction of emotion by way of the primitive sympathetic response" (1920, p. 25; Freud, 1921c, p. 84).

Freud attributes this "imitation" and "contagion" to the suggestive influence of the mass, and the particular suggestibility of its members (1921c, p. 88). This suggestibility has its origin in the identification of the individual members with each other, while each is at the same time identifying with the leader (or the mass ideal) and by this, giving up his own ego-ideal.

The most dangerous aspect is that for the individual it is perilous to be in opposition to the group; it feels safer to follow the example of those around him and perhaps "even 'hunt with the pack'. In obedience to the new authority he may put his former 'conscience' out of action, and so surrender to the attraction of the increased pleasure that is certainly obtained from the removal of inhibitions" (Freud, 1921c, p. 85).

I think that some of these characteristics described in relation to "group psychology" and the "mass-soul" can be observed directly in the current dynamics in certain network activities ("shit-storms"). The large, highly excitable group (mass) of users can turn a message into a big chorus of outrage, both "negative" and "positive". A tabloid newspaper report on the birth of a "New Year's baby" of a Muslim family triggered a shit-storm within hours, so the portal had to be closed and was countered by a subsequent "candy storm" of the civil society, initiated by an NGO.

Claustrum of the filter bubble

But in addition to the characteristics of the psychology of crowds and the projective mechanisms underlying anti-Semitic and racist attitudes, we have to understand the special condition individuals get into, which eventually leads them to look for specific slogans and leaders in order to help them grasp political problems and to withdraw into appropriate "echo chambers" and filter bubbles provided by social media and purposefully reinforced by far-right populist propaganda.

Right-wing propaganda seems to initiate certain paranoid anxieties by spreading selective news about invasion by strangers and refugees, such as their aggressive, greedy, and exploitive attitude against those who are invaded by them, sexual assaults by migrants, but also reports about planned legal equality for different social groups. These topics seem to cause a state of increasing existential threat, which brings the social media user to respond aggressively, to spread this propaganda to like-minded people. Several cycles of this communication bring about highly aggressively charged users, susceptible to radical slogans provided by leading figures.

In particular the fact that these "echo chambers" prevent any contact with "corrective" messages and the excitement of the lone user at being provided with a "truth" that he then shares with others likewise "inaugurated" adds an additional quality to the "knowledge" and provides immunisation against different viewpoints.

Some of the characteristics of a condition like this resemble Donald Meltzer's description of a state of mind he calls "life in the maternal rectum".

According to Meltzer's description, this psychic "claustrum" is dominated by an atmosphere of terror, exposure to sadism, and the nameless fear of being "thrown away". Viewed from the outside, it is an unconscious fantasy of a place in the maternal object where the object's debris is stored, a world where the internal father and his genitals are assumed to perform the heroic task of saving life. But after the secret or violent intrusion via anal masturbation or anal rape, the rectum of the inner mother "becomes a region of satanic religion ruled by the great faecal penis; the world of Orwell's 'Big Brother'. It is thus a world of groups or rather tribes, similar to Bion's [1952] basic assumptions groups" (Meltzer, 1992, p. 92).

The result of this dynamic, writes Meltzer, is humiliation, the compulsion to undignified behaviour, and the weakening of conceptual thinking as the basis of action. "Truth is transformed into anything that cannot be disproved; justice becomes talion plus an increment; all the acts of intimacy change their meaning into techniques of manipulation of dissimulation; loyalty replaces devotion; obedience substitutes for trust; emotion is simulated by excitement; guilt and the yearning for punishment takes the place of regret" (1992, p. 92).

Although this condition imprisons and is marked by claustrophobia, it provides, foremost, sadistic pleasure and a certain type of self-idealisation in the identification with the maternal object and the faecal penis.

Meltzer writes: "In fact, the great faecal penis is not an object, but a self-object, compounded of a bad (disappointing, deserting) object and a cold (minus LHK) part of the self, at part object level, therefore primitive" (p. 92).

With that he gives some hope for therapy by understanding that: "This great malignant object can be metabolized in its component parts of self and object, and by this the malignant character is dissolved." And Meltzer comes to an important point: "But the therapeutic task is a difficult one, for this compounded object is a master of confusion and cynicism, appropriating to itself the quality of the internal father, of heroism and protectiveness." The heroism is of particular interest, for it alleges to be a hero-of-the-resistance to the tyranny of ethical considerations, by definition, the crucial one going far beyond the ego centricity of the paranoid–schizoid position" (p. 93).

The experience of sitting in front of a screen, alone, bombarded and intruded upon by certain propaganda which forces itself into the consumer, seems to create this unique condition.

In November 2016, a German left-wing journalist Florian Klenk, writing in the online journal *Falter*, reported a meeting with a hate-poster who once posted "Can someone light this guy" in response to a tweet that there should be Turkish subtitles to the news on national TV, which led to a heated discussion on FPÖ's Facebook page. The journalist contacted the hate-poster and finally met him. It turned out that this man was a successful family man who increasingly got into one of these filter bubbles and echo chambers and became radicalised in the media. He was able to impressively describe the dynamic of being sucked into a highly disquieting world full of "fake news", designed to stir up particular emotions. During this meeting he distanced himself from his ideas and finally even apologised for the hate-post.

Conclusion

Social media provides us with a huge number of new possibilities for communication, for working together with a lot of positive effects and also politically in the fight against injustice in various fields.

But there are increasing demands for legal solutions to the use of data, for transparency of the algorithms and prosecution of the "weapons of math-destruction", and legal measures against "fake news" and political data-harvesting, especially after the fraudulent activities of Cambridge Analytica that were discovered in March 2018.

For psychoanalysts it should be of foremost interest to understand how we might use ideas of the unconscious processes to counteract this particular "mass building" of individuals who are isolated in front of a screen, exposed to a program that creates in them the illusion of being surrounded by "friends", while at the same time they are being intruded upon by a targeted, emotionalising propaganda directed at subjecting them to an imprisoning state of mind and to turning them into a voter for a far-right-wing party.

There are different approaches being explored as to how to reinstall rational thinking and interrupt the emotional automatism. For instance, a website in Norway requires answers to three questions concerning an article before it can be shared or commented upon.

There is a need for much more intensive research on the particular psychic states caused by social media, working together with teams of different professions on the legal requirements and safeguards (additional buttons, etc.) which should be developed in order to prevent those dynamics, analogous to the ban on subliminal advertising, in the hope of reconstituting open, properly informed "political minds" not misinformed by the seductive and isolating aspects of social media.

Notes

1. Bannon is an American media executive, political strategist, former investment banker, and former executive chairman of Breitbart News. He served as White House chief strategist in the administration of President Trump during the first seven months of his term. He also served on the board of Cambridge Analytica, the data analytics firm involved in a data scandal involving Facebook (Wikipedia).

2. Fact-check sites that wish to provide fact-checking for Facebook must be compatible with the code of ethics of the respected journalism institution Poynter and follow the guidelines of impartiality and disclosure of creditors and key employees. In addition, they must have a clear procedure for correcting their own research mistakes. "Algorithms are therefore quite capable of throttling false reports within their range and and taking factors such as fact checks into account when weighting the content" (Brodnig, 2017, p. 69).

3. Some authors speak of an information war ("Infowars") and it is interesting that both Google and YouTube are deeply embedded in the right spectrum. Disinformation strategies of Russian media and "troll factories", fake profiles that disseminate Kremlin-friendly propaganda online, are currently being discussed worldwide and have even led to the creation of an EU website: euvsdisinfo.eu, which reports on false reports or biased reports by pro-Kremlin media. Especially in election campaigns in Eastern Europe, but also in France, Russian influence seems to have come over disinformation and it is known that far-right-wing parties maintain good contact with Russia.

References

Bion, W. R. (1952). Group dynamics: a review. *The International Journal of Psychoanalysis, 33*(2): 235–247.

Brodnig, I. (2017). *Lügen im Netz: Wie Fake News, Populisten und unkontrollierte Technik uns manipulieren*. Vienna: Brandstätter.

Bundeszentrale für politische Bildung: http://bpb.de/politik/extremismus/rechtspopulismus/192118/was-versteht-man-unter-populismus

Fenichel, O. (1940). Psychoanalysis of anti-Semitism. *American Imago, 1B*(2): 24–39.

Fessler, D. M. T., Pisor, A. C., & Holbrook, C. (2017). Political orientation predicts credulity regarding putative hazards. *Psychological Science 28*(5): 651–660.

Freud, S. (1921c). *Group Psychology and the Analysis of the Ego. S. E., 18*: 65–144. London: Hogarth.

Gentzkow, M., & Shapiro, J. M. (2011). Ideological segregation online and offline. *The Quarterly Journal of Economics 126*(4): 1799–1839.

Le Bon, G. (1896). *The Crowd: A Study of the Popular Mind*. New York: Cosimo, 2006.

McDougall, W. (1920). *The Group Mind*. Cambridge: Cambridge University Press.

Meltzer, D. (1992). *The Claustrum: An Investigation of Claustrophobic Phenomena*. Clunie, UK: The Roland Harris Education Trust.

Simmel, E. (1946). Anti-Semitism and mass-psychopathology. In: E. Simmel (Ed.), *Anti-Semitism: A Social Disease*. New York: International Universities Press.

Sunstein, C. R. (2018). *#Republic: Divided Democracy in the Age of Social Media*. Princeton, NJ: Princeton University Press.

Volkan, V. D. (1999). Psychoanalysis and diplomacy: part I. Individual and large group identity. *Journal of Applied Psychoanalytic Studies*, *1*(1): 29–55.

CHAPTER FIFTEEN

Winner of the 2020
Gavin Macfadyen Memorial Essay Prize

Lord of the flies: a psychoanalytic view of the gang and its processes

Mark Stein

Introduction

In this chapter I argue that gangs—the antithesis of groups and teams—are not exclusively manifest in obvious and extreme examples such as the Mafia and street gangs, but are potentially in everyday, run-of-the-mill groups, teams, and organisations, and that this should cause us considerable concern. I suggest that, following a trauma, groups, teams, and organisations may develop gang-like aspects that attack healthy functioning, and that the gang and its evil are thus potentially in all of us.

I use psychoanalysis and its application to social and organisational dynamics to provide a theoretical framework for the understanding of the gang. I draw first on the psychoanalytic perspective of the school of Melanie Klein (1946) who, while building on the work of Freud (1984), has initiated a stream of psychoanalytic ideas that has subsequently been widely used and theorised. Most notable for this paper is the work of Bion (1967a, 1967b). Second, I draw on Kleinian writings that focus specifically on the gang. Having explored both the idea of a gang in society as well as the "gang" within the individual mind, key here is the work of Rosenfeld (1987). I also use other works on the gang in the Kleinian tradition such as Canham (2002), Steiner (1993), Waddell (1998, 2002, 2007), Waddell and Williams (1991), and Williams (1997). Third, I draw on the application of Klein's ideas to social and organisational dynamics in the work of authors such as Armstrong (2005), Bion (1961), Obholzer and Roberts (1994), and Petriglieri and Stein (2012).

I use William Golding's 1958 novel *Lord of the Flies* to illustrate my ideas about the gang. In using Golding's work to give shape to my theme, I take my cue from a long line of psychoanalytic authors, who, beginning with Freud, have drawn on novels, plays, poetry, and mythology to frame their thinking. Indeed, as early as the *fin de siècle* correspondence with Wilhelm Fliess that Freud engaged in at the outset of his career, he made multiple references to themes from Shakespeare, Goethe, Dante, and Sophocles, and, most especially, to the "gripping power of *Oedipus Rex*" (Freud, 1954, p. 223). It is important to note that Freud's use of such sources was not subsequently somehow "appended" onto his psycho-analytic thinking, but, alongside his clinical work, was pivotal in shap-ing his ideas from the very start of his career, with Sophocles' Oedipus myth providing a crucial spark that ignited much of his thinking around human development. As I have argued elsewhere, sources such as nov-els, plays, poetry, and mythology are especially helpful in psychoanalytic scholarship because, "in personifying human dilemmas … [they pro-vide] … eloquent, precise expressions of them" (Stein, 2005, p. 1406) and are therefore able to articulate some of the "more complex, painful and seemingly intractable aspects" (p. 1406) of human life. For these reasons, Golding's great novel, with its fine-grained account of ganging processes, is central to my account.

The outline of this chapter is as follows. Following this introduction, I provide a precis of William Golding's *Lord of the Flies* as a way of illus-trating the concept of the gang. Following that, using psychoanalytic ideas, I explore several themes as they present themselves in the novel. I argue that gangs are often formed in response to traumatic, unbear-able events experienced by their members. I then explore the healthy attempts to deal with these difficulties, following which I argue that such healthy attempts are undermined by the burgeoning gang. I pro-pose that, unable to deal with the trauma its members have endured, the gang uses splitting and projective identification to unconsciously and perversely project its most admired (but problematic) aspects into the leader, and follow this by exploring how it uses these same mechanisms to project its unwanted aspects into those whom it hates. I then argue that the gang is committed to destroying the sensory and communicative apparatuses that inform it of reality, and in their place, constructs a defensive delusional "reality" that must be sustained so that gang members can avoid facing the truth. Propped up by its delusional view of the world and by projective identification, the gang is likely to enact savage attacks on enemies inside or outside it, and this wreaks enormous damage on everyone, including, ultimately, the gang itself.

Precis of *Lord of the Flies*

I turn now to William Golding's *Lord of the Flies* in order to illustrate gang phenomena. While psychoanalytically inspired authors such as Canham (2002) and Waddell (2002) have already made important links to the gang-like aspects in Golding's novel, inspired by their writings I take this further in this chapter by using the novel as a central plank in the construction of a theory of the gang. *Lord of the Flies* is the story of a group of schoolboys who, while being evacuated from England to a place of safety during the Second World War, are involved in an aeroplane crash just off a deserted island. The pilot dies in the accident, and, in the absence of adults, the boys are forced to try to organise and fend for themselves.

Among the older adolescent boys are Ralph and "Piggy" (a nickname), who form a group in an attempt to create some order so that they can all survive and get themselves rescued. Ralph has clear memories of his father, while Piggy strongly recalls the aunt who brought him up following the death of his parents. Both Ralph and Piggy are determined to find ways to help the boys survive, with Ralph clearly being a leader, and Piggy being more of an innovative thinker within this group. Piggy proposes holding meetings governed by rules that are called together by someone blowing into a conch (shell), where turns to speak are determined by who has the conch in their possession at that time. Although his rules and the conch are to some degree adopted by the boys, they are constantly under threat, while Piggy himself is mocked and laughed at by many of the boys because he is overweight, and has poor eyesight and asthma.

There is also another older boy, Jack, who makes a powerful and ulti-mately dangerous bid for leadership. Head boy and chapter chorister at the school, Jack is highly rivalrous with Ralph in his ambition for leader-ship. Jack also dislikes Piggy, and is unhappy with the rules and the use of the conch. It is agreed initially that Jack and his group of choristers should go off and hunt for food, with Ralph's group (of which Piggy is a member) remaining to keep a fire going in order to attract the attention of passing ships. Over time, Jack and Ralph and their groups of followers are increasingly in conflict with each other.

The conflict between the two groups is shaped by a number of serious problems that confront the schoolboys. As well as struggling to main-tain some order and a capacity to think and organise themselves, they have little food, shelter, or protection from the elements. They cannot decide on their priorities and get into considerable disagreement about whether hunting for food, keeping a fire going, or building shelters is most important. Further, having no matches, the boys are hampered by being entirely dependent on Piggy's glasses to start a fire. To add to this, the "littluns" (younger boys) are terrified of an imaginary wild animal on the island (the "beastie"), with this fear escalating among the boys and increasingly dominating their thoughts.

Painting themselves with clay and charcoal, and almost naked, Jack's group of hunters become more and more gang-like, whipping themselves up into a frenzy so that they become obsessed with hunting and killing. When it is their turn to keep the fire going, they forget to do so, so that a passing ship is not aware that there is anyone on the island and sails on. Then, shouting "*Kill the Pig! Cut his throat! Kill the pig*" (Golding, 1958, p. 125—emphasis in original), they kill a sow and place its head on a stick. The pig's head on a stick—the *Lord of the Flies*—is intended both as a "gift" to the beast, and, later, as a way of terrorising the boys who are the enemies of Jack and his gang. In due course, the terror about beasts becomes widespread and begins to dominate the actions of the boys.

While Ralph's group maintains some capacity to continue to think and keep a sensible order, Jack's gang becomes increasingly vio-lent and dangerous, with Jack maintaining an iron rule over his follow-ers and expecting total obedience. The gang then turns from hunting pigs to attacking Ralph's rival group, as well as certain of their own gang members. Indeed, in a situation in which all the boys are profoundly vulnerable because of the lack of food, water, and shelter, Jack's gang becomes focused on attacking certain of the boys, and, in doing so, has largely given up on the real task of survival, ultimately putting all their lives at risk. Gang members steal fire from Ralph's group, take Piggy's glasses, and then murder him.

Further, a member of Jack's gang called Simon has a delirious, mysterious communication with the *Lord of the Flies*—the pig's head on a stick—who tells him that there is no beast and that "I'm part of you" (p. 158). Having stumbled across the body of a dead parachutist, Simon then runs frantically to tell members of the gang what he has seen, whereupon they murder him. The gang then captures, ties up, and tortures some of the boys, and tries to hunt Ralph, crush him with boulders, or smoke him out of his hiding place, causing a fire that burns a vast amount of foliage so that "the island was scorched up like dead wood" (p. 224). Just as they are hunting Ralph in order to try to kill him, the boys are rescued by the arrival of adults on the island.

The traumatic experience

Using psychoanalytic ideas, I now turn our attention to making sense of *Lord of the Flies*. In the context of war, the schoolboys have survived a plane crash and found themselves in a situation without adults; they have lost their parents, families, teachers, school, homes, and everything they have, and are therefore highly traumatised. Trauma may be understood as an injury to the mind caused by highly distressing events (Garland, 1998, p. 9) that are "etched" (Sklar, 2011, p. 2) into the psyche so that the victim is inclined to "relive the event … [but be] … unable to master the feelings it aroused" (Kahn, 2003, p. 366). While responses to trauma may vary, many of those who are traumatised may be inclined to experience deep feelings of vulnerability and anxiety, especially annihilation anxiety. Such anxiety may stay with victims, in varying degrees, for the rest of their lives and constitutes the "unbearable affect" (Stolorow, 2007, p. 9) of traumatisation.

As a result of their trauma, a phantasy is generated among the schoolboys that the adult world may have entirely collapsed and died: as Piggy says to Ralph, "Didn't you hear what the pilot said? About the atom bomb? They're all dead" (Golding, 1958, p. 9), a statement that gives voice to the phantasy that the adult world may have been completely killed off or destroyed. This refers not only to the parents, teachers, and other adults in the lives of the schoolboys, but also to adult functioning in general, foreshadowing the idea that effective leadership and authority may no longer be possible, and that chaos may reign on the island. Central to the contribution of the novel is thus the notion that the gang is born out of trauma and anxiety and in the absence—literally or metaphorically—of adult authority, where such authority is felt to have collapsed, died, or been killed off.

A key manifestation of the boys' trauma concerns their terror of wild animals or beasts. While this is especially felt by the littluns, as Golding puts it, "perhaps … [the littluns] … felt themselves to share in a sorrow that was universal" (p. 93), so that their fears symbolically expressed the anxieties of all the boys, as well as infecting all of them with terror. The boys become increasingly convinced of the existence of a "Beast from Water" (p. 81) and a "Beast from Air" (p. 103), with certain boys being persuaded that they had "seen the beast with our own eyes" (p. 108), a creature that has very specific characteristics so that, according to one version, it is known to be furry, with wings, eyes, teeth, and claws (pp. 108–109). The night becomes a particularly terrifying time, "full of claws, full of the awful unknown and menace" (p. 107).

In fact, there is no evidence at all of any dangerous animals or beasts, and the sighting of a pilot who had parachuted onto the island—"a sign … [that] … came down from the world of grown-ups" (p. 103)—was confused with a beast. Thus, the appearance of the "beast" may be understood as the return of a traumatic memory, the haunting of the boys' world by the world of the grown-ups that they had lost, a reminder of the "death" of the adult world that had left them bereft and ill-equipped to address the challenges ahead. To borrow from O'Shaughnessy (1964), the good, absent object (the adult world) has become a bad, present object (the beast), one that terrorises the boys, leading them to becoming obsessed with its destruction.

Healthy dependency and survival in the wake of trauma

In spite of the trauma of the plane crash and the perilous situation they face on the island, some attempts are made by certain of the boys to establish order and create a coherent, functioning group. The main initiative to create order comes from Ralph and Piggy, two of the older boys who have strong links with their pasts. Ralph and Piggy may be understood to have "resilience ... [which] ... is the capacity to withstand destructive impulses and experiences" (Waddell, 2007, p. 189), and, as best they can, recover emotionally from their trauma and resist engaging in ganging. Both Ralph and Piggy maintain a connection with reality and the adult world, and acknowledge their healthy dependency needs: indeed, Ralph and Piggy are the only two characters who make any significant reference to their families, and this connection helps them maintain a link with the adult world and adult functioning.

Ralph has powerful memories of his home, a hope that his father will rescue the boys, and, while exercising leadership, is also capable of feelings of longing, anxiety, and guilt, as well as having the capacity for self-reflection and self-criticism. Although his position is regularly under threat from Jack, Ralph is thus able to exercise his leadership over his group because he has a "link with the adult world of authority" (Golding, 1958, p. 61).

Piggy, like Ralph, also has strong memories of home, and these help him to hold on to a sense of hope and maintain a desire that life would improve one day. Piggy is also able to support Ralph at moments of despair: "Supposing I got like the others—not caring. What 'ud become of us?" (p. 153) asks Ralph, to which Piggy responds: "We just got to go on, that's all. That's what grown-ups would do" (p. 153). While Ralph and Piggy do not always get on very well, this interdependence constitutes a sign of effective work group and adult-like functioning. The capacities of both Ralph and Piggy, coupled with their abilities to work together, further enable considerable parental concern in them so that they are able to hold the littluns in mind and care for them as best they can.

While Ralph clearly intends to be leader, he also realises that he needs to work alongside Piggy because "Piggy could think. He could go step by step inside that fat head of his" (p. 83). Added to this, Piggy has "intellectual daring" (p. 142), the capacity to think creatively. Piggy makes many important suggestions, some of which are acted upon (such as the building of shelters), and others of which are dismissed (such as creating a sundial).

Together, Ralph and Piggy provide the possibility of boys working together in an organised, rule-based way, and thus "represent a struggle to stay as a group ... [and] ... organize a democratic assembly" (Canham, 2002, p. 119) that constitutes the boys' best chance of survival. In the absence of parents and other adults, they create a set of rules, because, as Ralph puts it, they "are the only thing we've got" (Golding, 1958, p. 99), so that, as mentioned earlier, turn taking in speaking is determined by who has the conch. Once again, these features suggest that Ralph's group is linked with reality, authority, and adulthood, thus increasing the possibility of survival.

Wanted identities and the appointment of a delinquent gang leader

Working against Ralph and Piggy and their relationship with reality and the adult world, however, are those who oppose these values, and, in particular, Jack and his burgeoning gang. Central to the functioning of the gang are, first, splitting (Klein, 1946; Rosenfeld, 1987), the primitive mechanism that involves radically separating out the wanted, "good" aspects from the unwanted, "bad" aspects, resulting in them appearing thoroughly separate and exaggerated; and, second, projective identification (Klein, 1946; Petriglieri & Stein, 2012; Rosenfeld, 1987), whereby certain of these wanted and unwanted aspects of members of the gang are unconsciously projected into others.

Importantly, Klein's concept of projective identification constitutes a broader idea than Freud's notion of projection because it involves not only projected feelings, but also parts or functions of the self that may be unconsciously split off and projected into the other (Mason, 2012, p. 303). Such splitting and projective identification of parts of the self are engaged in by people in order "to protect themselves from consciously experiencing unbearable feelings" (Petriglieri & Stein, 2012, p. 1222), and are thus mechanisms of defence (Braddock, 2011, p. 645), and this is particularly the case with the gang: splitting and projective identification protect gang members from having to face the reality of their situation, as well as the terrifying anxieties associated with it. These mechanisms are especially likely to be used for the evasion of trauma and the painful feelings associated with it because they absolve the gang of uncomfortable feelings of loss, anxiety, and guilt, and of the need to face the magnitude of the difficulties that confront it.

As indicated above, two types of splitting and projective identification—of wanted and unwanted elements of the gang—are involved. While in ordinary groups the splitting and projective identification are likely to involve more everyday aspects that are unconsciously projected, in a gang both wanted and unwanted aspects may include more extreme, perverse (Long, 2002), and sadistic elements. The first of these—the projection of the wanted characteristics—involves the perverse idealisation by gang members of their most disturbed and dangerous aspects, aspects that are then split off and projected into the gang leader. In particular, the gang leader embodies the idea there is no need to feel sad or to have to worry about anything, that the gang is entirely self-sufficient, all-powerful, and needs no one, and that a wonderful, pleasure-filled future awaits. To borrow from Rosenfeld, it is the "omnipotent destructive parts of the self" (1987, p. 106) that are split off, so that the gang leader is unconsciously felt to embody the most wanted, albeit disturbed aspect of each of the boys, and is as a consequence idealised and glorified.

Thus, having bolstered the ganging process by cutting the throat of a sow and placing its head on a stick, "Jack, painted and garlanded, sat there like an idol" (Golding, 1958, p. 164), surrounded by piles of pig meat on green leaves, fruit, and coconut shells, together with his admiring, albeit somewhat terrified, followers. This idolisation of Jack is a necessary element in binding together the gang to ensure that members can continue and indeed intensify their killing spree until all their enemies are done away with, with the phantasy that they can go on to enjoy a life filled with pleasure, albeit of a particularly perverse kind. Stoked up by the leader, central to this pleasure is vengeance, so that, as Steiner puts it, the gang increasingly becomes "expert in revenge ... [and promises] ... the ... destruction of ... enemies" (1993, p. 86).

Important in the recruitment of gang members is that they are enticed into the gang by the leader, being given the impression that they are entirely at liberty to join—and by implication, decline to join—according to their wishes: "Me and my hunters", proclaims Jack, "hunt and feast and have fun. If you want to join my tribe come and see us" (p. 154). Jack's gang thus presents itself as open and accessible to those interested in the pleasures of hunting and feasting, as well as representing "the temptation … to forget … [any] … responsibilities and … [lead] … a life free from … worries" (Canham, 2002, p. 119).

However, the reality is much different from this: rather than being free to join or leave, members are compelled to become involved with the gang and are forced into obedience, with some being captured, tied up, and beaten. In particular, the gang captures Sam and Eric, two of the littluns, forcing them to join up, as well as betray Ralph's hiding place so that the gang can pursue him with the intention of killing him. Thus, while claiming to lead a group that allows freedom of choice, Jack actually demands precisely the opposite, requiring total obedience from his followers, while terrorising and murdering those who oppose him. This tyranny involves the idea that there is no chance of escape and no possibility of any existence outside the gang (Williams, 1997, p. 56). It also involves controlling members of the gang to ensure that, to borrow from Rosenfeld, they "support one another in making the criminal destructive work more effective and powerful" (1987, p. 111), and "do not desert the destructive organization … or betray the secrets of the gang" (1971, p. 174).

As well as stoking up the idealisation of his followers, Jack thus also instills fear and obedience into them, whereby "Authority is perverted into dominance" (Dartington, 2010, p. 300): instead of the turn-taking and the use of the conch in the group led by Ralph, Jack operates in a highly authoritarian way in the gang, taking all the decisions himself, and making pronouncements that are followed by his acolytes raising their spears and exclaiming that "The Chief has spoken" (Golding, 1958, p. 155). As a consequence, an atmosphere of "intimidation, fear or reprisal and a coercion to conform" (Canham, 2002, p. 115) is created, so that the gang leader exercises a "tyrannical hold" (Waddell & Williams, 1991, p. 209) over the members.

Importantly, as Canham points out, Jack and his followers become "parodies of powerful grown-ups" (2002, p. 120), so that, having in phantasy "become" the parents, they feign certain aspects of mature parental and adult functioning, while simultaneously enacting the opposite, the delinquent gang. As well as the pretence of the boys being free to join the gang while effectively being coerced into it, another aspect of the parody of adulthood concerns how the boys address each other. In particular, at the outset, immediately after having proposed that the boys follow their school's rather formal and respectful traditions by calling each other by their surnames, Jack addresses Piggy by saying "shut up, Fatty" (Golding, 1958, p. 17). This demeaning of Piggy initiates a hateful, spiralling process that involves Piggy being regularly insulted, punched and smacked in the head, having his glasses stolen and then broken, and, ultimately, being murdered. Rather than having adult qualities, in reality Jack thus embodies a pretence of adulthood, becoming increasingly violent, vengeful, and tyrannical. To borrow from Darnley, Doctor, Gordon, and Kirtchuk, this is a scenario in which "the psychotic part ... [tries] ... to impersonate the non-psychotic part" (2011, p. 55), so that the gang pretends to embody adulthood while, in reality, perversely misrepresenting it; such psychotic aspects are explored further later in this chapter.

Unwanted identities and the creation of enemies

The counterpoint of the splitting and projective identification of the wanted identities is the use of these mechanisms in relation to unwanted identities, involving the projection of characteristics associated with disliked aspects of the gang. Such splitting and projective identification of the unwanted aspects of the gang into its enemies are therefore "likely to create fractures in relationships" (Stein & Pinto, 2011, p. 696) that deepen existing fault-lines and initiate new divisions because they involve the investment of these unwanted aspects in others. Hatred and violence are enacted on enemies both within and outside the gang, so that the bullying of these others becomes the gang's modus operandi (Waddell, 2007, p. 189).

However, as already mentioned, the gang embodies perverse elements so that, paradoxically, those who are attacked and bullied are hated precisely because they represent the good and healthy aspects that the gang has lost. Thus, while splitting and projective identification are likely to occur in all groups and teams, in a gang the targets are often perversely the most intact and integrated individuals, precisely because they represent what the gang has lost and cannot be. Specifically, the individuals who are targeted are those who are healthy enough to be (a) aware of their own vulnerability, (b) aware of the reality of what is going on, and (c) connected with the responsible, adult world. Those boys who are felt to be especially problematic are therefore those in touch with the truth of the catastrophe that has been suffered, and who provide a glimpse of the terrible reality that needs to be faced, so that they and their message must at all costs be thwarted and attacked. Indeed, to borrow from Bion, for those in this gang state of mind, there would appear to be "no problems other than the existence" (1967a, p. 88) of those who have had access to the truth, and these people must therefore be destroyed.

Thus, while there is a real need to hunt for food, such hunting becomes perversely twisted because Jack's gang cannot bear others who have the healthy qualities it has lost, and it becomes intent on hunting these individuals and attempting to destroy them. As Canham puts it, Jack's gang may be understood to be ultimately driven by an obsession or an "*idée fixe*, which is that their survival is dependent on killing the pigs which inhabit the jungle interior of the island" (2002, p. 119), and this *idée fixe* is soon transferred to the destruction and murder of people, a notion that hinges on the unconscious projection of unwanted aspects into specific individuals.

Some of those attacked are specific members within the gang, and this occurs in particular when the gang becomes engaged in a frenzied and ritualised dance, chanting once again that a beast should be killed, and its blood spilled. One of the gang members then pretends to be the pig and is at the centre of a circle of hunters who are chanting and taunting him. However, when this stops and he becomes a hunter again, "the centre of the ring yawned emptily" (Golding, 1958, p. 168), at which point, a "thing was crawling out of the forest. It came darkly, uncertainly" (p. 168) into the centre. This "thing" or "beast" is in fact another gang member, Simon, who has stumbled across the dead parachutist elsewhere on the island, and is "crying out something about a dead man on a hill" (p. 168). Simon is then turned upon and savagely murdered: "the crowd … leapt on to the beast, screamed, struck, bit, tore" (p. 169), so killing him.

There are particular reasons why, in representing that which is unwanted within the gang, Simon must be killed off. Simon is murdered because he is desperately trying to tell everyone that he has seen the dead parachutist, "a sign … from the world of grown-ups" (p. 103), and that there is no beast after all. He is also the boy who has a peculiar, hallucinatory communication with the mother figure of the sow's head on a stick, the *Lord of the Flies*, one that involves an "ancient, inescapable recognition" (p. 152). Because of this recognition and his connection to the adult world, Simon cannot be permitted to exist. What in particular cannot be tolerated is the idea that Simon carries the truth not only that there is no beast, but, as the sow's head "says" to him, "You knew, didn't you? I'm part of you" (p. 158). In other words, Simon must be killed off because he carries the knowledge that, rather than having a separate existence, the beast, being a residue of a traumatic memory, is actually within the boys themselves.

Similar destructive, projective processes occur in relation to those outside the gang, so that there is the development of an unrelenting desire to pursue members of the other group and capture or murder them. As already noted, with a central character in the other group having the nickname "Piggy", the ambiguity around which "pigs" are due to be killed becomes an increasingly menacing aspect of life on the island. This destructive frenzy reaches it apotheosis when, "with a sense of delirious abandonment" (p. 200), one of the gang levers a large rock from a cliff onto Piggy, who is knocked some forty feet onto another rock in the sea, so that his "arms and legs twitched a bit, like a pig's after it has been killed" (p. 201), and then drowns.

Importantly, while Piggy represents a number of human characteristics within the novel, as discussed, he also powerfully represents a connection with the adult world and with the truth. Piggy is the most adult-like of all the boys, taking seriously and trying to address the profound difficulties the boys face, with his conch and rules being emblematic of adult organisations and co-operation. He is also deeply aware of the precarious position the boys are in. For these reasons, the connection with adulthood and the truth, Piggy must be killed off.

Finally, because he too is in touch with the adult world and with the truth, Ralph must also be attacked with murderous intent. Ralph is particularly irksome to Jack because he challenges Jack's leadership, and this binds the two leaders together in an endless, destructive cycle. As Ralph comes to realise, "there was that indefinable connection between himself and Jack; who therefore would never let him alone; never" (p. 204). It is thus perhaps no coincidence that the arc of the story closes with Jack's gang ruthlessly pursuing Ralph with the intention of killing him. This speaks of the way in which, when ganging occurs, powerful projective processes lock rival leaders together so that the gang leader feels impelled to engage in unrelenting, murderous attacks on the leader who opposes him, not ceasing in this pursuit until that leader is destroyed.

Destruction of sensory and communicative apparatuses

A further issue is that, being intent on destroying both reality and also the healthy, dependent group that is aware of this reality, the gang must attack and dismantle all sensory and communicative apparatuses supplying information about the real world. A key sensory apparatus is Piggy's glasses, which, as well as the capacity to make fire, represent the ability to observe reality, with, as mentioned above, Piggy being most in touch with the real world of all the boys. Both literally and figuratively, Piggy is able to observe the reality of life on the island, and also witness the resulting vulnerability of the situation of the boys, and this cannot be tolerated by the gang. Thus, when Jack and his gang raid Ralph's group to steal Piggy's glasses, an important juncture in the establishment of the gang has been reached: "The Chief [Jack] ... *was a chief now in truth* ... From his left hand dangled Piggy's broken glasses" (p. 186—emphasis added). The theft and shattering of Piggy's glasses thus not only confirms Jack as a leader, but also represents the symbolic destruction and fragmentation of the perceptual apparatus that provides access to reality, and is therefore a crucial point in the establishment of the gang.

Further, as mentioned above, there is the communicative apparatus of the conch, effectively a "voice" to call the democratic assembly together, one that represents a link to the adult world and the possibility of organisation and order. When at the outset Piggy first sees the conch in the lagoon, he relates how he once knew a boy who had one: "He used to blow it and then his mum would come. It's ever so valuable" (p. 11). The conch thus signifies an important link to the world of the mother figure on whom the young child depends, as well as the world of adulthood, parenthood, and order. As Waddell puts it, the conch represents "the combined capacity of parenthood ... [and is] ... a resource for the thinking capacities" (1998, p. 131), as well as the communication of that thinking. As the gang has in phantasy usurped the adult world and "become" the adult authority, such links are felt to be intolerable, and the conch must therefore be destroyed. Thus, when Piggy is killed by a massive boulder levered from a high cliff onto him, the conch is also hit and "exploded into a thousand tiny white fragments and ceased to exist" (Golding, 1958, p, 200).

This process of the destruction of sensory and communicative apparatuses may be understood to involve psychotic thinking—that is, thinking dominated by psychotic processes, but which may be engaged in by people and groups who are not necessarily psychotic, but may indeed, at least in some ways, appear relatively normal. Key here is the two-part nature of psychosis, as noted by Darnley, Doctor, Gordon, and Kirtchuk (2011, p. 55): the first part is the denial, disavowal, or destruction of unacceptable reality associated with a psychic "catastrophe", trauma, or breakdown that cannot be faced; while the second part, described later in this chapter, involves the construction of a new and illusory substitute "reality" to replace the real world that is disavowed. Both parts are defensive and are necessary for the repression of memories and feelings in order to protect against "traumatic … [breaches] … which are powerful enough to break through the protective shield" (Freud, 1984, p. 301) in the mind.

Actions that enable this first aspect (the disavowal or destruction of reality) to take place are imperative because, to borrow from Rosenfeld, "Any contact with reality … inevitably … is felt as very dangerous" (1987, p. 87), so that all sensory and communicative apparatuses that convey such reality must be smashed into bits and fragmented. To borrow from Bion, the "capacity for judgement … [is] … split up and destroyed … and then ejected" (1967b, p. 100) … so that a "visual impression … [is] … minutely fragmented" (p. 99) into tiny particles. Alternatively, to draw on Darnley, Doctor, Gordon, and Kirtchuk, "the psychotic part … [attacks] … all aspects … responsible for the registration of … reality, minutely fragmenting and projecting all aspects of the mind" (2011, p. 56). Piggy's glasses and the conch must therefore be destroyed by being smashed to bits and fragmented so that they become useless, no longer having any meaningful use or function.

Regarding the communicative aspects specifically, in representing a dangerous contact with reality, both Piggy (who encourages thinking and conversation) and the conch (that makes it possible for people to communicate in an orderly fashion) may also be understood, to borrow from Bion, to be experienced by the gang as highly problematic "obstructing forces" (1967a, p. 90). Specifically, by "insisting on verbal communication ... [of reality they are] ... felt to be directly attacking the ... [psychotic] ... methods of communication" (Bion, 1967a, p. 91), and thus must be destroyed.

Construction of a new, substitute "reality"

The first part of the psychotic process (the destruction of unacceptable reality), as discussed above, is accompanied by a second aspect that involves the creation of a new, substitute, illusory "reality". This substitute reality involves delusions that provide a "patch" that appears to repair the rent between the ego, that controls the sensory and communicative apparatuses, and reality (Darnley, Doctor, Gordon, & Kirtchuk, 2011, p. 56). Together with the disavowal of painful realities, this construction of an illusory substitute reality may be understood as a defence, so that the painful issues are consigned to the unconscious. To draw again on Rosenfeld, this is psychotic because, "dominated by an omnipotent or omniscient, extremely ruthless part of the self" (1987, p. 112), a delusional, perverse world is created in which there is an experience of "complete painlessness and also the freedom to indulge in any sadistic activity" (p. 112).

The construction of this alternative, delusional reality is vividly illustrated by the functioning of Jack's gang. According to this substitute reality, the boys need not worry much about shelter, attracting the attention of passing ships, or looking after each other, but instead can indulge in hunting, playing war games, perverse destruction, and revenge. They are thus absolved of all moral responsibility, guilt, and anxiety, as well as the duty to work and to look after themselves and each other. Instead, they are led to believe that they can enjoy a life without pain, and a future that involves perverse pleasure and excitement, without struggle or hardship.

The transformation that enables gang members to create and enact this new reality involves them painting their faces and bodies with clay and charcoal, and, almost entirely naked, being psychologically "transported" to a different world, one dominated by perverse pleasures. As Jack explains, they would paint themselves—"You know, dazzle paint. Like things trying to look like something else" (Golding, 1958, p. 66), a change that made it possible for him to hide behind his mask and be "liberated from shame and self-consciousness" (p. 66). Those who join his gang are thus apparently freed from the anxieties about the catastrophe of their plight and are able to become "demoniac figures with faces of white and red and green ... [who] ... rushed out howling, so that the littluns fled screaming" (p. 154), "anonymous savages" (p. 155) in pursuit of hunting, feasting, dancing, and destruction.

Excited, almost naked, and disguised with painted faces and bodies, the boys then engage in a frenzied attack on a pig, killing it, and putting its head on a stick as a "gift" to the beast. Significantly, the pig they stumble across is a sow, a female pig "in deep maternal bliss" (p. 147), surrounded by her piglets suckling and sleeping. The gang of hunters, "wedded to her in lust" (p. 148), may be understood to have symbolically engaged in a highly sexualised and perverse act, with Jack "on top of the sow, stabbing downwards with his knife" (p. 149) and another boy plunging his spear "right up her ass!" (p. 149), so that the sow finally collapses with the boys "fulfilled upon her" (p. 149).

The killing of the sow is thus, in phantasy, a perverse attack on the mother, who is symbolically gang raped, murdered, and then eaten, so that the "gift" may also be understood to be the decapitated mother's head as a "present" to the father, and thus also a violent and perverse attack on the parents and their relationship. As I have argued elsewhere, the male gang generates a "macho culture which keeps out any trace of weakness, uncertainty, or vulnerability" (Stein & Pinto, 2011, p. 711), as well as feelings of affection, love, and gratitude. The brutal killing of the sow is therefore emblematic of a perverse triumph over the feminine and over the mother in particular, as well as the contemptuous destruction of the mother's world, the parental couple, and adulthood more widely. It also signifies the initiation of a new, illusory reality in which the gang has usurped the adult world, making it possible, at least in phantasy, for members to enjoy infinite pleasure in the absence of responsibility. This attack is a central message in the story because the book's title—*Lord of the Flies*—refers to the sow's head on a stick as a gift to the beast, and by implication to a violent and perverse attack on the mother and the parental union.

The increasingly gang-like way of thinking has considerable momentum because, together with the painting of the boys' faces and bodies, the smashing of the conch, and the murder of Piggy and Simon, the symbolic killing off of the mother and the parental couple transports the boys into a perverse world without limits or constraints. As Golding puts it, "The breaking of the conch and the deaths of … [the two boys] … lay over the island like a vapour. These painted savages would go further and further" (1958, p. 204), unleashing a destructive havoc that, in the absence of the arrival of adults on the island, would have been impossible to stop.

Conclusion

In conclusion, the view that I develop in this chapter locates the phenomena of gangs in a crucial, perhaps surprising place: especially following a trauma, ordinary groups, teams, and organisations may exhibit gang-like ways of thinking and acting that, in certain circumstances, lead them to become fully fledged gangs. Where such ganging develops, members are inclined to celebrate that which is perverse and dangerous so that the "success" of the gang pivots on the enactment of hatred, revenge, and destruction. It is suggested that this is of relevance to seemingly ordinary organisations such as governmental, business, public, and voluntary organisations because, as Armstrong argues, "Every organization contains a pathological version of itself" (2005, p. 81) that is latent and may in certain circumstances be activated, and this can also equally be said of groups and teams. These pathological versions may be unleashed—sometimes quite precipitously—by untoward, traumatic events, events that initiate processes that may unravel dangerously and with considerable speed. This is an important feature of *Lord of the Flies* because the gang emerges from a group of apparently ordinary, everyday schoolboys who suffer a catastrophic trauma, and as a result descend into anarchy and perverse destruction.

The account given in this chapter, as illustrated by Golding's 1958 novel, proposes that this descent into ganging involves splitting and projective identification so that a powerful, delinquent gang leader is invested with heroic and perverse aspects of gang members. To borrow from Steiner, this may involve sadistic elements in which members have "phantasied relationships with powerful, cruel figures" (1993, p. 48) that enable the gang to do its work. As a result, the gang may thus take "a psychotic form … [that offers] … a delusional world where freedom from pain and anxiety are promised" (p. 45). Such psychotic phenomena may sweep up even those ordinarily not much inclined to ganging:

as Waddell argues, ganging can involve "acting mindlessly in the gang of peers ... [even where individual members] ... would be unlikely to be able to do alone" (2007, p. 200). In this sense, the group/gang may have a greater capacity for psychosis than the individual.

It is important to add that these phenomena are probably more widespread than often acknowledged. In this context, Bell warns of "pretenders" (2011, p. 95) who are to be found in various individual, group, and institutional contexts within our societies. Such pretenders engage in processes of mimicry and imitation so that—in the absence of thinking—there is a pretence of thought, the attempt to "overthrow knowledge ... [and the] ... degradation of thinking" (p. 95). This may result in the creation of "cults ... [and] ... moral tyranny" (p. 95), delin-quency, ganging, and the perversion of the truth.

Worryingly, ganging dynamics are especially likely to emerge in sce-narios of "crisis and risk" (Stein & Pinto, 2011, p. 712) because of the likelihood of trauma in such situations. Indeed, precisely because of the widespread trauma that will inevitably be left in their wake, phenomena such as climate change, famine, wars, and pandemics could lead to the pervasive spread of ganging processes, and this should cause us much concern. The problem is deepened because, when the dust of a crisis has settled, or seems to have settled, there is often a failure to learn from experience, with "the real issues ... about gang culture ... [being] ... obfuscated" (p. 713), both because ganging phenomena may go unrec-ognised or are not properly understood, and also because the gang-like forces remain undiminished. As a result, the conditions for further ganging behaviour are sometimes set in train. It is against this perhaps gloomy background that my chapter has been written, with my hope being that I might be able to shed some light—and add to thinking—in relation to these difficult phenomena.

Acknowledgements

I would like to thank various people for their comments on earlier drafts of this text, including Jina Barrett, Tim Dartington, Angela Foster, Antje Netzer-Stein, Lionel Stapley, and Margot Waddell. I would also like to thank Stephanie Creary, Robin Ely, Elizabeth Hansen, Michael Jarrett, Sally Maitlis, Gianpiero Petriglieri, and Jennifer Petriglieri for the dis-cussion and comments on an early draft at INSEAD. I also owe much gratitude to William Halton, who has guided my writing projects over many years, and who has made a crucial contribution to this essay. The responsibility for the views expressed in this chapter are entirely my own.

References

Armstrong, D. (2005). *Organization in the Mind: Psychoanalysis, Group Relations and Organizational Consultancy.* London: Karnac.

Bell, D. (2011). Bion: The phenomenologist of loss. In: C. Mawson (Ed.), *Bion Today* (pp. 81–101). London: Routledge/New Library of Psychoanalysis.

Bion, W. R. (1961). *Experiences in Groups, and Other Papers.* London: Tavistock.

Bion, W. R. (1967a). On arrogance. In: W. R. Bion (Ed.), *Second Thoughts: Selected Papers on Psychoanalysis* (pp. 86–92). London: Maresfield.

Bion, W. R. (1967b). Attacks on linking. In: W. R. Bion (Ed.), *Second Thoughts: Selected Papers on Psychoanalysis* (pp. 93–109). London: Maresfield.

Braddock, L. (2011). Psychological identification, imagination and psychoanalysis. *Philosophical Psychology, 24*(5): 639–657.

Canham, H. (2002). Group and gang states of mind. *Journal of Child Psychotherapy, 28*(2): 113–127.

Darnley, B., Doctor, R., Gordon, J., & Kirtchuk, G. (2011). Psychotic processes in forensic institutions. *Psychoanalytic Psychotherapy, 25*(1): 55–68.

Dartington, T. (2010). *Managing Vulnerability: The Underlying Dynamics of Systems of Care.* London: Karnac.

Freud, S. (1954). *The Origins of Psycho-Analysis: Letters to Wilhelm Fliess, 1887–1902.* M. Bonaparte, A. Freud, & E. Kris (Eds.). New York: Basic Books.

Freud, S. (1984). *On Metapsychology: The Theory of Psychoanalysis: Beyond the Pleasure Principle, The Ego and the Id, and Other Works* (Pelican Freud Library, Vol 11). A. Richards (Ed.). London: Penguin.

Garland, C. (1998). Thinking about trauma. In: C. Garland (Ed.), *Understanding Trauma: A Psychoanalytical Approach* (pp. 9–31). London: Duckworth.

Golding, W. (1958). *Lord of the Flies.* London: Faber and Faber.

Kahn, W. A. (2003). The revelation of organizational trauma. *Journal of Applied Behavioral Science, 39*(4): 364–380.

Klein, M. (1946). Notes on some schizoid mechanisms. In: *Envy and Gratitude and Other Works 1946–1963* (pp. 1–24). London: Hogarth, 1975.

Long, S. (2002). Organisational destructivity and the perverse state of mind. *Organisational and Social Dynamics, 2*(2): 179–207.

Mason, A. (2012). Vicissitudes of projective identification. In: E. Spillius & E. O'Shaughnessy (Eds.), *Projective Identification: The Fate of a Concept* (pp. 301–320). London: Routledge.

Obholzer, A., & Roberts, V. Z. (Eds.). (1994). *The Unconscious at Work: Individual and Organizational Stress in the Human Services.* London: Routledge.

O'Shaughnessy, E. (1964). The absent object. *Journal of Child Psychotherapy*, *1*(2): 34–43.

Petriglieri, G., & Stein, M. (2012). The unwanted self: Projective identification in leaders' identity work. *Organization Studies*, *33*(9): 1217–1235.

Rosenfeld, H. A. (1971). A clinical approach to the psychoanalytic theory of the life and death instincts: An investigation into the aggressive aspects of narcissism. *The International Journal of Psychoanalysis*, *52*(2): 169–178.

Rosenfeld, H. A. (1987). *Impasse and Interpretation: Therapeutic and Anti-therapeutic Factors in the Psychoanalytic Treatment of Psychotic, Borderline, and Neurotic Patients.* London: Tavistock and the Institute of Psycho-Analysis.

Sklar, J. (2011). *Landscapes in the Dark: History, Trauma, Psychoanalysis.* London: Karnac.

Stein, M. (2005). The Othello conundrum: The inner contagion of leadership. *Organization Studies*, *26*(9): 1405–1409.

Stein, M., & Pinto, J. (2011). The dark side of groups: A "gang at work" in Enron. *Group & Organization Management*, *36*(6): 692–721.

Steiner, J. (1993). *Psychic Retreats: Pathological Organizations in Psychotic, Neurotic and Borderline Patients.* London: Routledge.

Stolorow, R. D. (2007). *Trauma and Human Existence: Autobiographical, Psychoanalytic and Philosophical Reflections.* New York: Routledge/Taylor & Francis.

Waddell, M. (1998). The scapegoat. In: R. Anderson & A. Dartington (Eds.), *Facing It Out: Clinical Perspectives on Adolescent Disturbance* (pp. 127–141). London: Duckworth.

Waddell, M. (2002). The psychodynamics of bullying. *Free Associations*, *9*(2): 189–210.

Waddell, M. (2007). Grouping or ganging: The psychodynamics of bullying. *British Journal of Psychotherapy*, *23*(2): 189–204.

Waddell, M., & Williams, G. (1991). Reflections on perverse states of mind. *Free Associations*, *2*(2): 203–213.

Williams, G. (1997). *Internal Landscapes and Foreign Bodies: Eating Disorders and Other Pathologies.* London: Duckworth.

Index